the vegetarian epicure

the vegetarian epicure

by anna thomas

illustrations by julie maas

vintage books

a division of random house / new york

Vintage Books Edition, April 1972

Copyright © 1972 by Anna Thomas
All rights reserved under
International and Pan-American Copyright Conventions.
Published in the United States by Random House, Inc.,
New York, and simultaneously in Canada by
Random House of Canada Limited, Toronto.
Originally published by Alfred A. Knopf, Inc., in 1972.

Library of Congress Cataloging in Publication Data
Thomas, Anna.   The vegetarian epicure.

1. Vegetarianism. I. Title.
[TX837.T46 1972b]   641.6'5   73-39176
ISBN 0-394-71784-8

Manufactured in the United States of America
D98765

for my parents

contents

the vegetarian epicure

introduction

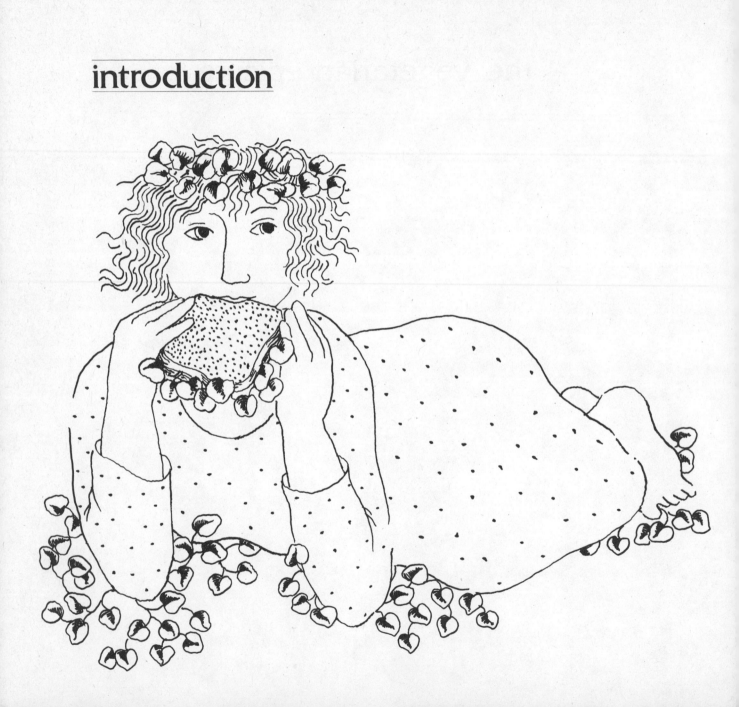

Good food is a celebration of life, and it seems absurd to me that in celebrating life we should take life. That is why I don't eat flesh. I see no need for killing.

There are increasing numbers who, like myself, are for one reason or another rejecting meat, fish, and fowl and turning to a vegetarian diet. Certainly we don't have to kill to nourish our bodies. All the proteins, vitamins, and minerals that we require in order to live and to be healthy are easily available in the endless variety of plant life, and in those gifts animals give us painlessly, such as milk and eggs.

The proposition that meat is necessary to so-called "gourmet" cooking is nonsense. My idea of a fine meal is one with which a fine vintage wine will be happy. That is not to say that this is a necessary test: vegetarian eating is much too various to be thus measured. But cooking and eating (and drinking) my way through this book in that epicurean spirit, I found the possibilities of vegetarian cuisine inexhaustible.

Many of us today turn to vegetarianism through enlightened self-interest. Among its advantages is the primacy of plants in the food chain. Plants are eaten by animals, certain of which are eaten by other animals, and so forth. The closer we stay to the beginning of the food chain, the more food is available to support the burgeoning population of this earth.

In these strange 1970's, ominous and dramatic new reasons are compelling people to reexamine their eating habits. More and more foods are being "processed," becoming the products of factories rather than farms. Chemical nonfood "additives" alter the look of foods and prevent visible spoilage, but the nutritive value of treated foods is hugely diminished—and their cost to you increased. Cattle and poultry are treated with silbesterol (a sex hormone) to promote growth—and profit—resulting in unknown danger to human consumers, including the possibility of various types of cancer.

The concentration of the pesticide DDT, banned at last by the U.S. Government in 1970, is so high throughout the world that none of us can escape having some of it in our bodies. All plants are likely to contain at least traces, but DDT is cumulative, so the body of an animal will contain all the DDT of all the plants and other animals it has eaten.

Much fresh-water and sea life, including tuna, swordfish, and shellfish, has been found to contain dangerous levels of mercury. Like DDT, mercury is not easily eliminated from the body. It can cause irreversible brain damage and death.

But this is a book about joy, not pollution. I hope that even if you are still in the habit of eating meat and fish, you will try some of the different ways and means of cooking suggested here. You might find yourself gradually and happily seduced.

People have approached me, puzzled, and asked how vegetarians eat. Their puzzlement is genuine. They try to imagine their own meals without meat and shudder. But when I imagine their meals I shudder too, because the standard American diet is so appalling in its lack of imagination. Even in finer cooking, the variety is largely limited to the preparation of the main course, almost without exception meat or fish. The menu is thus rigidly standardized. There is one important item: the entrée. In a very secondary place, really playing the role of uninspired accompaniment to the meat, are such things as salad, vegetables, and bread. The standard menu is served with but little change from day to day or week to week, the "square" meal certainly is.

Where meals are served in courses, the parts are still fitted into a relentless, unchanging pattern: soup, main course, salad, dessert. The first thing to do in considering the vegetarian cuisine is to get free of these stereotyped ideas. Otherwise, you may find yourself falling into the trap of "substitutions." Many vegetarian cookbooks have done this, imposing the old structure onto the vegetarian diet and trying to find "meat substitutes." They make a fundamental mistake (to say nothing of the fact that the food is apt to be stodgy rather than fresh and light).

Vegetarian cookery is not a substitute for anything. It is a rich and various cuisine, full of many marvelous dishes with definite characteristics not in imitation of anything else—certainly not in imitation of meat. The vegetarian menu lends itself to many structures. It is not the slave of the "main course," even as it does not avoid that arrangement when it seems fitting and useful. But it can also consist of several equally important courses, or several dishes served at once.

These ideas are neither new nor bizarre. We are all familiar with the Swedish smorgasbord. Many Oriental menus consist of several harmonious dishes. In Thailand, all the courses of a meal are served at once, in a half-moon arrangement around the plate, and one eats in whatever order seems appealing.

I think the only rules about arranging meals which need to be taken seriously are the rudimentary ones of pleasing the palate and maintaining good health. Many people seem worried about providing sufficient protein in a vegetarian diet; I haven't found it difficult. Any dish consisting in large part of eggs, milk, cheese, or other milk products is high in protein. Lentils, soybeans, and wheat germ are three of the most concentrated protein foods known to us, bar none. Peas, almost all beans, and whole grains are also extremely good protein sources. Buckwheat groats are phenomenal! Nearly all nuts are rich in protein, as are many seeds.

In fact, it is the possibility of endless variety that helps create a whole new style of eating—a new set of nonconventions. In the section on menus I suggest a few of the many combinations and arrangements possible with just the recipes in this book. I hope it serves as a starting point, leading quickly to even better ideas of your own with which to titillate your appetite.

I love to eat well, and I find there is a special added joy for the vegetarian epicure: the satisfaction of feeling a peaceful unity with all life.

entertaining

The sharing of food has always been, to me, both a serious and a joyful proposition. Feeding people graciously and lovingly is one of life's simplest pleasures: a most basic way of making life better for someone, at least for a while. Yet, sadly, so few people can find joy in cooking for their friends or family: for men it seems a threat to masculinity, for women a prison.

I was fortunate in that I seemed always to be surrounded by true hosts. My parents and relatives—old-fashioned Europeans—do not consider entertaining guests or offering refreshment a social chore; rather, it is a pleasant duty, an opportunity to create a little ease. To send a guest away unfed is sacrilege to them. On festive occasions, the banquets which appeared were astonishing.

I delight in the thought that, in our house, friends always feel welcome, and always leave refreshed. Sharing food is a large part of this, and whatever the culinary persuasion of my friends may be, I enjoy planning meals for them, preparing the food and serving them myself. As often as not, I am sharing not just food but a whole new way of eating. I think I can say, without boasting, that our friends come away from the experience delighted. For those of you who feel a little timid about breaking new ground for your friends, let me recount this very short story:

It was the evening of a dinner party for which I had been preparing all day. Among the guests was a couple I had not met before, and whom I sincerely wanted to please. As we were sitting down to dinner, the man—a brash New Yorker who doesn't mince words (you know the type)—announced, in loud though not unpleasant tones: "I just want you to know, out front, that I can't stand vegetarian food." I smiled, did my best to appear unperturbed, and served the first course—pea soup with butter dumplings. "But I love good soup!" he declared, hurling his words out through the table conversation. "I *love* good soup!"—and he proceeded to down it with gusto. So it went, right on to the fresh berry tarts, of which everyone present took seconds. The point is, very few people dislike good food it seems, and if you give them just that, chances are they won't even notice they haven't consumed their usual ration of meat.

We've all been to perfect dinner parties—the ones where the guests enjoy one another, the conversation is good, each course pleases the palate and is exquisitely timed, time itself vanishes, and only harmonious presence flows on effortlessly—until it all is suddenly over. The guests go home and the beautiful ruin of a table remains. Friendships bloom at such dinners, optimism is restored, and one begins to notice the extraordinary color of the wine. The chemistry of such a gathering is elusive. It has been my personal experience, however, that serving a menu that is somewhat foreign to the guests greatly enhances the possibilities of success. In addition to being well fed, they are intrigued and flattered.

Planning a good menu is a fine-pointed skill, particularly in the vegetarian cuisine which has not been studied with seriousness until recently. Each meal has an architecture! It may all hit the table at once, or it may be arranged in a series of courses. One or several dishes may be central.

When I serve a variety of dishes at a supper, I always try to arrange them in courses. Each separate course is so much more appreciated when it enjoys unshared attention! When five or six preparations are served at once, unfortunately, we have a tendency to eat too much too fast, with notable loss of enjoyment. How far more interesting to savor not only the separate tastes and textures but the arrangement of them in time. There are more dimensions here than one suspects. Hot and cold set each other off, as do heavy and light, mellow and piquant, and colors play on our senses all the while. In the summer, a chilled soup awakens discouraged appetites at the beginning of a meal, and almost any dinner can finish gracefully with a fresh fruit salad or some such light pause before dessert.

The number of courses and their design and placement are naturally dictated by several considerations, not the least of which is the work involved. If you are doing all the cooking and serving, it is an excellent idea to plan no more than one or two dishes which require last-minute attention. Many hot dishes, of course, can be largely prepared in advance and finished just before serving. The amount of food served in toto should be satisfying rather than impressive. Overstuffing is a sure enemy of enjoyment. Along the same line, one is not likely to appreciate the fine subtleties of a good meal when sodden with liquor. A moderate *aperitif,* however, or a glass of chilled sherry before dinner may be salutary. Guests are almost certain to follow your lead in this matter.

After-dinner drinks are another consideration, of course. In fact, after dinner is a time universally neglected in the planning of an evening at home. I was guilty of this omission myself before the considerable experience of doing this book. Testing hundreds (it seemed like thousands) of recipes in my own kitchen was an unlikely proposition. I did it, over a period of time, by having at least one dinner party a week. Our friends were the guinea pigs, and I can safely report that a good time was had by all, though few of our friends are vegetarians. During the course of this mad social whirl I had ample opportunity to study the dynamics of a dinner party, and the following took place with astounding regularity.

At the end of the dinner—coffee and dessert duly considered and leisurely disposed of—we would all retire to the living room (swearing that we shouldn't be hungry again for a day or so), and engage in all sorts of argument and storytelling. About two hours later, curiously, mouths would go dry and tongues somehow slow in their wagging.

So, the two-hours-later course came to be. This may consist of a great bowl of strawberries and a pot of cream, or maybe hot chocolate on a cold night, accompanied by thin slices of the torte that couldn't be finished earlier, or a platter of nuts and dried fruits with mulled wine. This two-hours-later course is especially recommended if grass is smoked socially at your house. If you have passed a joint around before dinner to sharpen gustatory perceptions, you most likely will pass another one after dinner, and everyone knows what that will do—the blind munchies can strike at any time.

menus

Devising a menu, whether for a dinner party or a simple family meal, is one of the happiest tasks of the cook. I love the thought of beginning each time anew—the possibilities, the feeling of anticipation.

A well-designed meal is suited to the season, to the location, and to the tastes of the diners. As I have said, the parts should contrast and complement one another in a lively way, but the result should be a harmonious whole.

There are basic aesthetic considerations: The food presented at the table should be appealing to the eye. The palate should find variety in rich and light, sharp and mild. But also consider time. Preparing a meal should be a pleasurable experience, and nothing can spoil it more neatly than overwork. Simplicity is desirable from an aesthetic point of view, particularly if you are doing the preparation alone.

Finally, try to do most what you do best, and give your creative temperament free play—within reason. Your own good sense will keep you from serving two or three courses rich with cream and eggs, or a sweet tart for dessert after a dinner consisting largely of a savory tart—so indulge your imagination.

I've composed a number of menus from the recipes in this book and list them here as a guide. For new vegetarians in particular, and for epicures of every persuasion, I hope they prove useful and inspire many more individual combinations. They are arranged—albeit loosely—in order of complexity, beginning with simple—though fine—meals and progressing to more elaborate menus requiring longer preparation time. Happy eating to you.

first: almost-one-dish suppers

There really is no such thing as a one-dish meal. The recipes thus heralded in our cookery books almost always are followed by the suggestion of a salad, bread, or whatnot else (to be served alongside or after). And so, while we may have a simple and well-arranged meal after following this sage advice, it obviously will not be a meal in one dish, nor should it be, for that is not a meal. None of that here. We call this honorable institution by its proper name: the almost-one-dish supper.

The requirements are simple. First there is the one dish, which is hearty, nourishing, and delicious. Then we have the qualifying "almost," those auxiliary delicacies which crown and complement the whole and add the word "meal" to what otherwise would remain one dish.

To retain the simplicity, the complementing dishes should not be elaborate: a salad if the dish is hot; breads and buns of all descriptions; natural foods requiring no preparation, such as fruits, cheeses, and certain raw vegetables.

Here are some of my suggestions for the almost-one-dish supper, many of them being adaptable to almost any number of people, and all of them being adaptable in general.

We can start by ignoring all the suggestions we have just set forth. Our simplest supper, recommended for summer nights, is the great Greek Salad. It is elegantly composed of every possible raw and pickled vegetable and generously decorated with Feta cheese. The menu looks like this:

GREEK SALAD
Crusty Bread, Black or White
chilled Retsina
Fruit, Pastry, Coffee or Tea

Although I don't generally presume to recommend wines, Retsina is indisputably demanded by the salty Feta cheese. Together the two make a rare bit of eating. If you believe in cans, you might also add a few rice-stuffed dolmades to this repast with no additional fuss.

While on the subject of rare bits, let us pass on to Welsh Rabbit, or Rarebit, as it is also known. There are scores of various "rabbits," and the choice of toasted breadstuffs with which they can be paired is even greater.

TOMATO RABBIT
over Slices of Toasted Herb Bread
Fresh Fruit Salad
Rice Pudding
Coffee

The Rabbit's elegant Swiss cousin is the Fondue, an easy and festive dish for a party, even a party of two. The bread should be French, but the rest is easily variable.

Raw Vegetable Relish Tray
CHEESE FONDUE NEUFCHÂTELOISE
Cubed French Bread
Tossed Green Salad
Pastries or Fruit
Coffee

One of the greatest wintertime suppers ever served is a hearty, thick soup. Minestrone alla Milanese is as lively a soup as you're likely to find, combining more than a dozen ingredients. It needs only the simplest embellishments.

MINESTRONE ALLA MILANESE
Mixed Grain Bread
Tossed Green Salad
Fruit and Cheese
Coffee

Tarts and pies have long been favorites as almost-one-dish meals, and two of my favorites among them follow here in pleasant company. The Pizza Rustica is an especially rich and filling dish, so choose the antipasto with care, avoiding the oily marinated vegetables often found there.

Antipasto Platter
PIZZA RUSTICA
Crisp French Rolls
Chilled Fresh Fruit Compote
Coffee

ONION TARTE LYONNAISE
Gazpacho Salad
Fresh Berries with Brandy and Kirsch
Coffee or Cappucino

The two menus below are very American offerings, the types of food associated with the earliest New England settlers. I especially like the combination of Stuffed Pumpkin and Spicy Sweet Potato Pie in one dinner. Whereas pumpkin and sweet potatoes may be of like character in the raw state, they come to happily different conclusions here.

STUFFED PUMPKIN
Cranberry-Cumberland Sauce
Spicy Sweet Potato Pie
Coffee

BAKED BEAN CASSEROLE
Hot Scallion Cornbread
Fruit Ambrosia
Coffee

Great pasta has always been able to carry a meal gallantly with little but well-chosen accompaniment. Here are two pastas, one from Greece and one from Italy, doing just that.

PASTITSIO
Sesame Ring
Salad Marocain
Fresh Fruit
Coffee

PASTA E FAGIOLI
Hot Herb Bread
Tossed Green Salad
Baked Cup Custard
Coffee

large and small dinners

The dinner menus that follow vary in complexity from just slightly more time-consuming than the almost-one-dish suppers to truly elaborate meals. They are all designed in courses. I feel that they can be more easily and gracefully served that way, and each of the foods can be more completely enjoyed. I want to stress that a dinner served in courses is not necessarily larger or more difficult than a dinner served all at once. Often it simply means that you have more time to enjoy each dish and can give it more attention.

Marinated White Beans
Garlic Bread
Tossed Green Salad with Zucchini
Stuffed Manicotti
Whole Fresh Fruit

Tomato Soup Supreme
Soybean Croquettes
Cranberry-Cumberland Sauce   Potatoes in Wine
Fresh Fruit Salad

Eggplant with Capers
Trenette con Pesto
Hot and Cold Salad
Zabaglione

Chilled Dill Soup
Savory Cheese and Onion Pie
String Beans Vinaigrette
Mazurek, Fresh Fruit

Leek Salad Vinaigrette
Fromage Romanesque   Mornay Sauce
Hot Tomatoes à la Provençale
Linzertorte

Almond Soup
Camembert à la Vierge
Potato Salad Vinaigrette   Cherry Tomatoes
Chilled Fresh Fruit Compote

Bryani
Potato Raita   Watercress Raita
Fresh Fruit Salad
Ginger Sherbet

Cheese Ramequins
Stuffed Baked Eggplant
Raw Mushroom Salad
Apple Pudding

Little Vegetable Tarts
Cheese Soufflé   Herb and Wine Sauce
Salad of Lettuce Hearts with Melted Butter
Cottage Pudding

The following menu begins with Orange Curry, which is a very thin, clear liquid. I suggest that it can just as well be sipped through the meal. The remaining dishes are served all at once, most of them as cooling condiments for the spicy curry and dal.

Orange Curry
Vegetable Curry
Saffron Rice
Spiced Dal
Banana Raita
Fruit Salad
Mango Chutney   Cashews
Ginger Cheesecake

Ratatouille
Baked Walnut and Cheddar Balls Béchamel
Marinated Mushrooms Oriental
Fresh Fruit Salad
Tarte aux Poires

Mushrooms Berkeley
Onions Monégasque
Gazpacho
Cheese Fondue Neufchâteloise
Summer Fruit Tart

Baked Polenta
Pimiento Peppers in Oil   Sesame Eggplant
Lasagne
Hearts of Butter Lettuce   Citrus Dressing
Lemon Ice

Creamed Artichoke Soup
Mushroom-Stuffed Pierogi
Asparagus Soufflé   Dill Sauce
Oriental Citrus Squash
Strawberries, Figs, Cookies, Coffee

Parsleyed Eggs on the Half-Shell
Marinated Mushrooms Oriental
Asparagus Pastry
Salad Marocain
Apricot Mousse

Asparagus Soup
Homemade White Rolls
Parmesan Crêpes   Creamed Black Mushroom Sauce
Vinaigrette Salad
Platter of Tomatoes, Avocados, Scallions
Fresh Fruit and Nuts

tools

I've been asked a number of times if fine vegetarian cookery isn't more complicated and time-consuming than other kinds. The answer is that all good cooking takes time and careful attention, whatever the ingredients. There are always certain dishes which can be prepared in almost no time. I can make a cheese fondue in fifteen minutes and a lovely omelet in only two or three. For the most part, however, good eating requires a certain investment of time and effort. Moreover, those people who have learned what a fascinating experience cooking can be consider this time spent in pleasure as much as in work.

What many people don't seem to realize is that there are certain specialized tools, many of them quite inexpensive, which can multiply the potential of a kitchen in a grand way. Recipes which have a forbidding look about them can, as often as not, be quite satisfactorily tamed if the right equipment is used. One need not be fabulously wealthy in order to have a kitchen that is functional as well as a very comforting place to be. My own kitchen, which is small and quite simple, is the best example I know of—in it I have successfully prepared every recipe in this book.

Since this is not really a book for those who have never seen a kitchen before, I will describe only briefly the most basic utensils. Every good kitchen needs an assortment of skillets, saucepans, casseroles, baking dishes, and mixing bowls in a variety of sizes. Heavy metals are a worthwhile investment in saucepans and skillets, and an enameled pan for boiling eggs and potatoes is an important acquisition. In fact, enameled cast-iron is my personal preference for most skillets and pots. I also recommend heavy stainless steel, particularly if it has a copper base, as copper is the best heat conductor. Avoid aluminum and remember that copper must always be lined.

As for cutlery, it is perhaps the single most important item in culinary equipment. An assortment of sharp, clean knives, preferably with carbon-steel blades, is indispensable. A large, finely serrated knife for bread, and an extremely thin, sharp vegetable knife are of prime importance. Keeping a whetstone for knife-sharpening is a very good idea, for clean and sharp blades can greatly reduce the preparation time of many dishes.

Also found in any usable kitchen are a good set of measures, in cups and spoons, some baking sheets and cake pans, and at least one cutting board. A simple food scale is a big help.

These are the most fundamental items to anyone who prepares and cooks simple foods. As your ideas move in the direction of more interesting and rewarding cookery, other items take their places among the essential.

For making sauces or soufflés, a wire whisk and a batch of wooden stirring spoons are essential. There is nothing which whips egg whites as well as the classic balloon whisk, and I also use it for the initial stirring of most thickened sauces. I can happily report that no sauce in my kitchen has been plagued with lumps since I discovered the whisk. For the gentle stirring that follows, as well as for the stirring of any soup or liquid of delicate composition, the old-fashioned wooden spoon is unrivaled. I keep separate assortments for sweet and savory liquids.

Also helpful for most saucemaking, as well as for melting and reheating, is a double boiler. Enamel or glass are recommended, especially for any liquids of high acidity, such as vinegar or citrus juices. Beware of double boilers the top part of which is narrow and deep, for they do not distribute heat evenly.

Several strainers and sieves, both fine mesh and coarse, are necessary. Having the proper one on hand, and rinsing it right after using it will save time. I also keep some cheese-cloth and muslin for fine straining. You can buy it dirt cheaply in any yardage shop.

Please do not consider a peppermill a luxury. Freshly ground pepper is quite a separate experience from stale, commercially ground pepper. Don't miss it. In the same spirit, equip your kitchen with a good-sized pestle and mortar (preferably of marble) and a heavy, solid garlic press. You may have to go to a specialty shop to find the proper press or mortar, but it's worth a good look around: weak presses fall apart on the first self-respecting clove of garlic, and mortars are usually too small or grind their own enamel into your herbs and spices. Avoid these pitfalls and have fresher and more aromatic seasonings than any tin will ever provide.

The preparations of soups, fresh vegetables, pasta, and rice are a large part of vegetarian cookery. A good colander, a ladle, a slotted spoon, and at least one giant pot are used constantly in these preparations. The steaming basket for vegetables is a marvelous invention: vegetables retain much more of their color, flavor, nutritional value, and integrity when steamed rather than boiled. Not indispensable, but very helpful, is an automatic vegetable slicer.

If you enjoy baking, whether breads or pastries, you will require yet another set of simple tools. An inexpensive pastry cutter is worth having even if you make one pie a year, for it reduces the time of crust preparation by half. A rolling pin and a large breadboard are basic, and a flour sifter, if kept for that purpose only, requires no washing and is immensely useful.

As you find the types of cookery that suit you most, you will probably begin collecting more specialized gear. Chafing dishes, custard cups, various molds, and little individual *gratin* dishes are all nice to have around; but if your budget is limited, I advise careful assessment of priorities.

There is one slightly more costly gadget that I do very strongly recommend: a good electric blender is nothing short of an uncomplaining kitchen slavey. Flawless purées are a matter of two or three minutes, difficult mortar sauces such as a pesto can be accomplished in seconds, and a large part of all grating, chopping, and mashing can be done away with. A perfectly adequate blender can be purchased for a little more than twenty dollars—you needn't be dazzled by a huge array of speed settings, for seven or eight will do very well—and after you have one for a few weeks you will be certain that you could never do without it again.

Take care in equipping your kitchen. If you enjoy cooking, you spend a good part of your time there, and it should be one of the most comfortable and cheerful rooms in the house and the time spent in it should be rewarding. Keeping this in mind, look for quality in the utensils you choose. Good tools will last and will repay your investment many times over in the hours that are saved preparing good food.

bread

When there is very little else left to believe in, one can still believe in an honest loaf of fragrant, home-baked bread. How many people, I wonder, have never tasted bread? It may seem absurd, but I'm sure there are many people today who don't know the taste of true bread. This wasn't so in earlier times, when whole grains were coarsely ground between millers' stones and baked regularly into large, richly dark and crusty loaves; bread was still revered as the staff of life. But now, large enterprising firms call themselves bakeries and lightly take the name of bread in vain, attaching it to that inflated, chalky mass that never knew a crumb and is scorned even by molds, no matter how stale it gets.

Accept no substitutes. A true bread is a noble thing: it has a crust, it has color and texture, and a real and rich flavor of its own. (If it was made in your own kitchen with your own hands, it may also have magic healing properties.) And while the making of real bread is suspected to nourish the soul, the eating of it certainly nourishes the body.

Somehow, making a yeast dough is a frightening prospect to many people; it need not be. There are several basic techniques to be learned, but they are uncomplicated and can be mastered in one or two bakings. If you take the trouble, you will be richly rewarded, for bread is made of grain, and grain does not taste like frothy plaster-of-Paris. Grain tastes as though it grew in big fields of good soil, waved around in clean-air breezes, drank up lots of sunshine and some rain, and, finally, was harvested in golden ripeness.

The basic techniques of baking with yeast are used in the creation of almost any loaf, and I shall go over them briefly here to avoid repeating myself in each individual recipe.

Flours, of course, differ greatly one from the other, and so it is impossible to give exact measurements in a bread recipe. You will soon learn to recognize a good bread dough by feel and by sight. After the addition of the right amount of flour, and after sufficient kneading, the dough should be firm, smooth, and very elastic: it will draw together strongly and the surface will blister when stretched.

To achieve this perfect dough, first consider the yeast: it is a living organism, and too much heat can kill it, while cold will prevent its growth. Before dissolving the yeast, therefore, test the water by dripping some on your wrist. If it feels warm without being uncomfortably close to hot, the temperature is right. Luckily, most dry, packaged yeast will tolerate a fairly good range of temperatures, unlike some moist cake yeast.

When the yeast is properly dissolved and combined with flour, liquid, and other ingredients as directed, attaining the right consistency is the next consideration. When the dough is too stiff to stir with a spoon, a little more flour—perhaps a handful or two—can be added to the bowl and worked in with the hand before turning the dough out. The dough, at this point, need not be smooth, nor all the flour absorbed. The slight kneading in the bowl is only to make it a little stiffer and thus prevent its spreading all over the board when you turn it out.

The breadboard that you use for kneading should be large—two by three feet is a good size. If you haven't a board this size, a good, flat, clean surface, such as a formica-covered kitchen counter or a piece of marble, can be dusted with flour and used instead.

To knead the dough, spread at least half a cup of flour, maybe a little more, on the board and turn the dough out onto it. Sprinkle more flour over the dough and some on your hands; then begin kneading. Be very careful at first, for the dough will be sticky and will need constant dredging in the flour on the board. Press down on it with the heels of your hands and fold it over; press down again, pushing away a little, and then fold over from the other side, and repeat. This is the basic kneading movement and you will soon find the variation which suits you best. The amount of flour which is to be added now depends on the individual bread dough—and each is an individual!

Add a little at a time as long as the dough continues to absorb it and become sticky. Turn the dough over frequently as you knead it to keep it from sticking to the board, and work it vigorously with your hands until it is absolutely smooth, elastic, and does not stick with normal light handling. This may take ten to fifteen minutes. It is very important to sufficiently knead the dough, for it is kneading which develops the gluten in the flour and gives the bread lightness and texture.

At this point, you usually form the dough into a ball, place it in a buttered bowl (turning it over so that the top is buttered too), and leave it to rise. Cover the bowl with a towel and place it in a fairly warm place—about 85 to 90 degrees is perfect—for the prescribed amount of time. I usually put mine on top of the oven, over the pilot light; another good place is inside the oven—turn it on for about one minute, turn it off, and put the dough in. Again, directions can approximate, but the dough itself will tell you when it is ready. The time varies with the amount of yeast and the kinds of flour used; darker, heavier flours are always slower to rise. If it is to be doubled in bulk, eye it carefully (to learn its size) when you first put it in the bowl, and don't touch it again until it is twice its former volume.

After the dough has risen, it is punched down. Of the whole process, this may be the greatest fun: just make a fist and sock it into the dough, then watch it deflate around your hand. Some doughs need to rise again after the first punching down, others are formed into loaves at that point.

I have found that the easiest way to form an ordinary loaf is this: Roll or press out the dough on a lightly floured board into an irregular oblong, wider at one end than the other. Starting from the narrower end, roll it tightly toward the wider end, then seal by pinching the ends together. Pat it into just the right size and place it in a buttered loaf pan, pinched seam down. When you become experienced in handling bread dough, you will find great enjoyment in making braids, twists, and other interesting shapes from the appropriate doughs.

The bread rises again after it is shaped—this time it does not take as long and should be almost but not quite double in bulk. Leave some of the rising for the actual baking or the bread will have neither the correct shape nor consistency. **Always preheat the**

oven. Check the loaves near the end of the specified baking time. If they are not a deep golden brown or darker, they will not be harmed by an extra five minutes in the oven.

Technically speaking, bread should be cooled before it is sliced, but I have never been known to resist for more than five minutes myself. If you slice some off while it is still steaming (as you shouldn't but probably will) the slice will have a few sticky places from the pull of the knife. Never mind—it will be delicious anyway, as wicked things are wont to be. Really hot bread is not as healthful to eat as warm or cool bread, however, so at least try not to glut yourself with half a loaf right away.

YEAST BREADS

french bread

Here is the world's simplest bread—we call it *pain ordinaire*—but it is simply beautiful to look at and to eat. A slender, long loaf, wrapped in the subtle, golden armor of a true, hard, French crust, and poised in solitary splendor on a bread-board, is fitting decoration for the most festive table. Broken or sliced, light as baby's breath inside, only a sliver of butter is needed and you have a master-piece in purity of taste.

1   heaping Tbs. butter
1   heaping Tbs. salt
1   heaping Tbs. sugar
2   cups boiling water
1   Tbs. dry yeast
⅔   cup lukewarm water
About 6 to 6½ cups unbleached, hard-
      wheat, white flour
Yellow corn meal

In a very large mixing bowl combine the butter, salt, sugar, and 2 cups of boiling water. Stir a little as it dissolves. Sprinkle the yeast over ⅔ cup lukewarm water in a little bowl and allow it to dissolve.

When the butter mixture is also luke-warm, combine the two and mix well.

Now start adding the flour, a little at a time. When you have added about 4 cups and the dough is beginning to get quite thick, beat it vigorously for about 10 minutes with a wooden spoon. Then add flour until the dough is too stiff to mix with the spoon.

Turn it out onto a large, floured board and knead, adding a little more flour as nec-essary, until it is satiny smooth and very elastic. Form it into a ball and put it away in a warm place to rise for about 1½ hours; the dough should double in size. Punch it down and let it rise again until doubled; this time it will only take about 1 hour.

Prepare the baking sheet by buttering it and sprinkling yellow corn meal lightly over the butter.

Divide the dough into 3 parts and shape each part into a very long, very slender loaf. Do this by rolling out each part into a rectangle about 14 inches to 15 inches long and 8 inches to 10 inches wide. Roll up the long side of the rectangle tightly until it is all a narrow, even loaf about 1½ inches wide. Seal the seam and the ends by pinching, and place the three loaves on the baking sheet.

Cover them with a dry tea towel and let them rise until they are almost double in size. Brush the tops of the loaves with cold water and, with a very sharp knife,

make 3 or 4 diagonal slashes across the top of each one.

Bake them in a preheated 400-degree oven for almost 1 hour; every 15 or 20 minutes, brush the tops with more cold water. This helps make the crisp, hard crust for which French bread is famous. Keeping a shallow pan of hot water in the oven while the loaves are baking also helps.

white bread

1   large potato
1½ cups milk
1½ Tbs. butter
1   package dry yeast
¼ tsp. ginger, ground
4   tsp. sugar
1   Tbs. salt
6 to 6½ cups unbleached white flour

Peel the potato and cut it up into large pieces. Boil it in a small amount of un-salted water until it is soft. Pour off the water—reserving ½ cup of it—and mash the potato with a little of the milk and butter until it is smooth.

Put the potato water in a small bowl, and when it has cooled to lukewarm, sprinkle the yeast and ginger, along with a tea-spoon of sugar, over it. Scald the rest of the milk, and combine with the remaining butter, salt, and the rest of the sugar. As it cools, begin stirring it, bit by bit, into the mashed potato. This should give you a smooth and creamy mixture—hardly anybody likes potato lumps in their bread.

When this mixture is somewhat cooled and the yeast mixture is foamy, mix them together in a large bowl and add 4 cups of flour. Stir vigorously with a wooden spoon. Add more flour, stirring until the dough can no longer be stirred with a spoon.

Turn the dough out on a well-floured board and knead for 10 to 15 minutes, adding flour as it is needed, until the dough is elastic and smooth. Beware of adding too much flour. If the dough is getting quite stiff, but still sticking, wash your hands and rub them with butter, as well as the board. This way your bread will not be too dry from too much flour.

Place the dough into a large buttered bowl, turn it over once or twice so that it is buttered on all surfaces, cover with a tea towel, and set aside in a warm place to rise until it has doubled in size. The first time this should take about 1½ hours. Punch it down and let it rise again, about 1 hour this time. Knead it down, divide into 2 parts, and form loaves. Place them in buttered loaf pans, cover again with a towel, and let rise about ½ hour or until almost double.

Put into a preheated 450-degree oven, and after 10 minutes, turn the heat down to 350 degrees for the next 45 minutes. The loaves should be a deep brown in color and have crisp crusts.

The same dough makes superb dinner rolls. After punching it down the second time, form the dough into a long roll about 2 inches in diameter. Cut across in pieces about 3 inches long. Place them on a buttered cookie sheet, cover with a towel, and let rise about ½ hour. Bake in a preheated 450-degree oven for 10 minutes, then turn the heat down to 350 degrees and bake another 30 to 35 minutes.

whole wheat bread

2   cups milk
3   Tbs. butter
1   Tbs. salt
3   Tbs. honey
2   Tbs. yeast
⅓   cup lukewarm water
½   cup wheat germ
5½ to 6½ cups whole wheat flour

Heat the milk to the scalding point and add to it the butter, salt, and honey. Put it all in a large mixing bowl and let cool to lukewarm.

Dissolve the yeast in the lukewarm water and, after a few minutes, add it to the lukewarm mixture in the bowl. Add the wheat germ and about 3 cups of flour and stir vigorously with a wooden spoon until the batter is smooth. Add more flour and keep stirring until the dough is too stiff to stir with the spoon. Turn it out on a floured board and knead—adding more flour as necessary to keep it from sticking—until it is very smooth and elastic.

Turn it into a buttered bowl, flip it over, and cover the bowl with a towel. Leave it in a warm place to rise until double in bulk—about 1 hour. Punch it down, cover, and let it rise again.

Knead a few times again and shape the dough into 2 loaves. Place them in buttered or oiled baking pans, cover, and leave to rise until almost double—about 45 minutes at the most. Bake for 45 minutes at 375 degrees. The loaves should be golden brown.

white oatmeal bread

1 large potato
1½ cups milk
1½ Tbs. butter
1 package dry yeast
¼ tsp. ground ginger
4 tsp. sugar
1 Tbs. salt
approximately 6 cups white flour
1 cup rolled oats, uncooked

This is a variation on White Bread and, to me, tastes even more delicious. Proceed exactly according to the directions for White Bread, adding the rolled oats right after you mix in the first 4 cups of flour. You will, of course, need slightly less flour to get a dough of the proper consistency. As with the other, part or all of this dough may be used to make dinner rolls.

whole wheat onion bread

Prepare the dough exactly as for Whole Wheat Bread and knead in 1 onion, sliced and cut into ½-inch slivers, after the first rising. Everyone I've seen try this bread has loved it.

whole wheat oatmeal bread

Proceed exactly as for Whole Wheat Bread, but mix in 1 cup of rolled oats in place of 1 cup of whole wheat flour. I personally prefer the texture of this bread to the simple wheat variety.

challah *(Jewish Egg Bread)*

1   package yeast
2   tsp. sugar
1¼ cups warm water
4½ to 5 cups hard-wheat, white flour
2   tsp. salt
2   eggs
2   Tbs. melted butter or oil
1   egg yolk
sesame seeds or poppy seeds

Dissolve the yeast in ¼ cup of the water and add the sugar. Sift 4 cups of the flour together with the salt into a large mixing bowl and add the 2 eggs, the melted butter or oil, and the rest of the water, as well as the yeast mixture.

Stir vigorously until all is well-blended. Dust a large board with about ½ cup flour and turn the dough out to knead. Knead in as much of the remaining flour as needed to make a smooth, elastic, non-sticky dough.

Grease a large bowl and put the dough into it. Cover and leave it to rise in a fairly warm place for about 1 hour. Punch it down and let it rise again until double in bulk.

On a lightly floured board, shape the Challah: first divide the dough into 2 parts—one slightly larger than the other. Then cut the larger part into 3 equal pieces. Roll the pieces into strips and form a fat, even braid. Place it in the middle of a buttered baking sheet. Now repeat this procedure with the smaller piece of dough, and place the second braid on top of the first.

Cover with a light tea towel and let rise for about ½ hour. Brush the loaf heavily with the egg yolk and sprinkle it generously with poppy or sesame seeds. Bake at 375 degrees for about 50 minutes.

You will have one very large and impressive Challah, golden brown and shiny.

swedish rye bread *(with a difference)*

This bread is dark and richly flavored, yet very light in texture, due to the magical powers of the low-starch gluten flour.

2 Tbs. dry yeast
1 cup warm water
⅔ cup hot water
2 Tbs. butter
⅓ cup unsulphured molasses
1½ Tbs. sea salt
1 Tbs. caraway seeds
1 Tbs. anise seeds
1 Tbs. dried, grated orange rind, or
    2 to 3 Tbs. fresh
yellow corn meal

Dissolve the yeast in the warm water. In a large bowl, melt the butter in the hot water and add the other ingredients, and finally the yeast mixture. Sift together:

2½ cups rye flour
2 cups pastry whole wheat flour
1½ cups gluten flour

Add most of the flour to the liquid, stirring it well to make a stiff dough. Put out some of the flour on a large board, and turn the dough out to knead. When you have kneaded it until it is smooth and elastic, place it in a greased bowl, cover with a towel, and let rise in a warm place until double in size, 1½ to 2 hours.

Punch down, form into nice loaves, place on a baking sheet which you have greased and dusted with corn meal and, covering again, let them rise until almost double. Then bake in a preheated oven of 350 degrees for about 45 to 50 minutes.

This makes 2 loaves.

honey wheat berry bread

This is the best bread I have ever made, and if you like whole wheat breads, you will surely agree. A superb loaf—delicious even when eaten dry, without butter.

½ cup dry wheat berries
water as needed
1⅔ cups scalded and cooled milk
1 Tbs. dry yeast
⅓ cup pure honey
2 Tbs. melted butter
2 tsp. salt
5½ to 6½ cups whole wheat or pastry
    whole wheat flour
½ cup wheat germ, toasted with honey

Simmer the wheat berries in about 2 cups water for 2½ to 3 hours while you start the bread. Add more water if necessary.

Scald the milk and let it cool to room temperature, or mix condensed milk with hot water to get the same result more quickly. In ¼ cup warm water, dissolve the yeast. Put it into a large mixing bowl and add, in this order, the milk, the honey, the melted butter, and the salt.

Stir in 4 cups of the flour and beat with a wooden spoon until the dough is very smooth and elastic. Add another 1½ cups flour and the wheat germ, and stir as well as you can, for now you will have a very stiff dough.

Sprinkle some flour on a large board and turn the dough out to knead. Add a little more flour if necessary, but don't let your dough get too stiff. Greasing your hands with butter helps overcome sticky-dough problems if you are not yet an old hand at kneading.

When the dough is satiny smooth and pulls together well, put it in a large greased bowl, cover, and let it rise until double in bulk, about 1½ hours. Then punch it down, put it back on the board, and knead in the cooked wheat berries, which should be soft enough to chew easily. Divide the dough into 2 parts, form it into loaves, and place them in greased loaf pans. Cover them again with a towel and let rise in a warm place until almost double—about 45 minutes this time. Bake in a preheated oven at 375 degrees for about 45 minutes.

sesame ring

1   package yeast
1¼ cups lukewarm water
4 to 4½ cups unbleached white flour
1   egg
2   tsp. salt
2   Tbs. melted butter or oil
1   egg yolk
4   Tbs. sesame seeds

Dissolve the yeast in ¼ cup lukewarm water and put it aside for a few minutes.

Pour 4 cups of white flour into a large mixing bowl. Add to it the egg, the yeast, the remaining water, the salt, and the oil or butter. Stir vigorously until the dough is smooth and somewhat elastic. Add a little more flour to make a stiff dough.

Turn the dough out onto a lightly floured board and knead until it is very elastic and smooth. Form the dough into a ball and put it into an oiled bowl, turning it over once so that all the surface is lightly oiled. Cover the bowl with a tea towel and set it aside to rise for about an hour; it should double in size.

Punch down the dough, knead it a few more turns, then form it into as smooth a ball as possible. With your fingers, poke a hole through the center of the ball. Pull apart the dough carefully into a donut shape, making it even and pulling up dough from the sides into a tightly pinched circular seam. Place the ring in a buttered pan, cover with a tea towel, and leave it to rise until nearly double.

Brush the top with beaten egg yolk and sprinkle a dense layer of sesame seeds over the entire visible surface of the loaf. Bake at 375 degrees for about 50 minutes. Serve with your finest Greek dinner.

monday pumpernickel

Start the week with this bread. Monday won't look so bad and the rest of the week will look better when you fortify yourself with this delicious, dark loaf—also very high in protein.

1 package dry yeast
¼ cup lukewarm water
2 Tbs. butter
1 Tbs. caraway seeds
1 Tbs. powdered lemon peel (or 2 Tbs. fresh grated)
1 Tbs. salt
2 Tbs. molasses
⅓ cup currants (not raisins)
2 cups milk
2 cups rye flour
2 cups whole wheat flour
1 cup pure, flaked bran (not the ready-to-eat cereal)
½ cup wheat germ
½ cup gluten flour

Dissolve the yeast in the lukewarm water. Put the butter, caraway seeds, lemon peel, salt, molasses, and currants in a large mixing bowl. Scald the milk and add it to the mixture in the bowl. When the butter has melted and the milk cooled to lukewarm, mix in the yeast, then the rye flour and half of the whole wheat. Stir vigorously with a wooden spoon until smooth. Add the bran, wheat germ, and gluten flour, and stir again. The dough should be very stiff now. Pour out some of the remaining whole wheat flour on a large board and turn the dough out on it. Dust it with more flour and knead, using the rest of the flour to keep it from getting sticky.

When it is smooth and elastic, form into a ball and put in a large, buttered bowl; turn over once, cover with a towel, and leave in a warm place to rise until double—about 1½ to 2 hours.

Punch down the dough and form into 2 loaves. Place them seam down on a lightly floured baking sheet, cover again with a towel, and let rise until almost double—about 1 hour. Brush the loaves with cold water and bake for 50 minutes in a preheated 375-degree oven.

Each loaf has about 83 grams of protein.

mixed grain bread

2   cups boiling water
1   Tbs. salt
2   Tbs. butter
1 to 2 Tbs. molasses
1   cup yellow corn meal
1   cup rolled oats
½   cup lukewarm water
2   packages yeast
1   cup rye flour
2   cups whole wheat flour
white flour as needed (about 1 cup)

Glaze:

beaten egg yolk, or water and Postum

Combine the boiling water with the salt, butter, and molasses in a large mixing bowl. Stir in the corn meal and oats, and, while this mixture cools to lukewarm, dissolve the yeast in the warm water. After about 10 minutes, add the yeast to the corn meal mixture.

Sift in the rye and whole wheat flour, stirring vigorously. Add enough white flour to make a stiff dough and turn out to knead. Add more white flour as needed to keep the dough from sticking.

When the dough is smooth and elastic, form it into a ball and place it in a large, buttered bowl. Turn it over once so that all sides are buttered, cover with a towel, and leave in a warm place to rise until double in bulk. This should take about 1½ hours.

When the dough has doubled, punch it down and form 2 loaves—either oblong or round. Place them on a baking sheet which has been greased and sprinkled with corn meal. Allow the loaves to rise until not quite twice their original size. This will take about ½ hour.

Just before putting them in the oven, brush the loaves with beaten egg yolk or a mixture of equal parts cold water and Postum. If you brush them with the water and Postum, brush them again once or twice during the baking; this repeated brushing with water will give your loaves a hard, shiny crust, and the Postum will add a dark color and flavor.

Bake for about 45 minutes at 375 degrees.

herb and onion bread

Here is the fastest yeast bread I know, and a delicious one. I like to bake it late in the day, to serve still warm with dinner. The aroma of herbs is the greatest appetizer you could devise. For 1 loaf:

½ cup milk
1½ Tbs. sugar
1   tsp. salt
1   Tbs. butter
1   package yeast
½ cup warm water
2¼ cups white or whole wheat flour
½ small onion, minced
½ tsp. dried dill weed
1   tsp. crushed, dried rosemary

Scald the milk and dissolve in it the sugar, salt, and butter; cool to lukewarm. In a large bowl, dissolve the yeast in the warm water. Add the cooled milk, flour, minced onion, and herbs, and stir well with a large, wooden spoon.

When the batter is smooth, cover the bowl with a towel and let the dough rise in a warm place until triple in bulk—about 45 minutes. Stir down and beat vigorously for a few minutes, then turn into a greased bread pan. Let it stand in a warm place about 10 minutes before putting it into a preheated, 350-degree oven. Bake about 1 hour.

black bread *(Peasant Bread)*

3   tsp. Postum
2   cups hot water
4   Tbs. dark molasses
2   cups fine, dark breadcrumbs, toasted
      (or 1½ cups crumbs, ½ cup wheat
      germ)
2   packages yeast
½   cup lukewarm water
1   tsp. sugar
½   tsp. ground ginger
3   cups rye flour
¼   cup melted butter
2   tsp. salt
1½ cups white flour

Glaze:

1   tsp. Postum, dissolved in 2 tsp. cold
      water

Pour the hot water into a large mixing bowl and dissolve in it 3 teaspoons of the Postum and the molasses. Add the breadcrumbs and mix.

Dissolve the yeast in the lukewarm water, adding the sugar and ginger. Stir the yeast mixture and let it stand for about 15 minutes. When the breadcrumbs are cooled to lukewarm and the yeast is spongy, mix them together and stir in the rye flour.

To this very dry mixture add the salt and melted butter. Spread the white flour on a large board, and put the dark mixture on it. Turn the bowl over it and leave it covered this way for about 15 minutes.

Knead it vigorously for at least 10 minutes, using as much of the white flour as necessary to keep the dough from sticking. When it is smooth and stiff, put it in a greased bowl, turn it over once, cover with a towel, and let rise in a warm place until double in bulk, about 1½ hours.

Turn out onto a very lightly floured board and shape into 1 large loaf, either quite long or round but, in any case, as high as you can make it: it will spread out as it rises again. Place it on a buttered baking sheet, cover, and let rise again about 30 minutes. It should be nearly double in bulk.

Before baking, dissolve 1 teaspoon of Postum in 2 teaspoons cold water and brush the loaf with this mixture. Bake about 40 to 45 minutes at 400 degrees.

pepper-cheese bread

1 package yeast
¼ cup lukewarm water
1 Tbs. sugar
1 tsp. salt
1 tsp. fresh-ground black pepper
¾ tsp. dry basil, crushed
2 cups whole wheat flour
3½ to 4 cups unbleached white flour
2 Tbs. melted butter
1½ cups warmed milk
1 egg
¼ tsp. Tabasco sauce
4 oz. sharp Cheddar cheese, grated

Soften the yeast in the lukewarm water with 1 teaspoon sugar. In a large mixing bowl, combine remaining sugar, salt, pepper, basil, and 1½ cups whole wheat flour.

Beat the egg with the softened butter, warm milk, and Tabasco sauce. Add it to the flour mixture and stir, then add the yeast and stir again until it is smooth.

Add the remaining whole wheat flour and enough white flour to make a stiff dough, flour a board, and turn the dough out to knead. Use only what flour is necessary to keep it from sticking while you knead. When the dough is smooth and elastic, put it in a large buttered bowl, turn it over once, cover with a towel, and leave in a warm place to rise until double—about 1 hour.

Punch it down and knead in the cheese, little by little. The dough should be very elastic and hard to knead now; this is good.

When the cheese is evenly distributed, form 2 loaves and place them in lightly greased pans. Cover with a towel again and let rise until nearly double. Bake in a preheated 400-degree oven for 15 minutes, then lower the heat to 350 degrees and bake for 35 minutes more.

QUICK BREADS

irish soda bread *(Whole Wheat)*

1¼ cups yogurt ⎫ or 1¾ cups
½ cup water ⎭ buttermilk
1   egg
1¼ tsp. baking soda (1 tsp. if using
       buttermilk)
3   tsp. baking powder
1¼ tsp. salt
2   cups white flour
2   cups whole wheat flour
¼   tsp. ground cardamom or coriander

Sift together all dry ingredients into a large mixing bowl. Beat the yogurt and water (or buttermilk) with the egg, and stir into the flour mixture. Turn the dough out on a lightly floured board and knead for a few minutes, until it is smooth. Divide the dough into 2 parts and form each into a flattened round. Place the rounds in 2 small, buttered cake pans and press them into the edges. Across the top of each loaf, make 2 crossing slashes, each about ½-inch deep. Bake for 35 to 40 minutes at 375 degrees.

This bread is best served warm (not hot), cut into wedges which are then split and buttered.

For an interesting variation, add a cup of currants to the dry ingredients before stirring in the rest.

sweet oatmeal raisin bread

1   cup unbleached white flour
1   cup rye flour
1   tsp. baking powder
1   tsp. salt
1   tsp. baking soda
2   Tbs. sugar
1   cup rolled oats
¼   cup molasses
1¼ cups yogurt
1   cup raisins

Sift together the dry ingredients and mix in the rolled oats. Beat the yogurt with the molasses until they are blended and smooth, then stir into the dry mixture until everything is thoroughly combined. Add the raisins and mix again, then pour into a greased loaf pan and let stand for about 20 minutes before baking. Bake in a preheated 350-degree oven for about 1 hour. This recipe makes 1 loaf, dense and moist—sweet enough without being too sweet. Try it with cream cheese.

milk and honey bread

A sweet bread for real honey fanciers. Serve it with cream cheese at tea time.

1   cup milk
⅔   cup honey
¼   cup butter
2   eggs
1½ cups white flour
1   cup whole wheat flour
1   Tbs. baking powder
1   tsp. salt
½   cup toasted wheat germ
1   cup walnut halves or chunks

Heat the milk and honey together until the honey is dissolved, then stir in the butter. When the milk and honey mixture is somewhat cooled, beat in the eggs.

Sift together the flours, baking powder, and salt. Add the wheat germ and gradually stir the dry mixture into the liquid. Stir in the walnuts, mix well, and turn into a buttered loaf pan.

Bake at 325 degrees for 1 hour.

cream scones

1 cup buttermilk
1 egg
2 Tbs. sugar
3½ cups unbleached white flour
2 tsp. baking powder
1 tsp. baking soda
½ tsp. salt
½ cup melted butter
⅓ cup currants

Beat together the buttermilk, egg, and sugar. Sift 3 cups of flour together with the baking powder, soda, and salt. Add about ⅔ of the flour mixture to the buttermilk and stir well. Gradually add the melted butter, incorporating it thoroughly into the mixture. Stir in the remaining flour mixture and the currants. A little more flour may be necessary to form a stiff dough.

Turn the dough out on a lightly floured board and knead for several minutes. Separate it into 3 equal parts. Shape each part into a thick circle about 4 to 5 inches across. Cut the circles into quarters with a sharp knife, and arrange the scones on a buttered cookie sheet. Bake in a preheated 400-degree oven for 20 to 25 minutes or until lightly browned on top. Serve warm with butter, preserves, honey, cheeses, and, above all, tea. (They are also delicious cold.)

12 scones.

popovers

3   eggs, beaten
1   cup milk
2   Tbs. melted butter
½   tsp. salt
1   tsp. sugar
1   cup unbleached white flour

Beat together the eggs, milk, melted butter, salt, and sugar. Beat in the flour, making the mixture perfectly smooth.

Butter muffin tins or custard cups. Fill the tins halfway with batter, or the custard cups ⅓ full. Place in a preheated 425-degree oven for 15 minutes, then reduce the heat to 350 degrees and bake another 15 to 20 minutes. Do not open the oven door during baking.

Popovers are best when served hot and fresh from the oven. They can be allowed to cool without falling though. Loosen them in the pan and tilt each one to its side, still sitting loosely in the cups. Pierce the sides with a sharp knife or skewer and leave them this way in the turned-off oven for about 10 minutes.

12 popovers.

hot herb bread

½   cup butter
1   Tbs. dried parsley, chopped
1   tsp. minced garlic
½   tsp. thyme
¼   tsp. powdered marjoram
1   long loaf fresh French bread

Let the butter soften, but do not melt it. With a spoon, work in the herbs until the mixture is smooth and well-blended.

Take a sharp bread knife and cut through the bread just to the bottom crust but not through it. Slice the whole loaf in this manner. Butter one side of each slice with the herb butter. Wrap the loaf tightly in foil and heat it in a medium-hot oven for about 15 minutes before serving.

corn bread

1¼ cups unbleached white flour
¾ cup whole-grain corn meal (stone-
      ground if possible)
4 Tbs. sugar
5 tsp. baking powder
¾ tsp. salt
1 egg
1 cup milk
2 Tbs. melted butter

When I first tried this recipe, I expected it to shoot right through the top of the stove from all that baking powder. It didn't, and I do recommend you try it because it is the most delicious corn bread I've ever eaten.

Sift together all the dry ingredients. Beat the egg with the milk and add it to the flour mixture along with the melted butter. Stir everything up well.

Spread the batter in a buttered 9-inch pie dish and bake in a preheated 375-degree oven for about 30 to 35 minutes, or until it is lightly browned around the edges.

Serve hot with butter.

Serves 4 to 6 generously—and that's the way you have to serve this bread.

soup

Good soups I hold in as high regard as great breads, and together they make some of life's sublime moments. Good soups always bring to my mind the romanticized image of the old world, which I fondly harbor against all reason: kitchens filled with the rich fragrances of foods prepared slowly and lovingly—before the time of instant, no-mess, no-fuss, no-meal packages.

A sure way to radically alter the atmosphere of your kitchen is this: find yourself a great soup kettle, four- or five-quart, at least. If it is an old one, so much the better. On a day when you plan to be at home, do one of the great all-day soups—maybe a bean soup or one which requires a special homemade broth. Tend it through the day as it simmers, and if you have the time and inclination, make some bread the same day. Now watch how your kitchen begins to acquire a soul. And at the end of the day, especially a cold one, warm your friends or family with a simple but rare meal; hearty soups need only a good bread and possibly a platter of cheeses or a salad as accompaniment.

Of course, there is a great variety of soups: hearty and delicate, long in preparation and short. If you are serving a number of dishes, seduce your dinner guests with a first course of some subtle and fragrant purée, elegantly garnished. For a pleasant summer dessert, serve a chilled fruit soup. Happily, any chilled soup and many hot soups can be prepared ahead of time.

potato peel broth *(also known as Garbage Soup)*

One of the most useful and delicious preparations I have found for the making of various soups is this hideous-sounding liquid. I never throw away a potato peel; if I don't have everything I need at the same time, I simply boil my potato peels in water and salt whenever they happen to come off the potatoes, and put away this potato water to complete the broth at another time.

peels from 6 to 7 large, healthy pota-
      toes
1   large onion
2   carrots
1   small stalk celery
1½ quarts water
a sprig of parsley
1   clove garlic (optional)
salt and pepper
MSG

Peel the potatoes, after washing them carefully, taking off strips at least ¼-inch thick. Peel the onion and quarter it, wash the carrots and celery, and cut them into large pieces. Put the potato peels and all the vegetables into a large pot with 1½ quarts of water, add a small sprig of parsley and, if you wish, a peeled clove of garlic. Simmer over a low flame for at least 1½ hours, or until all the vegetables are very soft. Add water as it evaporates, keeping everything covered. When the peels and vegetables are tender, either one of two courses may be taken: for a clear broth, simply drain off the liquid and correct the seasoning; for soups where the consistency of a very thin purée is desirable, remove the celery and garlic and press the rest through a sieve until only a dry pulp of peels remains.

Variations on this broth may be effected easily by the addition of various other vegetables, in small amounts, or by seasoning with herbs such as bay leaf or sweet basil. The basic broth should be fragrant, light brown in color, and delicious to the taste all by itself. It is used as the basis for several soups in this book, and you will no doubt find variations of your own.

This recipe makes about 6 cups.

garlic broth

Again—a very deceiving name, and a recipe that deserves some explanation. Garlic, the taste that terrorizes so many people when the pungent little bulb is raw, becomes gentle, delicate, even meek, when simmered slowly in a broth. The thought of using so much garlic all at once may give you pause. Bring together all your courage and do it, is my advice. This fragrant broth will probably become a staple in your kitchen as it has in mine.

fine, clear soup, serve the hot broth as is with some cooked noodles or rice. Fresh vegetables, such as thinly sliced carrots, sweet peas, cubed potatoes, or sliced zucchini may be added and simmered until tender for another soup. Try it also with little dumplings. This broth is excellent, of course, for sauces, risotto, cream soups, and many other recipes that call for consommé.

1½ qt. Potato Peel Broth (see preceding recipe)
1½ Tbs. olive oil
½ bay leaf
1 head garlic, broken into cloves and peeled (about 16 cloves)
¼ tsp. thyme
pinch of sage

Combine all ingredients and simmer slowly for 30 to 45 minutes. Discard the garlic cloves and the bay leaf.

The possibilities are now endless. For a

egg lemon soup

6 cups strong Potato Peel Broth (page 50) or Garlic Broth (page 51)
1 cup vegetable stock
salt and pepper
3 eggs
1 lemon
1½ cups cooked long-grain rice
lemon slices

Make a flavorful potato peel broth in the usual way, adding a little strained potato pulp if you wish. Add to this a cup of strong vegetable stock, or a spoonful of vegetable stock concentrate. (These commercial mixtures make questionable broths but excellent seasonings when used in moderation.) Finish the seasoning with salt, pepper, to your taste. Beat the eggs with the juice of one lemon. About 5 to 10 minutes before you want to serve the soup, add some of the hot broth to the beaten eggs—stirring vigorously—then return it to the pot, still stirring, and heat for a few minutes this way until the egg mixture is smoothly bound into the broth. Add the cooked rice and serve at once, garnishing each bowl with a paper-thin slice of lemon.

This will serve 6 and goes nicely with slices of black bread spread with dill butter. The bread and butter should be chilled.

spring vegetable soup

This is a very special soup. It requires the freshest, youngest vegetables: large, old string beans, peas that aren't really sweet, and great, gnarled carrots won't make this soup. Everything must be tender. The bell pepper and string beans must be cut into tiny pieces and the carrots sliced very thin. This soup has a marvelous, delicate fragrance and a slightly sweet taste. Serve it for a light supper with thick slices of homemade rye bread, followed by fruit and great cheeses.

3   cups Potato Peel Broth (page 50) or
      Garlic Broth (page 51)
2   medium carrots, sliced thin
½   cup fresh string beans, cut up
½   cup fresh sweet peas
½   onion, chopped fine
2   Tbs. butter
½   red bell pepper, chopped
the kernels from 1 fresh ear of corn
lemon rind, freshly grated
black pepper
salt
dill weed

Heat the potato peel broth in your kettle and add to it the carrots, string beans, and sweet peas. Let this simmer for 15 to 20 minutes; meanwhile, chop the onion and sauté it in the butter. After 15 to 20 minutes, add the bell pepper and corn to the soup. Let it simmer another 8 to 10 minutes—no more. Now add just a wee bit of freshly grated lemon rind—maybe ½ teaspoon—and the sautéed onions with the butter; grind in some black pepper, add a little salt if it's needed, and sprinkle in a small amount of dill weed. Let it all heat through for a few minutes and it is ready to serve.

Serves 4 to 5.

potage les deux champignons

3 cups light Potato Peel Broth (see page 50)
¾ lb. fresh mushrooms
3 Tbs. flour
3 Tbs. butter
1 cup heavy cream
2 Tbs. sherry
1 tsp. salt
pepper
parsley

Prepare potato peel broth, unless you have some on hand.

Actually, only one kind of mushroom is used in this soup, but a great interest in texture is derived from having some of the mushrooms cooked and some raw. So, wash them all carefully, set aside four or five for the garnish, and slice the rest.

Cook the mushrooms in the potato peel broth until they are very tender, then drain off the broth, which is now a very dark, aromatic mushroom stock. Slice the cooked mushrooms or liquefy them in a blender—anything between these two extremes in texture would be wrong.

Make a Velouté, following the method on page 83, from the mushroom stock, using 3 tablespoons of flour and 3 tablespoons of butter. Let it cook about 10 to 15 minutes, stirring often, then stir in the cream and the sherry, season with salt and freshly ground black pepper, and add a little chopped parsley. Add the sliced or liquefied mushrooms and let it all heat through. Slice thinly the whole, raw mushrooms which you set aside at the start of this operation, and float several of these slices on each bowl of steaming hot soup. Pass a pepper grinder.

This recipe makes 4 to 5 servings of a very intriguing soup.

corn chowder

1 very large potato or 2 small potatoes
salted water
½ onion, chopped
2 Tbs. butter
1¾ cup fresh corn kernels (about 3
    ears)
½ cup thin-sliced, fresh pimiento
2 cups milk
½ cup light cream
salt and pepper
paprika
1 Tbs. brown sugar
pinch of thyme

Peel the potatoes as thinly as possible
and dice into ½-inch cubes. Cook them
in salted water to cover for about 20
minutes, while sautéing the onion in
butter. When the potatoes are barely
tender, add all the remaining ingredients,
and simmer another 20 to 30 minutes,
stirring occasionally. The soup should be
slightly thickened and delicate in flavor.
Serve it very hot with Black Bread (see
page 41) or French garlic bread.

Serves 4 to 6.

barszcz (*Clear Borscht*)

4 to 5 small beets
1½ qt. Potato Peel Broth (see page
    50)
2 or more cups mushroom stock (from
    black mushrooms cooked for
    uszki) (see page 56)
2 Tbs. lemon juice
1 to 2 Tbs. sugar
salt and pepper
a few drops of wine vinegar (optional)

Wash the beets and cut off the greens
about 3 inches from the bulb—do not peel!
Boil them this way for about 30 to 45
minutes, or until just tender enough to
slip off the skins; take the skins off, holding the beets under cold running water
to do it. Cut the beets into julienne strips
and put them in the broth, together with
the strained mushroom stock. Season to
taste with lemon juice and a little sugar—
also salt, black pepper, and perhaps a few
drops of vinegar. Simmer for about 10 to
15 minutes to bind flavors. Serve in large,
shallow soup bowls with 4 to 5 hot *uszki*
in each bowl. Serves 8.

uszki *(Tiny Mushroom-Stuffed Dumplings for Barszcz)*

Filling:

½ lb. dried black mushrooms
1 whole yellow onion
6 Tbs. butter
salt
¼ oz. fresh mushrooms
1 to 2 slices dark bread
1 onion, finely chopped
seeds from 3 pods cardamom
good pinch dried thyme
1 tsp. dried dill
½ tsp. MSG
fresh-ground black pepper

Dough:

3½ to 4 cups flour
1 tsp. salt
2 eggs
1 cup water

Filling: Simmer the dark mushrooms in a quart or more of water together with the whole onion, 1 tablespoon butter, and some salt for about 1 hour. Drain, reserving the stock, and discard onion. Now wash the mushrooms very carefully and thoroughly until every speck of dirt and grit is gone. Strain the broth through muslin, until it is perfectly clear.

Put the mushrooms through the food chopper—with the fine blade—then put through the fresh mushrooms and finally the bread.

Melt 5 tablespoons butter in a large skillet. Add to it the cardamom seeds and thyme. After a few minutes, add the chopped onion and sauté it until it is soft. Add the ground mushroom mixture, the dill and MSG, salt, and lots of freshly ground black pepper. Sauté the whole mixture for 15 to 20 minutes, stirring very often, and add a few spoons of the mushroom stock if it seems too dry. The consistency should be about that of cooked oatmeal—a thick but moist mixture.

Dough: Mix the flour with the salt. Beat the eggs with the water and stir into the flour. Add a little more water, if necessary, to make a dough that is smooth but fairly stiff. Knead it awhile in the bowl with your hand—it will be sticky, so use a spoon to push it back when you squeeze it. Don't get both hands caught in it at once or you will never get loose!

Flour a large board and dump half the dough at a time in the middle of it. Sprinkle with more flour and start rolling it out, adding flour as necessary to keep it from sticking.

Roll it out as thinly as possible, less than ⅛-inch thick and *even*. Cut the dough into 2-inch squares. Place a spoonful of the filling in each square, and fold it over to make a triangle. Press the edges together very firmly, moistening with a little water if necessary. Now bring the two ends up to the center, give one a half-turn, and press them together. Sauté the *uszki* in butter until they are all deep golden brown on both sides—this much can be done ahead of time. Arrange them close together on a large baking sheet. Just before serving, put them in the oven at 325 degrees for about 15 minutes.

This recipe makes between 75 and 100 *uszki,* which is enough for about 15 serv-ings, theoretically. You must, however, count on people wanting a second portion. *Uszki* are also delicious reheated, served as an accompaniment to salad, or by themselves as hors d'oeuvres or first course.

This is a long trip, making *uszki*—it can take nearly a full day by itself, unless you are very light-handed. However time-consuming, though, this is a fail-safe recipe. Unlike many other great gourmet traditions, if you use the proper ingredients and follow directions carefully, this one can hardly go wrong.

corn and cheddar cheese chowder

1   large potato, peeled and diced
2   cups boiling salted water
1   bay leaf
¼   tsp. dried sage
½   tsp. cumin seeds
3   Tbs. butter
1   onion, finely chopped
3   Tbs. flour
1¼ cups heavy cream
kernels from 2 ears of corn
½   tsp. Bakon yeast (not a meat prod-
        uct)
chopped chives and parsley
¼   tsp. nutmeg
salt and pepper
1½ cups sharp Cheddar cheese, grated
        (4 oz.)
4 to 5 Tbs. dry white wine

Peel and dice the potato and boil it in the salted water with the bay leaf, sage, and cumin seeds until just barely tender— about 15 to 20 minutes. Melt the butter in a saucepan and sauté the chopped onion in it for a while; then add the flour. Mix well and add the cream, stirring with a whisk. Pour this sauce into the potatoes and their water, adding also the fresh corn kernels. Add the Bakon yeast, the chopped herbs, and the rest of the seasonings and let the soup simmer gently for about 10 minutes. Then stir in the grated cheese and the wine and mix well; heat until the cheese is completely melted, correct the seasoning, and serve.

This is a wonderful, hearty soup, recommended for cold nights and hungry people.

This recipe serves 4 to 6.

pea soup with butter dumplings

Soup:

4   cups shelled peas (about 4 lbs. fresh,
        unshelled)
4½ cups water
1   tsp. brown sugar
salt and fresh-ground black pepper
½   cup light Rhine wine
4½ Tbs. butter
4½ Tbs. flour

Dumplings:

6   Tbs. butter
2   eggs
½   cup flour
¼   tsp. nutmeg
salt

Soup: Cook the peas in the water and sugar until they are quite soft, about ½ hour. Then press the soup through a sieve or put it in the blender for a few moments. Season this thin purée with salt and pepper and stir in the wine.

Melt the butter in a skillet and stir in the flour. Let the roux cook over a very low flame for a few minutes, stirring constantly. Then stir in a cup or two of the soup and whisk until smooth. Return the thickened soup to the rest and blend well.

Dumplings: To make the batter, soften the butter as much as possible, short of melting it. Beat the eggs with the flour and beat in the butter. Season with salt and nutmeg. Drop the batter into gently boiling soup by half-teaspoons. When the dumplings have risen to the top, they will need 5 more minutes before they are done.

Serves 5 to 6.

potato soup

5   large russet potatoes, peeled and
       diced
3 to 4 leeks
3½ to 4 cups water (enough to keep it
       all covered)
1½ cups milk or cream
½   tsp. caraway seeds
2   Tbs. dill weed
1   tsp. salt
fresh-ground pepper
2 to 3 Tbs. sour cream
butter
garnish: chopped chives, parsley, or
       more dill (optional)

Peel the potatoes and use the peels for a potato peel broth—never throw them away! Wash the leeks and chop them up well, discarding the tough green ends. Cook these vegetables in the salted water about ½ hour, or until they are tender. Add the milk, caraway seeds, dill, and salt and pepper to taste. Let the soup simmer another 15 to 20 minutes, or until it begins to take on a rather thick consistency and the potatoes begin to fall apart a little. Now stir in a few tablespoons of sour cream and a tablespoon or two of butter; let it all heat through, and serve. You may garnish this soup with chopped chives, parsley, or more dill. It is a good, hearty soup. Louis, my paramour and unofficial taster, is a true connoisseur of potato dishes, and he finds it supremely wonderful.

This recipe makes enough for 4 to 6 servings.

minestrone

1½ qt. Garlic Broth (see page 51)
2   medium potatoes
3   carrots
3   small zucchini
5 to 6 tomatoes, firm and ripe
3 to 4 Tbs. olive oil
1   small onion
½   tsp. dried sage
1   tsp. dried basil
pinch of oregano and parsley
½   cup cooked peas or kidney beans
handful of broken spaghetti
salt and pepper
grated Parmesan cheese

Prepare garlic broth, as indicated on page 51, if you haven't some on hand.

Peel the potatoes and cut into fairly large cubes. Scrape and thickly slice the carrots. Wash and slice the zucchini. Scald the tomatoes, peel them, and cut into large pieces.

Heat the olive oil in a large kettle and add the onion, potatoes, and carrots. Sauté these vegetables for a few minutes, until the onion is soft, then add the garlic stock and herbs. Bring it to a boil, lower heat, and gently simmer for 15 minutes. Add the zucchini, part of the tomatoes, and the peas or beans. Simmer another 15 minutes. Add a little broken spaghetti, the rest of the tomatoes, season with salt and pepper and cook only until the pasta is *al dente*, another 12 to 15 minutes. Serve hot, and pass a bowl of grated Parmesan cheese.

6 to 8 servings.

minestrone alla milanese

This recipe makes enough soup for at least a dozen people, maybe more. Cut all amounts in half for a smaller group, or make it all and freeze half for another day. It is a meal in itself, served with just a good bread and cheese and fruit.

1½ cups dried kidney beans
3 to 4 cloves garlic
1   large onion, chopped
5   Tbs. olive oil
3   large potatoes, pale and clean-
        skinned
2   carrots
5 to 6 medium zucchini
1 to 1½ cups cut string beans
3 to 4 medium leeks, sliced (about
        ½ cup)
salt and pepper to taste
fresh parsley, chopped
large pinch of celery seeds
1 to 2 tsp. basil
1   tsp. oregano
large pinch of marjoram
½   head savoy cabbage
½   cup long-grain rice

6 to 7 tomatoes
1   cup grated Parmesan
3 to 4 Tbs. butter

Soak the beans overnight in enough water to keep them covered, then drain them and put them in a giant kettle (2-gallon, or larger) with 4 quarts of water. Add the garlic cloves, peeled and put through a press, the onion, and the olive oil. Simmer the beans for about 1½ hours.

Choose 3 large potatoes with healthy skins and scrub them thoroughly under running water. Cut them into large pieces, without peeling, and add them to the pot. Slice the carrots and zucchini thickly and add them also, together with the cut string beans and sliced leeks. Season with some salt and pepper, a little chopped parsley, a good pinch of celery seed, some basil, oregano, and a pinch of marjoram. Simmer again for about 45 minutes.

Slice thinly half a small head of savoy

cabbage and add it to the soup along with the rice. If you can get the large, beautiful rice of the Lombardy region of Italy, you will truly have Minestrone alla Milanese. After adding the rice, simmer the soup another 20 minutes. If it is getting too thick for your taste, add a little more water as needed.

About 5 minutes before the soup is ready to serve, add the tomatoes (cut into large wedges), the Parmesan cheese, butter, and a little more fresh parsley.

Serve steaming hot with a good bread and more Parmesan cheese if desired.

lentil-tomato soup

A hearty and nutritious soup—high in protein—that does not take long to make and tastes as though it took all day.

⅔ cup dried lentils
4 cups water
1 onion, chopped
4 carrots, chopped
2 stalks celery, chopped
a few Baco-bits (optional)
1 cup tomato paste
chopped parsley
garlic
salt and pepper
thyme
dill weed
tarragon
dry white wine (optional)

Put the first 6 ingredients into a large pot and simmer gently for about 3 hours, replenishing the water as needed. If you have a taste for it, try adding a little dry white wine. Then, tasting to see what quantity is right for you, add very small amounts of the herbs and spices.

Finally, stir in a cup of tomato paste and let it all heat through. 6 servings.

blonde lentil soup

3   stalks celery, cut in large pieces
5   medium carrots, sliced thick
MSG
5   cups water
1   onion, peeled and quartered

Make a broth by combining the above ingredients and cooking until vegetables are very tender; then discard the celery and onion. Put the carrots through a sieve and return them to the broth.

1   onion, chopped
3   shallots, minced
2 to 3 cloves garlic, minced
2   Tbs. butter
1   tsp. lemon rind, grated
1   bay leaf
1   cup dried Champagne lentils (blonde)
juice of 1 lemon
sweet basil
salt and pepper

Sauté the onion, shallots, and garlic in the butter. When the onions begin to turn brown, add them to the broth along with the lemon rind, bay leaf, and lentils. Let it cook for about 40 to 60 minutes, adding water to maintain the same consistency. Now add the freshly squeezed lemon juice, a little crushed sweet basil, and season with salt and pepper to taste. Let it simmer another 20 minutes or so and serve.

This is a soup with a rather exotic taste—delicious and high in protein. Enough for 4 good servings.

lentil soup creole

1   cup lentils
2   qt. boiling water
1½ tsp. salt
1   onion
1   stalk celery
1   small, green bell pepper
1   sweet red bell pepper
3   Tbs. butter
½ tsp. Bakon yeast
1   tsp. vegetable broth powder
1   tsp. brown sugar
bay leaf
4 to 5 Tbs. catsup or tomato purée
2   Tbs. flour
fresh-ground black pepper

Douse the lentils with the boiling water, add the salt and let them stand, covered, about an hour. Chop the onion, the celery stalk, and the bell peppers (you should have approximately 1½ cups bell peppers when they are chopped). Melt 3 tablespoons butter in a saucepan and add to it the Bakon yeast and vegetable broth powder. Add the diced vegetables, brown sugar, and a bay leaf, and sauté for a few minutes before adding it all to the lentils.

Cook over a very low flame for about 1½ hours. Mix together the flour and the catsup (or tomato purée). Add a little of the hot soup to this, stirring well, then return it all to the pot. Grind in some black pepper, heat through, and serve.

6 to 8 servings.

savory pepper soup

1   cup peppers, finely chopped
2   lb. ripe tomatoes
1   onion, chopped
1½ cups water
3   Tbs. butter
3   Tbs. flour
½ tsp. powdered lemon peel or 1½ tsp.
      fresh, grated lemon peel
salt and black pepper
1   cup cooked brown rice
sour cream
fresh dill or parsley

Pick out an assortment of small and medium sized hot peppers—yellow ones, orange ones, red, and green. Ten to twelve peppers should be enough. Wash them, cut them open, and discard all the seeds and pulp, unless you want a truly fiery soup. Chop the rest very finely. You should have a full cup of minced peppers.

Scald the tomatoes and peel them. Chop the onion. Now, the fast method is to put all the vegetables in the blender and purée them, then add the water and simmer the mixture for about 20 minutes. If you have no blender, chop the tomatoes, put all the vegetables in a pot with the water, and simmer until they are very soft and falling apart. At this point press the mixture through a sieve.

Melt the butter in a small saucepan and stir in the flour to make a roux. Cook it awhile, stirring always, and then pour in some of the heated soup. Whisk it to make a smooth sauce, pour it back into the soup and, stirring occasionally, continue to simmer very gently for another 10 minutes. Add the lemon peel, grind in fresh black pepper and add salt to taste. Stir in a cup of cooked brown rice, heat through, and the soup is ready.

Pour it steaming hot into bowls, and in the center of each one place a large spoonful of smooth, thick sour cream. Sprinkle on a little chopped fresh dill or parsley, and serve.

Serves about 4 people.

garbanzo bean soup

2   cups dried beans
salt
½ tsp. dried rosemary
3   Tbs. olive oil
3   cloves garlic, put through a press
3   Tbs. chopped onion (about ½ of a
       smallish onion)
2   Tbs. diced green chili (canned
       Ortega chilis are fine)
1   Tbs. Worcestershire sauce
3 to 4 Tbs. tomato paste
fresh-ground black pepper
1   cup shell macaroni

Soak the beans overnight, in enough water to keep them covered. The next day, add some salt and the rosemary, as well as more water if it's needed, and simmer for 2 to 3 hours, until the beans are tender.

Heat the olive oil in a small saucepan and add to it the crushed garlic and chopped onion. When the onion is transparent, stir in the diced green chili, the Worcestershire sauce, and tomato paste. Add this sauce to the beans and their liquid, and season with plenty of fresh-ground black pepper and some more salt if it's needed.

Add a little more water—just enough to make room for the macaroni. When it is simmering, pour in the macaroni and continue cooking until it is tender, another 20 minutes or so. Serve steaming hot with French bread.

Serves 6 to 8.

onion soup

1 qt. clear Potato Peel Broth (see page
    50)
4 large Spanish onions
5 oz. butter
2 cups water
1 small piece of bay leaf
¼ tsp. thyme (dried)
1 to 2 tsp. lemon juice
1 to 2 Tbs. brandy
salt and fresh-ground black pepper
sliced French bread
grated Gruyère cheese

Make potato peel broth, as described on page 50, if you haven't some already on hand.

Cut the onions into quarters and slice them. Sauté these slices in the butter very gently until they are very tender and golden. Pour over them the broth and water, the herbs, lemon juice, and brandy. Season with salt and pepper and let simmer slowly another ½ to 1 hour. The liquid will reduce slightly.

Just before serving: pour the hot soup into 1 large casserole or 6 individual ones. Top it with slices of French bread (one for each serving) and sprinkle over the toast an ample amount of grated Gruyère cheese. Bake the soup in a hot oven for 15 minutes, then serve immediately.

6 servings.

chestnut soup

1½ qt. rich soup stock (Potato Peel or
    Garlic Broth with vegetable sea-
    soning added—see page 50 or 51)
2   lbs. fresh chestnuts
3   Tbs. butter
3   Tbs. flour
⅓ cup red table wine
¼ cup brandy
salt and pepper
nutmeg
cayenne pepper
paprika

Make the stock as described on page 50
or 51, if you haven't some on hand.

Cut a cross in each chestnut with a knife
and put them in the oven to roast for
about 15 to 20 minutes at 375 degrees.
Chestnuts are ready when they can be
pierced easily with a skewer.

Peel the chestnuts and put them through
the food grinder with a fine blade.

Add the chestnuts to the soup stock and
simmer slowly for about ½ hour. In another pot, make a roux of the butter and
flour. Add the hot soup slowly, stirring
with a whisk until it is all well blended.
Add the brandy and wine, and season to
taste with salt, fresh-ground black pepper, and nutmeg. Add a pinch of cayenne,
if you are adventurous.

Let the soup simmer another 10 minutes
or so, stirring it often. When you serve
the soup, sprinkle a little paprika over
each serving. Very crisp croutons may be
passed in a separate bowl.

Serves 6.

creamed artichoke soup

2 cups hot vegetable broth (from
   cubes or powder)
8 oz. artichoke bottoms (drained
   weight)
¼ tsp. prepared mustard
3 tsp. lemon juice
garlic
salt and pepper
3 Tbs. flour
3 Tbs. butter
1 cup milk or light cream

Prepare some vegetable broth from cubes or powder, if you haven't some on hand.

Before you begin, you must know that for this soup you can use only the finest artichoke bottoms, smooth as molded custard. Old, rough bottoms are worthless, so pay the higher price, even though it may astonish you.

If you insist on using fresh artichokes for this recipe, you will need the bottoms of 10 to 11 large, cooked artichokes. If, like me, you prefer to go the jar route (in this case), wash the bottoms carefully in cool water to remove the strong taste of brine, then chop them and heat them with a few drops of water until they are soft. Pass them through a sieve and season the purée with the mustard, lemon juice, a little grating of garlic, and some salt and pepper.

Make a roux with the butter and flour and let it cook a few minutes. Add the 2 cups of hot vegetable broth, which should be lightly seasoned and delicate (broth from a powder is fine for this), and stir with a whisk until the sauce is smooth. Cook this Velouté for about 10 minutes, then stir it into the purée. Thin the soup with a cup of milk or light cream, correct the seasoning, and heat through. The soup should be served very hot and slivers of additional cooked artichoke hearts may be added in modest quantity.

This recipe is enough for 4 very discriminating gourmets.

asparagus soup

4½ to 5 cups strong Potato Peel Broth
  (thickened) (see page 50)
1½ lb. asparagus, cooked
1½ cups asparagus juice (from cooking)
½ cup light cream
2 to 3 egg yolks
salt and pepper

Start with 4½ to 5 cups of flavorful potato peel broth. If it is weak, use more and simmer slowly to reduce it until you have a good concentration of flavor. Add to this broth 1½ cups of the liquid in which the asparagus was cooked, or the liquid from the cans if you can't get fresh asparagus. Put half the asparagus through a sieve and add it to the broth. Also press through the sieve enough of the potato peels from the broth to make ½ cup purée.

Mix the potato purée well with the cream and egg yolks. Add a small amount of the hot soup to this mixture, whisking it to bind in the egg yolks; then return it all to the pot and continue to stir with the whisk for a few minutes as it simmers on a low flame. Season with salt and pepper, add the remaining asparagus spears cut into pieces, heat through, and serve.

This recipe makes approximately 6 servings.

creamed tomato soup with cognac

3   lb. ripe red tomatoes (15 to 16
        medium tomatoes)
1   large onion
3   oz. butter
sweet basil leaves
1   pint rich cream
1   tsp. brown sugar
4 to 5 Tbs. cognac
salt and pepper

Scald the tomatoes and slip them out of their skins. Cut them coarsely and pound them in a bowl. Chop up the onion. Melt the butter in a large soup pot; add the onions when it begins to turn brown. Stir them around a little and then add the tomatoes and about 1 teaspoonful of crushed sweet basil leaves. Let this mixture simmer about ½ hour, then put it through a sieve until only some dry onion and seed pulp is left to discard. Heat this mixture through.

In another pot, heat the cream with the sugar until it is ready to boil. Stirring quickly with a wire whisk, pour the heated cream into the soup, which *must not* be boiling. Now add the cognac, season well with salt and pepper, and the soup is ready to serve.

It is especially nice if you can serve a hot loaf of homemade French bread with it, or thin slices of buttered pumpernickel.

6 servings.

tomato soup supreme

1½ qt. Garlic Broth (see page 51)
1   tsp. crushed sweet basil
12 oz. pure tomato paste
¼   cup cognac
1   cup light cream
¼   cup condensed milk
2   Tbs. brown sugar
1   Tbs. lemon juice
1   Tbs. Worcestershire sauce
¼   cup butter
¼   cup flour
fresh parsley, chopped

Prepare garlic broth as described on page 51.

Add the basil to the broth and simmer it slowly until it is reduced to 1 quart. Then add the tomato paste, cognac, cream, and condensed milk. Stir until everything is perfectly blended, and simmer very gently for a short while. Season with brown sugar, lemon juice, and Worcestershire sauce.

In a medium skillet, heat the butter until it bubbles, and stir in the flour. Cook this roux over a very low flame for a few minutes. Then add some of the hot soup and stir with a whisk until you have a smooth sauce. Pour it back into the soup, stir again with the whisk, and heat gently without bringing to a boil.

Sprinkle with parsley and serve hot.

4 to 6 servings.

dill soup

thick peels of 5 to 6 potatoes
2 carrots
2 stalks celery
1 onion
2 eggs
¾ cup sour cream
½ cup chopped fresh dill weed
salt
peppercorns

1 carrot
½ stalk celery
½ small onion (optional)
salt and pepper
cream (optional)
2 eggs
¾ cup sour cream
½ cup chopped fresh dill weed or ¼ cup dried dill weed

Take the thick peels of 5 to 6 potatoes, 2 whole carrots, and 2 stalks of celery, cut in large pieces, and 1 onion, quartered. Cover with water in a large pot, about 1½ to 2 quarts. Add some salt and a few peppercorns, and let it simmer slowly about 2 hours. Replenish the water if it cooks down too much. When the vegetables are very tender, discard half the carrots, most of the celery, and about half the onion. Press the rest through a sieve until only the skin pulp is left.

Or:

1½ qt. Potato Peel Broth (see page 50)
1 whole potato

If you are starting with a potato peel broth, already made, add to it 1 whole potato, unpeeled and cut into pieces, 1 small carrot, and half a celery stalk, both also cut up. If you like, add half a small onion and let this simmer for an hour or two, then press it all through a sieve.

Proceed with either one or the other of these two purées. Season well with salt and pepper and, if it seems too thick for your taste, thin it with a little cream. Mix 2 beaten eggs with about ¾ cup sour cream and about ½ cup finely minced fresh dill weed, or ¼ cup dried dill weed. Add some of the hot purée to this mixture slowly, stirring all the while, until you have poured in about 2 cups. Now return it all to the pot, stir well as it heats through, and serve. Be careful not to let it boil after you have added the eggs and sour cream.

This soup is delicious hot and fantastic cold. If you are serving it hot, you may want to have a bowl of hot, crisp croutons alongside. If it is a hot day and the soup is to be served chilled, very thin slices of unpeeled cucumber in each plate do nicely as a garnish.

This makes about 5 to 6 servings.

gazpacho

1 small onion, chopped
1 large cucumber—peeled, seeded,
     and sliced
1 small bell pepper, seeded and diced
3 tomatoes, peeled and diced
3 eggs
⅓ cup olive oil
¼ cup vinegar
1 cup tomato juice
1 to 2 cloves garlic
2 Tbs. lemon juice
2 Tbs. brown sugar
¼ tsp. cayenne pepper
salt
1 tsp. dill weed
2 Tbs. prepared mayonnaise
4 to 5 large sprigs watercress

Garnish:
1 large, firm tomato
1 bell pepper
1 cucumber
croutons (optional)
watercress sprigs

Here's an odd Gazpacho: it's heated before it's chilled; the eggs set slightly, and
the soup is much thicker and altogether
more interesting for it.

Begin by puréeing all the vegetables in
a blender, together with the eggs, oil,
vinegar and tomato juice. (You may have
to do half at a time, depending on the
size of your blender container). Add all
the remaining ingredients except the
mayonnaise and watercress and empty it
into a pot. Heat very slowly, stirring constantly with a wire whisk, and simmer the
mixture this way for no longer than 2 to
3 minutes. Take it off the heat and continue stirring with the whisk occasionally
as it cools. Add the mayonnaise and put
back in the blender—at high speed—for
a very short time. Pour into a tureen or
serving bowl and chill. Sprinkle the
chopped watercress leaves over the top
before serving.

In a separate bowl, pass the garnishes: a
firm red tomato, coarsely chopped; a bell
pepper, coarsely chopped; a cucumber,
seeded (but not peeled) and cut into
cubes; possibly croutons sautéed in olive
oil; and more watercress leaves.

Serves 4 to 6.

iced cucumber soup

6 large cucumbers
1½ qt. water
3 Tbs. butter
3 Tbs. milk
3 Tbs. white corn meal
salt and pepper
½ cup finely chopped fresh chervil
or 3 Tbs. crushed dried chervil
1½ cups cream

Peel the cucumbers, cut them into 6 or 7 pieces, and put them in a pot of boiling water. Let them cook for about 15 to 20 minutes, or until they are soft enough to be mashed. Drain off the water and reserve it. Press the cucumbers through a sieve and discard the seeds.

To the cucumber purée add 1 cup of the reserved water and the butter. Let this mixture heat until it begins to simmer; meanwhile moisten the corn meal in the same amount of milk. Add the corn meal to the soup and, stirring often, let it cook another 15 or 20 minutes. Take it off the heat, add the chervil, cream, and salt and pepper to taste.

Chill the soup well before serving.

4 to 6 servings.

almond soup

2 cups blanched almonds
3 Tbs. butter
1 medium onion
grated peel of 1 or 2 lemons
peppercorns
seeds from 2 to 3 cardamom pods
½ tsp. caraway seeds
salt
1 cup heavy cream
½ cup long-grain, white rice
⅓ cup currants
1 pimiento pepper
1 cup small dark croutons, well toasted

For this soup, a blender is almost a necessity. Combine the almonds with about a quart of water (you may want to do half at a time) and blend at a high speed for a few minutes. The almonds should be rather finely ground and the water very milky. Pour the almonds and their liquid into a saucepan and heat gently.

Chop the onion and sauté it in the butter. When it begins to brown, add both butter and onion to the almond mixture. Add also the grated lemon rind, some whole peppercorns, the cardamom seeds, and the caraway seeds. Cover and simmer very gently for about 1 hour, stirring occasionally.

Press the mixture through a fine sieve, reserving the liquid, then return the pulp to the saucepan and add 3 cups of hot water. Simmer again for 1 hour, and once more press through the sieve.

Discard the dry pulp.

Season the almond stock with a little salt, and add the cream. This much can be prepared ahead.

About 20 minutes before serving, add the rice and the currants. Simmer the soup, covered, while preparing the garnish. Cut a fresh pimiento pepper into slivers, discarding the seeds and white pulp. Sauté these slivers, along with a cup of small, dark croutons, in a little butter or olive oil.

When the rice is just tender, ladle the hot soup into bowls and sprinkle over each one some crisp sautéed croutons and pimiento. Serves 4 to 6.

herb croutons

1 Tbs. thyme
2 Tbs. finely chopped dried parsley
1 clove garlic
salt and pepper to taste
¼ cup softened butter or Ghee (page 254)
8 to 12 slices stale brown bread

In a mortar, crush together the herbs, salt and pepper, and garlic until well blended. Mix them with the butter or ghee (clarified butter) and spread thinly on both sides of the bread slices. Cut the bread into cubes, arrange them on a baking sheet, and toast in the oven for about 15 to 20 minutes, tossing around occasionally so all sides are crisp. Serve hot with split-pea soup or other purées.

These may also be frozen for later use. Simply take them out and toast them again in the oven for about 10 minutes whenever you need them.

sauces

There is not a cuisine anywhere in which saucemaking does not figure largely. If any one thing can elevate one's cooking from edible menus to a magnificent repertoire of seductive dishes, it is the art of the sauce. The humble omelet becomes the basis for an endless parade of exquisite dishes simply by its combination with various sauces. It is the very sauce, "holding its breath," which creates the ethereal soufflé. From a variety of creamy sauces, the recipes for fascinating tarts and pastries are born. And so on, from the simplest garnish to the sauce which is itself the whimsical and savory body of the meal: the fondue.

With sauces, however, as with all fine things, employ delicacy in preparation and discretion in use. Better almost not to sauce at all than to oversauce. There are certain rich foods with which sauces would be too much. There are vegetables which, when they are young and fresh from the garden, are so happily flavorful and friendly in texture that they require only melted butter and some select herbs.

As to the making of sauces, it does require at times a delicate hand and a watchful eye, but, with a little concentration, any of us can easily have at least one of each. The basic formula for most sauces is simple enough: make a roux from equal amounts of butter and flour, and add to it those liquids and flavorings which determine your sauce. It is the method of doing this which is critical.

For prime results with the least risk, make your roux over hot water in a double boiler (or an improvised bowl on a pan of water). This very gentle heat allows you to cook it until the raw taste of the flour is gone without burning it. The liquid you will stir in should first be heated and, as you slowly pour it in, you should be stirring constantly. If egg yolks have been added to a sauce, do not allow it to boil for it will quickly reward you by curdling. The safest way to avoid trouble is to add a little of the hot sauce to the eggs first, then a little bit more, before you put the eggs into the sauce; but still be careful about not letting the sauce boil up again.

The sauces made with a roux are the Veloutés and the Béchamels. The second main category of sauce which figures in vegetarian cookery is the purée. These are sauces based on cooked vegetables or fruits, and range in texture from the true purée—a fine, creamlike preparation—to the hearty sauce which retains in part the individual textures of its ingredients. It is these sauces which so often fill the famous French omelets, and grace many pastas.

Finally, there are sweet sauces, marinades, and salad dressings. Master them, and you will be able to consistently prepare delightful and impressive meals from simple ingredients.

sauce velouté

This is an adaptation of the classic Velouté, and it works very well indeed. The secret is a delicious vegetable stock, spiked with a little mushroom and lemon flavor.

2½ cups strong, hot vegetable stock
4 to 5 peppercorns
3 to 4 dried dark mushrooms
squeeze of lemon juice
3 Tbs. butter
3 Tbs. flour
grated onion
salt
ground pepper

Heat the stock, adding to it the peppercorns, the carefully washed mushrooms (fresh mushrooms can be substituted, but you must use twice as many), and a few drops of lemon juice. Let it simmer, covered, for about 10 or 15 minutes, then strain through a cheesecloth. In the top of a double boiler, heat the butter and add the flour to make a light roux. After a few minutes, add a little grated onion and the hot stock, stirring with a whisk. Salt and grind in more pepper to taste. After it begins to thicken, the sauce should cook very gently another 10 minutes or so, then be strained through a sieve.

This sauce may be used as the basis for a number of variations.

enriched velouté

2 cups (approximately) Velouté (see above)
lemon juice
2 egg yolks
1 cup cream

Make a Velouté, seasoning it with a little extra lemon juice. To 1 cup of cream, add 2 lightly beaten egg yolks, and stir with a whisk as you gradually add the hot Velouté.

sauce béchamel

3 Tbs. butter
3 Tbs. flour
½ onion, minced
2½ cups hot milk
peppercorns
thyme
1 tiny bay leaf
salt
grated nutmeg

In the top of a double boiler heat the butter until bubbly. Add the finely chopped onion, and let it cook over very low heat for 3 or 4 minutes—stir in the flour and continue cooking a few minutes more, then begin adding the milk. Pour in the milk bit by bit and stir with a whisk while you do. The sauce will begin to thicken after a few minutes. Add a few peppercorns, some thyme, and a very small bay leaf or a piece of one. Sprinkle in a little salt and nutmeg, let it cook slowly for 10 to 15 minutes, then strain through a sieve.

Béchamel is the basic white sauce, and countless subtle (and strong) variations can be executed with it by the addition of particular herbs, spices, cheeses, and other ingredients. It will keep in the refrigerator in a tightly covered jar for a few days, but it is not recommended that you attempt to store it longer than that.

sauce mornay

2   cups (approximately) Velouté (see page 83) strongly flavored with mushrooms
½   onion, finely chopped
2   oz. Gruyère cheese, grated
1   Tbs. grated Parmesan
2   Tbs. butter
2   egg yolks
½   cup cream

Make the Velouté, using a stock very strongly flavored with mushrooms. Add the chopped onion, the grated cheeses and the butter. Cook at least five minutes, then strain. Stir the lightly beaten egg yolks into the cream and add it to the sauce. Beat the entire mixture with a whisk.

A Mornay sauce may also be made using Béchamel as the base. The Mornay made with Béchamel is paler, more delicate in flavor, and somewhat richer. Either sauce can be used on omelets, soufflés, and vegetables.

tomato and chili sauce

1   lb. tomatoes, peeled
2 to 3 Tbs. diced green chili pepper
½   onion
1   clove garlic
2 to 3 Tbs. olive oil
8 to 10 green olives, chopped
oregano
salt and fresh-ground black pepper

Put the tomatoes and chilis in a blender and blend for a moment only, or chop together the tomatoes and chilis. Chop the onion and mince the garlic. Heat the olive oil in a skillet and sauté the onion and garlic in it until transparent. Add the tomatoes, chilis, and olives.

Heat the sauce over a medium flame. Season with a little oregano, and salt and pepper to taste. Stir often. The sauce is ready after 8 to 10 minutes.

Serve on cheese pudding, omelets, or enchiladas.

Makes about 2½ to 3 cups of sauce.

sauce aurore

Béchamel (with more bay leaf) (see
    page 84)
2 bay leaves
2 cloves garlic
2 to 3 Tbs. tomato paste
a little red wine
powdered marjoram

Prepare Béchamel sauce according to the recipe, with this adjustment: crush 2 cloves of garlic into the butter when you melt it, and add 2 bay leaves. Sauté these herbs gently for a few minutes, then remove the bay leaves. Proceed according to the recipe, replacing the bay leaves when the milk is added.

When the Béchamel is ready, stir into it 2 to 3 tablespoons thick tomato paste, 1 or 2 tablespoons red table wine, and a good pinch of powdered marjoram. Stir with a whisk, heat for a few minutes more, and serve. Like Béchamel, this sauce can be stored for two or three days in a tightly covered container in the refrigerator, and should be reheated carefully in the top of a double boiler. It is delicious with steamed fresh vegetables and may be substituted for Béchamel in many recipes. Try Baked Walnut and Cheddar Balls Béchamel (page 199) with this sauce.

creamed black mushroom sauce

2½ to 3 oz. dried black mushrooms
3   cups water
8   small boiling onions
5   Tbs. butter
2   cups strong vegetable broth
3   Tbs. flour
1   cup cream
2   Tbs. good sherry
salt and pepper

Put the mushrooms in a pot with the water before you wash them and let them simmer gently, covered, for about ½ hour. Drain off the water and pour it through a fine sieve lined with cheesecloth, to catch the tiny particles of dirt; set it aside. The mushrooms have now given off much of their strong flavor and aroma, and can be very fastidiously washed without losing their taste down the drain. Wash them individually if you must, but be sure that all the dirt is gone, else you will be gritting your teeth at dinner time. If the mushrooms are in very large pieces, cut them up a little. Peel and slice the small onions and put mushrooms and onions into a large skillet with 2 tablespoons of butter. Sauté for a few minutes, then pour in the hot, strong vegetable broth, and leave it all to simmer on a low flame.

In a smaller skillet, melt 3 tablespoons of butter and stir in the flour. Let the roux cook a few minutes, stirring well—then add the cleaned mushroom stock and whisk until the mixture is smooth. When it just begins to thicken, add the cream and the sherry, salt and pepper, and continue cooking it slowly, stirring occasionally with the whisk, for about 10 minutes.

As for the mushrooms and onions in the pan, they should simmer very gently until the vegetable stock is all but gone. Then return them to the sauce and serve it very hot, spooning it out of a deep dish over rolled Parmesan crêpes, noodles, an omelet, or some other delicacy. This makes 1 quart of impossibly delicious mushroom sauce.

herb and wine sauce

2½ cups Potato Peel Broth or Garlic
     Broth (see page 50 or 51)
¾ cup white table wine
¼ tsp. dried rosemary
¼ tsp. dried dill
pinch tarragon
3 Tbs. butter
3 Tbs. flour
garlic juice
lemon peel (powdered or fresh)

Prepare the broth and cook in a small saucepan until it is reduced to 1½ cups. Add the wine and herbs, and continue simmering gently for at least 5 minutes more.

Melt the butter in a heavy, enameled saucepan or in the top of a double boiler. Add the flour and simmer for 5 to 10 minutes, stirring often. Gradually add the hot broth, stirring with a whisk as you do. Season with a few drops of garlic juice and a little lemon peel—be moderate here.

Allow the sauce to simmer gently for another 10 to 15 minutes, stirring often. You may strain the sauce to remove the herbs if you like, but this is not necessary.

Serve hot with soufflés, crêpes, or vegetables.

cranberry-cumberland sauce

2 lb. thick, whole-berry cranberry
    sauce
½ Tbs. dry mustard (more if desired)
juice and grated rind of 1 to 2 oranges
1 to 2 tsp. cornstarch
1 tsp. lemon juice
2 to 3 Tbs. sugar
grated cinnamon or cloves (optional)
grated lemon peel (optional)

Dissolve the mustard in the orange juice,
together with about a teaspoon of cornstarch. Add this mixture to the cranberry
sauce, along with the lemon juice, the
grated orange rind, and 2 tablespoons of
sugar. Heat the sauce, stirring constantly,
for about 10 minutes.

A little ground cinnamon or cloves may
be added, as well as some grated lemon
rind. Taste the sauce for seasoning, adding more sugar if needed. If the sauce is
too thin (this depends on the density of
the cranberry sauce you start with and the
amount of orange juice you add) dissolve
another teaspoon of cornstarch in a little
juice or water and stir it in.

Chill the sauce well before serving.

Serve as a relish with Soybean Croquettes
(page 130), Baked Walnut and Cheddar
Balls Béchamel (page 199), and similar,
delicately flavored dishes.

hollandaise sauce

3   egg yolks
¼ tsp. salt
¼ lb. butter
1   Tbs. lemon juice
white pepper

Beat the egg yolks until they are smooth and creamy, adding the salt. Melt the butter in a little saucepan with a pouring lip.

Drop by drop, add half the butter to the egg yolks, and continue beating all the while. Then alternately add butter and lemon juice—still beating—until all is used up. Season with some white pepper.

At this point the Hollandaise may be stored in the refrigerator for up to a day or two without curdling. When you are ready to use it, heat it gently in a double boiler until it just melts, then stir it lightly with a whisk, and serve immediately. Overlong heating may cause the sauce to curdle.

The sauce may also be served cold, either over vegetables or as a dipping sauce for them. It is delicious with eggs cooked in almost any style. To serve cold, simply stir it up a little after it has chilled in the refrigerator, and serve as you would mayonnaise.

Makes about ¾ cup.

white wine sauce

1½ cups Garlic Broth (or Potato Peel
        Broth) (see page 51 or 50)
1   cup dry white table wine
5 to 6 dried dark mushrooms
3   Tbs. butter
3   Tbs. flour
2   Tbs. cream
1   egg yolk
salt and pepper
dried powdered lemon peel (optional)

Combine the broth and the wine in a small saucepan, add the mushrooms, cover tightly, and simmer for about ½ hour. Strain through muslin and discard the mushrooms.

Heat the butter in a heavy enameled saucepan or the top of a double boiler. When it is bubbly, add the flour and let it cook for a few minutes over very low heat, stirring often. Gradually pour in the heated broth, stirring all the while with a whisk. After the sauce thickens, continue to stir often as it cooks over low heat for at least 10 more minutes. Beat the egg yolk with the cream and stir into the sauce. Season to taste with salt and fresh-ground black pepper. You may also add a tiny pinch of dried powdered lemon peel.

dill sauce

This light, smooth sauce is easy to make, keeps for a day or two in the refrigerator, and is super with asparagus soufflé.

3 Tbs. flour
3 Tbs. butter
1 cup hot vegetable broth (light)
1 cup milk
2 Tbs. chopped dried dill weed or 3 to
       4 Tbs. chopped fresh dill
2 to 3 Tbs. good dry sherry
salt and pepper

Make a roux with the butter and flour, then add the hot broth and stir with a whisk until smooth. Continue stirring while you add the milk and let it cook over very low heat, or in the top of a double boiler, for a few minutes. Add the dill weed and the sherry, season with salt and pepper, and cook gently about 10 minutes, stirring often. Serve hot in a sauceboat with a vegetable soufflé, an omelet, etc.

real mayonnaise

1 whole egg
½ tsp. salt
½ tsp. dry mustard
2 tsp. cider vinegar
⅛ tsp. Tabasco sauce
1½ Tbs. lemon juice
½ cup olive oil
½ cup peanut or safflower oil
1 Tbs. hot water

Put all the ingredients except the oil into the container of the blender and blend them thoroughly. Then—with the blender still on—begin pouring in the oil, gradually, in a very thin, steady stream. If the mayonnaise becomes very thick, push it down from the sides of the blender with a spatula and continue blending until all the oil is emulsified. Blend in a tablespoon of very hot water to stabilize the sauce. Store in the refrigerator.

provençale sauce

8 medium fresh tomatoes or 2 medium
    cans tomatoes
1 smallish onion
2 to 3 cloves garlic
olive oil
tarragon
parsley
salt
pepper
water or dry white wine

Scald the tomatoes, remove their skins, and chop them coarsely—or chop the drained tomatoes (reserving the liquid) from 2 medium cans. Chop the onion and mince at least 2 cloves of garlic. Toss the onion and garlic into a large skillet with a few tablespoons of olive oil and sauté until the onions turn golden. Then add the tomatoes, some crushed tarragon, a little parsley, and salt and pepper to suit you.

Let this mixture cook awhile, stirring a little to prevent burning, and then add the liquid from the canned tomatoes, or some water or dry white wine if you used fresh tomatoes. Simmer very gently for ½ hour longer, adding liquid if needed, and it is ready to serve right away or to store away in the refrigerator for future use.

Fine for pasta or omelets.

salads and dressings

Almost anybody can carefully follow directions and produce a good soup or a puffy soufflé, but when I am served a fine salad—crisp, pure, and simple—with an uncomplicated but well-blended dressing, I look with confidence to the cook and anticipate with relish whatever else might come from that kitchen. For it is the simple thing that must be made with utmost care.

Attention: First of all, a salad is a refreshment, not a confection. There are those who hold that the only true salad is the classic *Salade Verte,* lightly bathed in the simplest of vinaigrette dressings, and all else belongs to some other culinary genre. I personally do not subscribe to this extremist dogma, but I agree that the impeccable tossed green salad, if not the beginning and end, is at least the quintessence of salad. Not to be scorned, nevertheless, is the tastefully blended *Salade Composé* and, likewise, certain marinated vegetables of which I am so inordinately fond and which also can be honorably served as salad.

I forcefully draw the line, though, at some of the concoctions passed off as salads in numerous restaurants. Five pieces of syrupy canned fruit leaning on a mound of cottage cheese *is not* a salad, nor is a sticky little ball of mayonnaise-smeared macaroni pitifully exhibited on a plate of tired lettuce.

For a tossed green salad *par excellence,* use only the freshest, crispest of greens, taking off the first few layers of leaves if necessary. Romaine, Boston, Bibb lettuce, curly endive, and very tender young spinach leaves all are superb starting points. Lettuce leaves should be carefully washed in cold water and either patted dry or given a few good shakes in a salad basket. Once clean, they are to be used whole or, if exceedingly large, torn once or twice with the hands, but never cut with a knife. Small amounts of certain other crisp greens can be added for a more complex texture or taste; slivered bell peppers, fresh watercress, fennel, cucumbers, and celery all are recommended.

As to the dressing, it is to be prepared just before it is added to the salad, from the very best oils and vinegars, with a discriminating touch of herb or flavoring. Bottled dressings are neither desirable nor necessary. A delicious dressing can be made in the salad bowl itself: first rub the bowl with garlic, then add the cleaned lettuce and pour over it a few spoons of pure olive oil. Toss a few times; add just a little wine vinegar and some salt; coarsely grate in a liberal amount of black pepper, toss again, and serve.

simple vinaigrette sauce

(French Dressing)

¼ cup white wine vinegar or herb
    vinegar
1 Tbs. lemon juice
¼ tsp. dry mustard or 1 tsp. prepared
    Dijon mustard
salt and fresh-ground black pepper
½ cup olive oil

Mix together the vinegar, lemon juice, mustard, salt, and pepper. Add olive oil, a little at a time, beating with a whisk until the mixture emulsifies. This sauce may also be made in the blender: simply put all ingredients into the container and blend at high speed for a very short time.

This makes about ¾ cup dressing.

fancy vinaigrette sauce

Simple Vinaigrette Sauce
1 Tbs. chopped parsley
1 Tbs. chopped onions or chives
1 tsp. capers
1 clove garlic, put through a garlic
    press

Make Simple Vinaigrette Sauce as directed. Add the chopped parsley, chopped onion or snipped chives, garlic, and capers. Mix well or blend again, as you prefer.

Note: The amount of oil can be increased if a milder sauce is desired.

Other variations on vinaigrette sauce are done the same way. You may add a sieved, hard-cooked egg for a thicker sauce, or any one of a number of fresh or dried herbs. If you use dried herbs, let them soak a while in the olive oil before using. Especially nice in salads are dill, oregano, basil, and tarragon—but beware of the tarragon, for a little goes a very long way.

sharp vinaigrette

This is my favorite among vinaigrettes. The large amount of fresh garlic, along with the mustard, gives it a sharp bite that I particularly enjoy in my salads.

½ cup olive oil
¼ cup white wine vinegar or tarragon
        vinegar
2   Tbs. Dijon mustard
¼ tsp. salt
fresh-ground black pepper
2 to 3 large cloves garlic

To make the sauce, either whip all the ingredients together in a blender at high speed for several minutes, or follow the old time-honored process:

Combine the vinegar, mustard, salt, pepper, and the garlic, either minced or pressed. Beat in the olive oil gradually with a fork or a whisk until the mixture emulsifies.

Remember—whole fresh garlic cloves must be used or the sauce won't be sharp.

vinaigrette dressing for fruit salads

¼ cup cider vinegar
¼ cup water
3 to 4 Tbs. lemon juice
½ cup safflower oil or olive oil
pinch of salt
½ tsp. capers
1   clove garlic
¼ tsp. paprika
⅛ tsp. crushed tarragon
⅛ tsp. crushed basil
⅛ tsp. powdered marjoram

Blend all the ingredients at high speed for a few minutes. Use this dressing sparingly on fresh fruit salads.

herb vinegar

Occasionally I have some good red wine left over after dinner. Most wines are no longer really drinkable a day or two after being opened, but neither should they be wasted. Here is what I do with mine: a superb mate for the finest olive oil.

1 pt. red wine
1 pt. cider vinegar
2 to 3 peeled and cut garlic cloves
tarragon
peppercorns
thyme seeds
oregano or sweet basil (optional)

Mix the red wine and the cider vinegar. Add the garlic, along with a small branch of tarragon (or some dried tarragon), a few peppercorns, a good pinch of thyme seeds and, if you like, a little oregano or sweet basil, although these last are not necessary.

Pour it all into a bottle, stop it with a cork, and put it away for a few weeks. You will have a most deliciously flavored wine vinegar.

tossed green salad with zucchini

1 small head butter or Boston lettuce
1 large head crisp Romaine
4 medium zucchini
about ¾ cup Fancy Vinaigrette Sauce
    (see page 97)

Wash the lettuce and zucchini. Shake or pat dry the lettuce. Slice the zucchini into ¼-inch slices and drop them into boiling salted water for about 5 to 6 minutes; drain in a colander and pour cold water over them.

Rub a salad bowl with garlic. Break the Romaine and the butter lettuce into the bowl, add the zucchini slices, and, just before serving, pour the dressing on and toss until everything is evenly coated. Grind in some black pepper or pass the pepper grinder.

6 servings.

hearts of butter lettuce, citrus dressing

Here is a crisp, tart salad, guaranteed to refresh the palate after a heavy, rich meal. I like to serve it at the end of those sumptuous Italian pasta feasts.

For 6 to 8 people, take 3 or 4 crisp heads of Boston or butter lettuce and strip off the first few layers of leaves. Take apart the remaining leaves, wash them, and shake them dry or drain in a colander. One heart of Romaine, torn into large pieces and mixed with the butter lettuce, adds an interesting touch. Add to this a small amount of *fresh* chopped parsley.

To dress the salad, squeeze on the juices of 1 lemon and 1 small lime, add a little salt, and toss. Serve the salad and pass with it a pepper grinder and a small pitcher of olive oil for those who will.

salad of lettuce hearts with melted butter

Only the finest, crispest hearts of Boston and Romaine lettuce for this salad.

3 to 4 very fresh lettuce hearts
3 to 4 Tbs. clarified butter
2 Tbs. lemon juice
1 Tbs. lime juice
garlic clove, minced
lots of fresh-ground black pepper
crushed rosemary and dill (optional)

Wash the lettuce carefully, dry it, and chill. Melt the butter and add to it the lemon juice, lime juice, garlic, and perhaps a bit of rosemary and dill. When all has heated through, set it aside to cool to lukewarm. Then pour it quickly over the lettuce, toss until each leaf glistens, grate on a lot of black pepper, and serve at once.

A salad like this is best as a course in itself—the last one after heavier foods.

Serves 4 to 6.

raw mushroom salad

1 lb. very fresh button mushroo̶~~m~~
½ cup olive oil
¼ cup wine vinega
2 Tbs. capers
½ small fresh pimi
    coarsely grated
pinch of cayenne pe
salt and pepper
1 large, crisp head
    lettuce or Rom
hard-cooked eggs (o
more fresh sliced pim

Wash the mushrooms
them. Make a marina
vinegar, cayenne, pim
seasoning it with salt
the marinade over the
toss them lightly. Set t
hour or two at least, an

Wash the lettuce and te
medium-sized pieces.
amounts of the lettuce
plates, depending on how
the servings to be. (If thi
course, I suggest rather s

ey should be slightly
ound of the marinated
o of each plate of let-
th additional pepper
or sliced hard-cooked

salad marocain

3 to 4 large, firm tomatoes
2 large bell peppers
3 Tbs. olive oil
1 tsp. cumin seeds
1 Tbs. white wine vinegar
fresh-ground pepper
salt
1 Tbs. chopped fresh parsley

Scoop out the seeds from the peppers and cut all the vegetables into cubes. Drain them in a colander for a few minutes, then remove to a salad bowl.

Heat the olive oil in a small pan and add the cumin seeds. Let them cook in the oil for 2 to 3 minutes and remove from heat. When the oil is somewhat cooled, add vinegar, grind in some black pepper, and add a little salt. Mix this dressing well, pour it over the vegetables, and toss. Put the mixture away to cool in the refrigerator for about ½ hour before serving. Sprinkle the chopped parsley over the top at the last moment.

Serves 4 to 5.

leek salad vinaigrette

8 medium leeks

Vinaigrette Dressing:

½ cup olive oil
¼ cup white wine vinegar with
     tarragon
1 clove garlic, put through a press
fresh-ground black pepper
salt
½ tsp. Dijon mustard

Trim the leeks, cutting off the root and most of the green tops. Wash them carefully and cut into slices. Drop the leeks into boiling salted water for 7 to 10 minutes, or until they are just barely tender. Drain the leeks immediately and rinse with cold water.

Make a vinaigrette sauce, beating together the olive oil, wine vinegar, garlic, pepper, salt, and mustard. A little more oil or vinegar may be added for a more bland or tart sauce, according to your preference. Pour about ⅔ cup of this sauce over the leeks and chill very well.

Serves 4 to 6.

cucumbers in sour cream

These are cucumbers trying to become dill pickles and not quite making it. They have a freshness and delicacy pickles can't claim, and a piquant flavor that ordinary cucumber salad doesn't know.

4 to 5 medium cucumbers
1½ Tbs. salt
2   Tbs. sour cream
1   Tbs. chopped chives
2   Tbs. chopped fresh dill
1   clove garlic, put through a press
fresh-ground black pepper

Peel the cucumbers, quarter them lengthwise, and scrape out the seeds. Now slice the long strips at an angle, into even little disks. Add the salt, mix well, and set aside for 1 hour. Then rinse the cucumbers thoroughly and press out excess liquid.

Stir in the sour cream, chives, dill, garlic, and enough fresh-ground black pepper to suit you. Chill at least 1 hour, stir again, and serve.

Serves 4 to 6.

string beans vinaigrette

1   lb. fresh green beans
½   medium onion
1   small clove garlic
⅓   cup fresh-grated Parmesan cheese
6   Tbs. olive oil
2   Tbs. white wine vinegar with
      tarragon
½   tsp. salt
fresh ground black pepper

Garnish:

tomatoes, olives

Wash the beans, snip off the ends, and cut them French style. Drop them into boiling salted water and cook until just tender. Drain.

Finely chop half of an onion and mince a clove of garlic. Combine the beans with the other ingredients and mix well. Chill and serve with tomatoes, olives, and other fresh or marinated garnishes of your choice.

Serves 4 to 6.

polish tomatoes

About 6 firm, ripe tomatoes
1 small onion, minced
sweet basil
dill weed
salt and pepper
pinch of parsley
4 Tbs. olive oil
3 Tbs. wine vinegar

Wash and thickly slice the tomatoes. Put them in a bowl with the minced onion, some crushed basil, dill weed, a little parsley, and some salt and pepper. Toss them until the slices are evenly coated with the herbs. Now add the oil and vinegar, and toss again. Serve well-chilled. This dish is excellent with a hot, creamed dish, with quiche, or with an omelet.

In Poland, of course, the tomatoes grow this way.

gazpacho salad

2 bell peppers, seeded and thinly sliced
4 firm tomatoes, finely diced
2 cucumbers, seeded and chopped
     (not peeled)
1 onion, peeled and chopped
salt and pepper

Vinaigrette Dressing:

about ½ cup olive oil
about ¼ cup wine vinegar
2 garlic cloves, put through a press
pinch of ground cumin
chopped parsley
2 tsp. chopped shallots

Garnish: fresh watercress sprigs

In a deep glass or crystal bowl, arrange the vegetables in thin layers, sprinkling each layer with a little salt and pepper. Start with a layer of bell peppers, then tomatoes, cucumbers, onions, and over again until all the vegetables are used up.

Make the vinaigrette dressing and pour it over the salad. Chill the salad for several hours and garnish with watercress.

Serves 6.

greek salad

1 crisp head lettuce
olive oil
lemon juice or vinegar
salt and pepper
1 lb. Feta cheese (or more to taste)
oregano
1 medium cucumber
2½ cups whole cherry tomatoes
½ lb. Greek olives (¼ lb. black, ¼ lb.
     green)
1 small green bell pepper
sliced avocado and sliced onion
     (optional)

A well-made Greek salad is perhaps the most resplendent centerpiece a table can have. This salad is never tossed! Rather, it is carefully constructed, step by step, in the most elegant design you can create. Here is my method:

First, choose a large oblong or oval platter. Line it with the outer leaves of a crisp head of lettuce. Tear the remaining leaves into small pieces, season them with a little olive oil, lemon juice or vinegar, and some salt and pepper. Arrange the lettuce in a mound on the platter. Break the Feta cheese into pieces or slice it, and sprinkle some olive oil and chopped oregano on it. Slice a cucumber, without peeling it, and sprinkle the slices with salt and pepper. Just within the edge of the platter, make a ring of overlapping cucumber slices, interspersed here and there with a few cherry tomatoes. Inside that ring, arrange the pieces of Feta cheese in a smaller ring. Continue with the green olives. In the center, pile the remaining cherry tomatoes with the black olives.

Slice the bell pepper, onion, and avocado, and decorate further with these vegetables, as your imagination suggests. The finished product should be almost too beautiful to eat. Sprinkle with a little more olive oil and lemon juice, a bit of oregano, and place in the center of the table.

Now, eat it Greek style: Rather than ruining it instantly, by serving onto individual plates, each guest simply spears what he wants from the platter and eats it. So it comes apart as it came together—bit by bit—and everybody eats as much as he likes of whatever he prefers.

hot and cold salad

crisp hearts of butter or Boston lettuce
    (enough for 4)
3 to 4 oz. of a mild cheese, cut in sliv-
    ers
Vinaigrette Sauce (page 97 or 98)
12 to 15 tiny, pickled, cocktail onions
½ lb. fresh mushrooms
3 to 4 Tbs. butter
salt and fresh-ground black pepper

Wash and dry the lettuce and put it in a large bowl. Add the slivered cheese; put away to chill a little. Have ready the Vinaigrette (about ½ to ¾ cup), the onions, and your pepper grinder. Wash and slice the mushrooms.

Just before serving, heat the butter in a skillet and begin sautéing the mushroom slices. Pour the dressing over the chilled lettuce, and toss until every leaf is evenly coated. Put the dressed salad on individual plates; place 3 to 4 small onions at the side of each one.

Stir the mushrooms often, and after 6 to 8 minutes on a hot flame they should be quite ready. Pile some mushrooms over each plate of lettuce, give each one a good grate of pepper, and serve immediately.

The effect of the hot mushrooms on the cold lettuce is a delight, but there can be no waiting around or the lettuce will wilt and the mushrooms cool.

Makes 4 servings.

potato salad vinaigrette

6   large waxy potatoes (white rose)
salted water
1½ cups milk

Vinaigrette Dressing:

6 to 7 Tbs. olive oil
3 to 4 Tbs. white wine vinegar
salt and pepper
1   whole clove garlic
3 to 4 crisp green onions

Peel the potatoes and boil them whole in enough salted water to cover; about 45 minutes to 1 hour should be enough. As soon as they are tender (don't over-cook) take them out and, while they are still warm, very carefully cut them into cubes. Treat them very gently or they will fall apart.

Put the cubes in a bowl and pour the milk over them. The potatoes should be covered. Soak them in the milk for about 20 minutes, then drain. (The milk that is left from this procedure is delicious to drink.)

Rinse the potatoes quickly with cold water and drain again. Make a vinaigrette dressing with 6 to 7 tablespoons of olive oil and 3 or 4 tablespoons of white wine vinegar, a crushed clove of garlic, some salt, and fresh-ground pepper. Add 3 or 4 finely chopped green onions. Pour the dressing over the potatoes, lift them gently a few times so that all are coated, and chill well before serving.

6 servings.

jerusalem artichoke salad

This is very like a potato salad, but with a more interesting taste and not quite so mealy. It is served chilled and makes a fine summer supper dish.

1   lb. Jerusalem artichokes
whites of 2 hard-cooked eggs
1   large red bell pepper
1   large dill pickle
green olives
pickled pearl onions
1   crisp stalk celery
⅔   cup fresh green peas, steamed
      quickly
salt and pepper

Steam the artichokes 10 to 15 minutes, peel, and then chop them along with the egg whites, the bell pepper, the pickle, olives, and onions (to your taste—I use about a dozen each of olives and onions), and the celery. Mix all the ingredients (don't forget the peas!), and season with salt and pepper. Set it aside to chill while you make this sauce:

Old-Fashioned Mayonnaise Sauce:

yolks of 2 hard-cooked eggs
2   Tbs. lemon juice
1   Tbs. safflower oil
¼   cup mayonnaise
¼   cup sour cream
2   tsp. Dijon mustard
salt and pepper

Mash the egg yolks, alternately add the lemon juice and the oil—a few drops at a time—creaming until smooth. Now add the mayonnaise, sour cream, and mustard; mix well, add salt and pepper to taste. Pour this sauce over the salad and toss it up until it is well mixed, being careful not to mash the softer ingredients of the salad. Chill well.

Serves 6

french vegetable salad

2   large new potatoes, washed and
        peeled
3   large carrots, washed and peeled
1   cup fresh green or yellow string
        beans, washed and cut
1   cup newly shelled peas
½   head fresh cauliflower
1   large cucumber
about 1 cup Simple Vinaigrette Sauce
        (well salted, with a little garlic
        added) (see page 97)
salt and pepper
chopped fresh parsley
1 to 2 Tbs. capers (optional)

Dice the potatoes and carrots into cubes about the size of two peas. Cook them in boiling salted water, together with the cut string beans and the peas, for about 6 to 7 minutes. They should be just barely tender, still firm.

Break the cauliflower into tiny flowerettes and cook it the same way, until it is just only tender and still a little crisp.

Peel the cucumber, seed it, and dice it.

When the cooked vegetables are cool, toss all the vegetables together and season well with Simple Vinaigrette Sauce. Add a considerable amount of fresh-ground black pepper and some salt. Chill the salad for an hour or two. Toss again and turn it out on a platter. Garnish with fresh chopped parsley and perhaps some capers.

Serves 6 to 8.

marinated vegetable salad

1 lb. cut green beans, or a mixture of green and wax beans, cooked
1 lb. kidney beans, cooked
12 oz. marinated artichoke hearts
3 to 4 oz. pitted ripe olives
1 small onion, preferably red, thinly sliced
4 to 6 oz. pickled mushrooms
½ lb. garbanzos or chick peas, cooked
2 oz. pimientos, chopped
1 Tbs. capers
¼ cup chopped fresh parsley
1 Tbs. chopped green onion or chives

Dressing:

½ cup olive oil
¼ cup herb vinegar
¼ tsp. tarragon, crushed
¼ tsp. chervil, crushed
pinch of cayenne pepper
salt and fresh-ground black pepper
1 clove garlic
1½ tsp. MSG (optional)

Combine the first eleven ingredients in a large bowl. Prepare the dressing in a blender by whipping all the ingredients together for a few moments. In the absence of a blender, crush the herbs in a mortar, put the garlic clove through a press, and shake all the ingredients together in a jar.

Pour the dressing over the mixed vegetables, toss lightly but thoroughly, and cover the bowl. Leave it to marinate overnight in the refrigerator.

This is a marvelous antipasto salad for any kind of pasta, is also delicious with cheese dishes, and travels very well on picnics. The quantity is rather huge—it serves about a dozen people—but it keeps well for a week or so if stored in the refrigerator and tightly covered.

marinated cauliflower à la grecque

1 cauliflower
2 cups water
¾ cup olive oil
¼ cup cider vinegar
½ cup lemon juice
¾ tsp. dried fennel seed
½ tsp. dried chervil
½ tsp. dried thyme seed
1 small bay leaf
¾ tsp. ground coriander
8 to 10 peppercorns
¾ tsp. salt
1 stalk celery, sliced
2 cloves garlic, put through a press

Wash the cauliflower, trim off the green leaves, and break or cut it into small flowerettes. Now put all the ingredients together in a fairly large pot and heat them to boiling. If your cauliflower is especially large, add a little water so that the marinade covers the cauliflower.

Let it boil about 10 minutes, then take it off the heat and allow it to cool. Turn it into a bowl and chill it at least 24 hours. Drain and let the flowerettes rest in the colander for a few minutes so that excess oil drips off. Serve on a platter with other cold and pickled vegetables, or by itself, either as an appetizer or a salad.

holiday vegetable salad

This is the greatest of all composed salads, in my personal estimation. We eat it traditionally on Christmas Eve and other large occasions. The recipe given here makes a rather enormous amount of salad, but I suggest making the full amount: it tastes even better a day or two old, and keeps very well up to a week.

½ lb. mushrooms
6 to 8 waxy potatoes
4 tart green apples
2½ cups diced dill pickles
4 whole eggs and 3 egg whites
1½ cups peas
1½ cups carrots
½ cup tiny pickled cocktail onions
½ onion, finely chopped
vinegar from mushroom marinade
olive oil
wine vinegar
salt and fresh-ground black pepper

Mayonnaise Sauce:

3 hard-cooked egg yolks
6 to 8 Tbs. olive oil
3 to 4 Tbs. lemon juice
1 tsp. sugar
¼ cup sour cream (more if desired)
1 Tbs. prepared French mustard
salt and pepper

Garnish:

red and green peppers
radishes
green and ripe olives
raw carrots
fresh parsley

The day before you want this salad, prepare the mushrooms: wash and slice them, and pour over them a marinade of hot cider vinegar with a bay leaf and about a teaspoon of pickling spices. Cover and set aside for 24 hours.

Boil the potatoes in their jackets, let them cool, then peel and dice them. Peel, core, and dice the apples. Chop 4 whole hard-cooked eggs and the whites of 3 others, reserving 3 yolks for the sauce. Slice the cooked carrots.

Combine all these things in a giant mixing bowl and add to them the dill pickles, the slightly cooked peas, the pickled onions, and the fresh chopped onion. Drain the mushrooms, reserving the marinade, and add them to the salad.

Season this mixture with salt, fresh-ground black pepper, some olive oil, some wine vinegar, and a little of the mushroom marinade—be careful not to pour in the whole spices. Toss the salad lightly to combine all ingredients. Taste and correct the seasoning.

Prepare the mayonnaise sauce: If you have a blender, you're home free. Put the egg yolks in first with the olive oil, lemon juice, and sugar. Blend at high speed until the olive oil emulsifies and the mixture is smooth. Add the sour cream and mustard, along with salt and pepper, and blend again. The sauce should be thick and pale yellow in color.

Add a few spoons of this sauce to the salad and toss until it is thoroughly blended. Be certain that the salad is cor-

rectly seasoned—it should not be bland. Choose a beautiful large serving bowl and empty the salad into it. If the size is perfect, the salad will come almost to the top when it is leveled. Smooth the top, pressing it gently with a fork until it is as nearly flat as possible. Spread the remainder of the sauce over it evenly.

Now enjoy yourself. Take some fresh pimiento pepper or green ones, fresh parsley, thin slivers of radish or carrot, little slices of olive; take any colorful or lovely vegetables you can find and decorate the top of the salad in the most exquisite manner possible.

Serves 10 to 12 generously.

marinated lentil salad

⅔ lb. dried lentils
1 large onion, finely chopped
salt and pepper
flakes of cayenne pepper
4 Tbs. olive oil
2 cloves garlic, pressed
2 bay leaves
2 qts. water
3 Tbs. wine vinegar
1 Tbs. lemon juice

Dressing:

½ large onion, finely chopped
½ to ⅔ cup chopped fresh parsley
1 tsp. prepared mustard
salt and pepper
3 Tbs. (approximately) olive oil
juice of 1 lemon

Garnish: stuffed olives, tomato wedges,
        parsley sprigs

Soak the lentils overnight and drain them (unless they are presoaked). Take out about 1 cup of the lentils and put it into approximately ½ quart of water, with a little chopped onion, some salt and pepper, and a few flakes of cayenne pepper. Let simmer about 1½ hours.

For the remainder of the lentils: In a large pot, sauté the chopped onion in 2 tablespoons of the olive oil until it is transparent. Add the garlic, bay leaf, 1½ quarts of water, some salt, and the lentils. Simmer this also about 1½ hours. When the lentils are tender, drain and rinse them, keeping the two kinds separate until they are cool. Then mix them together, add 2 tablespoons of olive oil, the vinegar and the lemon juice, salt and pepper to taste, and set aside overnight.

To make the dressing, combine the onion, parsley, mustard, salt, and pepper in a bowl, mixing thoroughly. Then add the olive oil, bit by bit, beating continuously until the sauce thickens. Then add the lemon juice, beat again, and pour over the lentils, mixing it in. Chill well, then pile the lentils on a platter and garnish all around with stuffed olives, wedges of tomato, and sprigs of fresh parsley.

This dish is very high in protein, and serves at least 6, with generous portions.

marinated bean salad

1½ cups cooked green string beans, cut into 1-inch pieces
1½ cups cooked yellow wax beans, cut into 1-inch pieces
1½ cups cooked red kidney beans
1½ cups cooked garbanzo beans or chick peas
1 large onion, sliced into ½-inch slivers
⅔ cup olive oil
⅔ cup sharp wine or cider vinegar
salt and lots of fresh-ground black pepper
2 to 3 Tbs. sugar
chopped pimiento and green pepper (optional)
chopped fresh herbs, basil or mint (optional)

Combine all the beans in a large mixing bowl. Mix the rest of the ingredients to make the dressing, and pour it over the beans. Toss until everything is thoroughly combined. Cover the bowl and refrigerate overnight.

This recipe makes 6 to 8 servings.

pimiento peppers in oil

4 large sweet red peppers
10 to 12 marinated black olives, Greek or Italian
1 very well-smashed clove of garlic
salt
olive oil
lemon juice

Roast the peppers in a hot oven, turning them often but not breaking the skin, until the skin is blackened—it should take about 20 minutes.
Let them cool very slightly and, when you can handle them, remove the skins and discard the seeds and cores. Cut the peppers into strips.
Cut up the olives into slivers and discard the pits. Combine the pepper strips with the olives, sprinkle on some salt and pressed garlic, add just a small spoon or two of olive oil, and a little lemon juice. Mix well with a wooden spoon or your hand, to avoid tearing the strips, then arrange them on a plate and serve with antipasto.
They may be served warm or cold.
Makes 6 to 8 servings.

frozen fresh fruit salad

2   cups diced, peeled fresh fruit (I rec-
      ommend peaches, nectarines, straw-
      berries, firm bananas, seedless
      grapes; use one kind or a combi-
      nation, as you prefer)
2 to 4 tsp. sugar
16 oz. cream cheese
1   tsp. powdered ginger
¼   tsp. salt
2   Tbs. lemon juice
⅓   cup heavy cream, whipped
½   cup chopped nuts (optional)
salad greens
additional fresh fruit

Set refrigerator control at lowest point.

Peel and dice the fruit you have chosen; sprinkle with just enough sugar to slightly sweeten. Let stand while preparing the rest.

Cream together the cheese, ginger, salt, and lemon juice. Fold in the whipped cream and fruit. If you want to add nuts, add them at this point.

Pour the mixture into a mold, into ice-cube trays, or into small, individual molds, and freeze; about 3 hours should be enough. When firm, remove from molds by dipping the molds, almost to the top, in hot water for a moment, then turn over onto a plate. Buttering or oiling the molds before putting in the mixture is helpful. If you froze the salad in ice-cube trays, slice to remove. Serve on salad greens with additional fresh fruit. Vinaigrette dressing may be served separately.

About 8 servings.

fruit salad

This is not the sort of dish for which a specific list of ingredients can be given. They must change with the seasons, for a fruit salad is not much good if the fruit is not fresh. That is the only rule: *fresh* fruit.

The dressings that may be served with fruit salads vary. I like to serve a fruit salad with no dressing at all—with the right kind of fruit this works very well. Sour fruits can be sprinkled first with sugar, then with a little wine or liqueur. Sour cream is also used as dressing for fruit, but it should be used very sparingly. Finally, vinaigrette, unlikely as it may sound, goes very well with certain fruit salads. I have included here a special recipe for vinaigrette to be used on fruit (see page 98).

Here are a few suggestions for combinations of fruit:

strawberries
sliced bananas
sliced oranges

nectarines
plums, pitted
apricots, pitted

large chunks of pineapple
seedless grapes
tart apples, cut and cored, but not peeled
strawberries

grapefruit sections
orange sections
sliced pears

garden salad

The Garden Salad evolved from our great passion for salads in general and our marked disinterest in anything else on hot summer evenings. It started in the spring as a nice and unassuming little salad. April turned to May and tender young peas appeared. In June, avocados were plentiful, tomatoes beautiful, and ourselves inspired. By the time we were celebrating midsummer's eve, we suspected that there wasn't a real salad to be had outside our house. The garden salad that we serve now is ever full of glorious surprises, always changing, always a splendid supper dish. Most important: in spite of its many ingredients, it remains that noble thing—a salad. Saladly crisp and gardenly various is the garden salad.

Suggested salad greens (you choose):

Romaine lettuce
butter or Bibb lettuce
tender young spinach
iceburg lettuce
Belgian endive
curly endive
red leaf lettuce
garden lettuce

Most-favored ingredients:

fresh shelled peas
green bell pepper
firm fresh mushrooms
avocado
green onions
tomatoes
tart green apples
cucumbers
radishes

Often appearing:

cubed cheeses
Baco-bits
Chinese pea pods
alfalfa sprouts
sunflower seeds
green olives
pimiento pepper
pine nuts

Always:

Vinaigrette Sauce (pages 97–98)

The leafy greens should constitute about

one half of the salad—with vegetables and other ingredients making up the other half.

Wash the greens carefully and dry them. Tear the leaves into manageable pieces. For a salad that will serve 4 to 6 people the way we eat salad, and 8 to 10 the way most people eat salad, I use the equivalent of 1½ to 2 good-sized heads of lettuce.

To that amount of lettuce, add ½ to 1 cup of fresh shelled peas, depending on how much you like them. Slice up a bell pepper into slivers. Wash about 10 good-sized, firm, fresh mushrooms and slice them very thinly. Peel an avocado and cut it up into bite-size pieces. Chop 3 or 4 green onions. Cut 3 or 4 firm tomatoes into sixths or eighths. Wash and quarter 1 tart green apple and slice it. Peel and slice 1 medium cucumber and thinly slice a small handful of radishes.

The amount of any of these ingredients can be adjusted according to your taste.

Toss together the greens and other ingredients. If you like cheese in salad, cut about 4 oz. of a preferred cheese into cubes and toss with all the rest.

I have used sharp Cheddar, Swiss, Gruyère, Fontina, Monterey Jack, Roquefort, and Feta, all with excellent results.

At this point we usually also add imitation bacon bits, green olives and, on those special occasions when we have them around—pine nuts. These are particular flavors which appeal very much to some and not at all to others, so try a little at first and then suit yourself.

I think the best way to dress this salad is in the bowl. Pour on some olive oil, toss; add wine vinegar, toss again; add salt and pepper and whatever herbs you prefer to find in your salads, toss again; taste, add, taste, adjust, taste, and so forth, until you have the perfect salad. If you prefer, of course, you can make a separate vinaigrette dressing and pour it on all at once. I like to use plenty of garlic, some chopped basil and oregano, and a little tarragon and dill with my vinaigrette in this salad. A pepper mill should be passed as the salad is served.

curried lentils in pineapple

1   pineapple
1½ Tbs. butter
2½ cups cooked lentils (about 1 cup
     dried)
½ tsp. salt
¾ tsp. cumin seeds
½ tsp. mustard seeds
½ tsp. turmeric
½ tsp. ground coriander
pinch of cayenne
2   tomatoes, firm and large

Vinaigrette Sauce:

2   Tbs. white wine vinegar
3   Tbs. olive oil
1   tsp. Worcestershire sauce
1   tsp. prepared French mustard
1   clove garlic
¼ cup dry white wine
salt and fresh-ground pepper

Cut the top off of a large, ripe pineapple and put it aside; carefully hollow out the whole fruit. Discard the core, drain off the juice, and cut the fruit into small chunks. Turn the shell over and let it drain, upside-down, for at least ½ hour.

Heat the butter in a skillet and add the spices to it. After a few minutes, add the cooked, drained lentils and mix them well with the heated spices. Cool.

Cut the tomatoes into bite-size pieces. Mix together the chopped pineapple, the tomatoes, and the lentils.

Prepare a vinaigrette sauce with the olive oil, white wine vinegar, 1 clove of garlic, the mustard, and the Worcestershire sauce. Add the white wine, and season with salt and lots of fresh-ground black pepper.

Pour the sauce over the lentil mixture and toss until everything is evenly coated. Fill as much of this mixture as will fit into the pineapple shell and replace the top. Serve the rest alongside in a bowl. Chill very well before serving.

another way

Here is another way to serve this dish: Slice 3 pineapples lengthwise, without removing the tops. Scoop out the fruit from all 6 halves. Use the fruit of 2 pineapples, increasing other ingredients in proportion and reserving the remaining pineapple for another use. Prepare the recipe and pile large servings into the pineapple shells.

Serves 6.

vegetables

The most delicious story ever told about a vegetable is Lewis Carrol's *Alice's Adventures in Wonderland,* an affectionate account that opens to us the nature of that most illustrious of vegetables—the psychedelic mushroom. The influence of the vegetables with which we are here concerned is not as far-reaching, but their beneficence in matters gastronomical is known. In ingestion, the well-treated vegetable pleases the palate, and in digestion, it gives no cause for rue.

French and Chinese cuisines are the two that are included always, with an ever-changing third member, whenever the "three great cuisines of the world" are named. They are—not coincidentally—the schools of cooking in which vegetables have been treated with the greatest care and success.

French and Chinese cooks have always recognized the true and signal characters of garden-fresh vegetables. They have understood, also, this happy coincidence: the treatment which allows vegetables to retain most of their nutritive value is the same treatment which preserves the freshest, loveliest taste and most desirable texture.

Soaking and overcooking—the two largest sins committed against the purity of fresh vegetables—are strictly avoided by all French and Chinese cooks worthy of their stations. For the simplest kind of vegetable preparation, I recommend steaming or sautéing. The shorter the cooking time, of course, the more nutritive value and flavor is retained. If a vegetable must be boiled, be certain that the minimum amount of water is used, and that it boils vigorously before the vegetable is added. Likewise, the pan in which the vegetable is to be sautéed should be sizzling. Vegetables that are to be peeled should be peeled as thinly as possible, because much flavor and many vitamins often lie directly under the skin.

Vegetables are no small matter. (The seven of spades, a gardener for the Queen of Hearts, was nearly beheaded for bringing the cook tulip roots instead of onions.) The vegetables presented to you here believe wholeheartedly in their own importance. They combine smartly with eggs, cheese, and with one another; they are on intimate terms with herbs and spices, and you will find them frequenting the tastiest crusts and custards. Certain of them are capable of gently dominating the table, alone or in discriminating combination with other glories. All are prepared to please you.

beets in citrus sauce

1½ to 2 lb. very young beets
1¼ cups liquid from beets
1   lemon
1   Tbs. orange peel, freshly grated
2½ Tbs. sugar
½   tsp. salt
½   tsp. ground cloves
2   Tbs. frozen orange juice concentrate
1½ Tbs. cornstarch
1   Tbs. butter

Cook the beets whole until just tender. Drain, reserving liquid, peel and slice thin. (Or slice equivalent amount of canned beets.) Pour liquid from the beets (either from the can or the cooking water) into a pot, add the grated peel and the juice of 1 lemon, the grated orange peel, sugar, salt, cloves, and frozen orange juice concentrate. Dissolve the cornstarch in just enough water to make a smooth paste and add that also. Beat the mixture lightly with a whisk and cook until it becomes clear.

Add the sliced beets and the butter, heat it through, correct the seasoning, and serve very hot. Serves 6 to 8.

artichokes vinaigrette

To cook artichokes:

Wash them and remove the tough outer leaves; trim off the stem and the pointy tops of the remaining outer leaves. Put them into a large kettle of vigorously boiling salted water, to which you have added a little olive oil and a little lemon juice. Cover and let cook for about 40 minutes, or until a leaf will slip out easily. When they are tender, take them out and turn them upside-down to drain. They may be served hot or cold, and a sauce should be passed in a bowl for dipping. I recommend vinaigrette, or lemon butter with some fresh herbs.

To eat the artichoke, pull off one leaf at a time, dip it in the sauce, and eat the tender, meaty part of the vegetable at the base of the leaf. When leaves are gone, scrape off the fuzz (choke), and eat the heart.

(See also Creamed Artichoke Soup—page 70.)

greek stewed artichokes

6 to 8 tiny artichokes or 4 large ones
2   lemons
¾   cup olive oil
1   onion, finely chopped
4   large carrots
12 to 16 tiny whole onions
4   large potatoes
1   tsp. flour
1   bunch fresh dill, chopped, or 1 Tbs.
      dried dill
salt and fresh-ground black pepper

Trim the artichokes, cutting off the stem, the tough outer leaves, and the tops of the other leaves. Scrub them, rub them with lemon, and put them into well-salted water to keep them from turning black.

Put the olive oil in a very large, fireproof casserole or skillet and sauté the chopped onion in it while you prepare the other vegetables. Scrape the carrots and cut them into 1-inch pieces. Peel the whole small onions. Peel the potatoes and cut them into about 6 pieces each.

Add all the vegetables except the artichokes to the hot oil and turn them over and over for a few minutes until the potatoes begin to turn golden. Add the flour and dill and stir very well.

Take the skillet off the heat and arrange the artichokes in it, fitting the onions and pieces of carrot and potato around them. Squeeze in the juice of 1 lemon, add some salt and pepper, and add enough hot water to just cover the vegetables. Put on a tight-fitting lid, and bake at 375 degrees for 50 minutes to 1½ hours, depending on the size of the artichokes. The water should be simmering gently.

Serve very hot. The liquid becomes a delicious sauce, just a bit thickened by the potatoes.

This recipe makes 4 to 6 servings.

asparagus pastry

flaky pastry or Pastry Brisée (see page
    286), for one crust
about 2 lb. asparagus
1½ cups rich Sauce Béchamel (see page
    84)
2   oz. grated Swiss or Gruyère cheese

Make pastry for one shell, line a shallow
pan with it, and bake it for 20 minutes
or until just brown.

Clean the asparagus, discard the hard end
pieces, and cut into 1-inch pieces. Steam
it until it is tender (10 minutes for very
young asparagus; longer for older—only
testing will tell). Now put the asparagus
into the pie shell, pour the Béchamel over
it, sprinkle on the cheese, and put it into
a medium oven to bake until it is browning on top. Serve very hot. This is an
elegant and unexpected dish, which has
completely won the guests who've eaten
it at my table.

To prepare ahead: Have crust ready.
Steam asparagus and leave tightly covered. It will get cool, but if it doesn't dry
out, you're all right. Have the Béchamel
and cheese ready in separate containers.
About 15 minutes before you want the
dish ready, arrange asparagus in the pie
shell, pour the sauce over, sprinkle on the
cheese, and put into a moderate (300 to
325 degrees) oven for about 15 minutes.
It should heat through very well and be
browning on top. This way, you are gone
from the table only a minute and the
pastry is ready at precisely the right moment.

baked beans à la charente

1   lb. dried white beans
salted water
1   medium onion stuck with 2 or 3
      cloves
2   cloves garlic
½   tsp. thyme
1   bay leaf
¼   cup butter
1   small onion, chopped
1   cup thick tomato paste
1   cup cooking liquid from beans
2   Tbs. dried parsley
¼   cup cognac
½   cup dry red table wine
salt and black pepper to taste
1   tsp. Worcestershire sauce
optional: 2   tomatoes
                1   eggplant
                olive oil

Soak the washed beans overnight in water to cover. Then, pour them into a large pot, adding more water, the onion stuck with 2 or 3 cloves, the garlic, thyme, and bay leaf. Simmer gently for 1½ to 2 hours or until the beans are tender. Drain, reserving 1 cup of the liquid; discard the onion, bay leaf, and garlic.

Melt the butter in a skillet and sauté the chopped onion until it is tender. Add the tomato paste, the parsley, the liquid from the beans, the cognac, and the wine. (Use a good wine and a good cognac—it is very important to the flavor of the beans.) This sauce should simmer for at least 15 minutes, or until it is slightly thickened and reduced. Season it with a little salt, lots of fresh-ground black pepper, and a little Worcestershire sauce.

Pour the drained beans into the sauce and mix well. Rub a large casserole lightly with olive oil, then pour the beans into it. Now, if you want to be fancy, slice the eggplant (without peeling it) into ½-inch slices, and also slice the tomatoes. Brush the eggplant slices lightly with olive oil and put them under the broiler for a few minutes. Dust all the slices with salt and pepper and overlap them—alternating eggplant and tomato—in a circular fashion on top of the beans. Cover the casserole and bake at 325 degrees for 1 to 1½ hours. Serve hot. Makes 6 servings.

herbed soybean casserole

slightly less than 1 cup dried soybeans
    (2½ cups cooked)
1   cup cooking liquid from beans
3   Tbs. butter
½ tsp. thyme
1   Tbs. crushed dried parsley
2   cloves garlic, crushed
1   small onion, finely chopped
½ tsp. dill
pepper
3   medium tomatoes
2   large crookneck squashes (about ¾
    lb. together)
½ cup grated Parmesan cheese

Wash the dried beans carefully and soak overnight in salted water. Add more water if necessary and cook for 3 to 4 hours, or until beans are tender. Drain, reserving 1 cup of the cooking liquid.

Melt the butter in a large pan and sauté the onion in it for a few minutes, then add all the herbs. Sauté a few minutes more, and add the beans and the cup of cooking liquid. Let them simmer in the pan until the liquid is somewhat reduced, about 10 to 15 minutes. Meanwhile, butter a large casserole, wash and slice the tomatoes, and wash the squashes and slice them very thinly, but do not peel them.

Add the grated Parmesan to the beans and stir well. Pour half the beans into the casserole, cover them with a layer of tomato slices, then a layer of squash slices. Now pour the rest of the beans in and repeat the layers. Put a few pieces of butter on top and grind on some black pepper. Cover and bake for 2 hours at 300 degrees.

Serves 4 to 6.

baked beans with chutney

2   cups dried pinto or navy beans
1   cup cooking liquid from the beans
1   onion, finely chopped
½   cup chutney (or ⅓ if very hot), finely
       minced
1½ tsp. dry mustard
½   cup honey
salt
fresh-ground black pepper
optional: ⅓ to ½ cup yogurt

Wash the beans well and put them in a large pot with 1 quart of water. Bring to a boil, turn the heat down, cover, and let simmer at least 1½ hours. Drain off the liquid, reserving a cup of it.

In a small bowl, dissolve the dry mustard in the bean liquid, add the finely chopped onion, the minced chutney, and salt and pepper to taste. Stir this into the beans. Pour the beans into a casserole or baking dish, and pour the honey evenly over the top. Cover and bake at 325 degrees for 1½ hours. Remove the cover and bake another ½ hour.

Serve steaming hot out of the casserole, with a moist, mild-flavored bread and a large, refreshing salad. This recipe serves 4 to 6 people.

An interesting variation on this recipe is the addition of a few spoons of yogurt just before the beans are taken out of the oven. If you are a yogurt fancier, this will delight you: it seems to heighten the spicy, hot flavor of the dish. If you are not a yogurt fancier, try it anyway with some leftover beans, and you may become a convert.

soybean croquettes

2 cups cooked soybeans (see page 128)
1 small onion
1 to 2 cloves garlic
4 cloves shallot
4 Tbs. butter
1 cup milk
4 Tbs. flour
½ tsp. crushed rosemary
½ tsp. thyme
1 Tbs. parsley
4 Tbs. wheat germ
salt and pepper
MSG
1 beaten egg
crushed cereal or breadcrumbs

Mash the soybeans by putting through the meat grinder or a vegetable mill. Mince the onion, garlic, and shallots, and sauté in 2 tablespoons of the butter just until the onion is transparent. Melt the other 2 tablespoons butter in a small skillet while heating the milk. Stir the flour into the melted butter and add the hot milk, stirring over a small flame until you have a smooth, thick sauce. Add to this the sautéed onion mixture.

In a mortar, crush together all the herbs. Now, combine in a large bowl the ground soybeans, the white sauce, the herbs, and the wheat germ. Add salt and freshly ground black pepper to taste, and a dash of MSG.

In a shallow dish, beat the egg with a little milk. In another dish, put the breadcrumbs or crushed cereal. Shape the soybean mixture into croquettes (buttered hands help), or if that is too much of a bother, shape into ovals. Dip the croquettes first into the egg, then lightly into the breadcrumbs, then the egg again, and the breadcrumbs once more. Make sure they are well coated. Place them in a greased, shallow baking dish and bake in a very hot oven (410 degrees) for 20 to 30 minutes.

This is enough for 4 to 6 servings.

Serve the hot croquettes with Cranberry-Cumberland Sauce (see page 89) or with applesauce and sour cream.

baked bean casserole

2 cups dried pinto beans
pinch soda
2 onions
2 cloves garlic
2 Tbs. olive oil
1 bay leaf
salt
3 to 4 cups broth (Potato Peel Broth—
      see page 50—or vegetable broth)
½ cup tomato paste
1 Tbs. hot mustard
1 tsp. MSG
pinch of cayenne pepper
½ cup molasses
1½ tsp. powdered ginger
1 tsp. Bakon yeast
2 Tbs. Worcestershire sauce
3 Tbs. wine vinegar
4 carrots
3 Tbs. butter
3 crisp green apples
fresh-ground black pepper

Soak the beans overnight in water with a pinch of soda; then simmer for about 2 hours together with 1 peeled onion, the garlic, olive oil, bay leaf, and some salt.

At the end of 2 hours, drain the beans. The skins should crack easily when blown upon.

Make a sauce of 1 cup of the broth, the tomato paste, 1 chopped onion, the mustard, MSG, cayenne, molasses, ginger, yeast, Worcestershire sauce, and vinegar. Mix the beans thoroughly with the sauce.

Scrape the carrots and cut them into large pieces. Cook the carrot pieces in butter in a tightly covered skillet.

Peel and core the apples and slice them in rings.

In a bean pot or a heavy casserole, make a layer of beans, salt and pepper them, then a layer of carrots and apples, another layer of beans, and so on, until the ingredients are used up. Pour enough broth over it to just reach the top of the beans. Cover tightly and bake for 7 to 8 hours at 300 degrees. Every 2 or 3 hours check to see if the beans are drying out, adding more broth as necessary.

Serves 6 to 8.

savory baked garbanzo beans

1   cup dry garbanzo beans
pinch of soda
3   ripe tomatoes
1   large, fresh green pepper
1   onion
2 to 3 Tbs. olive oil
2   cloves garlic, chopped fine
sweet basil
tarragon
parsley
salt and pepper

Soak the beans in water overnight with a pinch of soda. The next day, drain and rinse the beans, and cook them in enough water to keep them covered for about 1 hour.

Remove the skins from the tomatoes by dipping them for an instant into very hot water and then peeling them. Chop the tomatoes into fairly large pieces. Slice the green pepper in very thin matchstick pieces. Peel, quarter, and thinly slice the onion.

Throw all of these very thin slices into a pan with some hot olive oil; add also the chopped garlic, and let it sauté for a few minutes. Add some crushed sweet basil, a small amount of crushed tarragon, and the chopped tomatoes. Let this mixture simmer a minute or two while you drain the beans and remove the skins that have come loose. Finally, combine the beans with the tomato mixture, put it all into an attractive, ovenproof dish, cover tightly, and bake for 1 hour at about 325 degrees.

This makes 4 to 6 servings, and is also delicious cold.

marinated white beans

1 cup small white beans, dried
1 qt. water
½ cup olive oil
1 bay leaf
2 whole cloves garlic
salt

Marinade:

½ cup olive oil
½ cup tarragon vinegar (or plain white
    wine vinegar)
3 to 4 Tbs. chopped parsley
½ tsp. dried crushed oregano
½ tsp. dried crushed basil
¼ tsp. dried crushed tarragon
salt and pepper

Wash the beans and soak them overnight. Combine the beans with the water, olive oil, garlic, bay leaf, and some salt. Simmer gently until they are just tender, 1½ to 2½ hours. Of course, the only way to tell is to try a few: they should be reasonably tender but not mushy or soft. When they are done, drain them, and remove the bay leaf and garlic cloves.

Mix together all the ingredients for the marinade, place the beans in a bowl, and pour the marinade over them. They should be just covered. Cover the bowl and refrigerate overnight.

These beans are delicious served with any kind of Italian pasta or similar dish. They are eaten cold, and this recipe makes enough for 6.

baked soybeans with chutney

1   cup dried soybeans
⅓   cup finely minced chutney (mango
       is preferred)
6   oz. tomato paste
1½ tsp. dry mustard
1½ cups liquid from beans
16 to 20 small boiling onions
3   Tbs. molasses

Wash the dry beans carefully and soak overnight in salted water. Add more water if necessary and cook for 3 to 4 hours, or until beans are tender. Drain, reserving 1½ cups of the cooking liquid.

Combine the chutney, tomato paste, and mustard, and mix well. Add the beans, the peeled onions, the molasses, and the liquid, and simmer in a pot until the sauce is slightly thickened. Pour it all into a casserole or bean pot; cover and bake for 1 to 1½ hours in a 325-degree oven. Serve hot.

The chutney gives a spicy flavor that is quite strong; if you prefer rather sweet baked beans, add a little more molasses.

Serves 4.

eggplant tomato casserole

1   large eggplant (about 1½ lb.)
1½ tsp. salt
2   eggs, beaten
2   Tbs. melted butter
fresh-ground black pepper
2 to 3 Tbs. chopped onion
½   tsp. crushed oregano
½   cup dry breadcrumbs
2   large tomatoes, sliced thin
2   oz. Cheddar cheese, grated
¼   cup grated Parmesan cheese
paprika

Peel and slice the eggplant. Put the slices in a pan with the salt and about an inch of boiling water and cover tightly. Cook about 10 minutes and drain. Mash the eggplant and mix in the eggs, melted butter, pepper, onion, oregano, and breadcrumbs.

Butter a shallow, 1½-quart baking dish. Cover the bottom with half the tomato slices. Spoon in all of the eggplant mixture and spread evenly. Arrange the rest of the tomato slices on top. Mix together the cheeses and sprinkle over the top layer of tomatoes. Add a sprinkle of paprika and bake at 375 degrees for about 45 minutes. Serves 6.

stuffed baked eggplant

3   small eggplants (they should be the
      size of little cantaloupes)
2   red bell peppers
4 to 5 Tbs. olive oil
salt and pepper
minced garlic
2   onions
3 to 4 sprigs fresh parsley
basil
3 to 4 tomatoes
Topping:
1   cup ground walnuts
½   cup wheat germ
¾   cup grated Parmesan cheese
2   Tbs. melted butter
1   cup milk or light cream

Slice each eggplant in half lengthwise and cut out the meat, leaving ¼ inch in the skin. Dice up the eggplant into fairly large pieces, and the red bell pepper into small ones, reserving about ⅓ of one of the peppers for decoration.

In a large skillet heat about 3 tablespoons of the olive oil, and sauté the eggplant and diced bell pepper in it, tossing the pieces lightly until they are evenly coated and the eggplant begins to get soft. Season it with salt and pepper, and a little minced garlic if desired. Divide this mixture evenly between the 6 eggplant shells, pressing it down into them.

Chop the onion, the parsley, and the tomatoes. Sauté the onions in the remaining olive oil, adding the chopped fresh parsley and some crushed sweet basil, along with a little minced garlic. When the onions just begin to get soft, add the chopped tomatoes, simmer a few minutes, then spread the mixture on top of the eggplant pieces in the shells and pat it down. The eggplant shells should now be full to the top but not overflowing.

Finally, combine the wheat germ, ground nuts, and Parmesan cheese; moisten with the melted butter and enough milk to make a soft paste, and spread a thin layer of the mixture on top of each eggplant half. Decorate this crust with the reserved red pepper, sliced into thin strips.

Bake the eggplants in an oiled dish for about 45 minutes at 350 degrees. Serve very hot. 6 servings.

eggplant with capers

1 large eggplant, cut up in small cubes
3 Tbs. olive oil
1 clove garlic, minced
1 onion, quartered and thinly sliced
½ to ¾ cup chopped celery
1 Tbs. tomato sauce
water, as required
3 to 4 Tbs. capers
12 black pitted olives
6 green stuffed olives
2 to 3 Tbs. wine vinegar
1 Tbs. sugar
salt and pepper to taste
lemon slices

A large, nonstick skillet with a cover is best for this.

Sauté the eggplant in 2 tablespoons of the olive oil. When it begins to get soft, remove from the pan, and put it aside. Add the third tablespoon of olive oil and sauté the garlic and onion until the onion is golden. Then add the celery, the tomato sauce, and a few tablespoons of water. Cover, and let this steam for 10 to 15 minutes, stirring occasionally. Add a little water if necessary.

Now, return the eggplant to the pan, add the capers, chop and add the olives. Heat the vinegar with the sugar and add that also. Salt and pepper to taste, and let simmer gently for another 10 to 15 minutes, being careful not to let it burn.

Serve it hot or cold, with slices of lemon (my own preference is well-chilled).

Serves 6 to 8 as appetizer.

eggplant parmigiana

1   medium eggplant, sliced thick
flour
1   egg beaten with some milk
dried breadcrumbs, wheat germ, or
        cracker meal
olive oil
½   lb. Swiss cheese or Mozzarella,
        sliced
6   oz. tomato paste
white or red wine as needed
pinch of oregano
clove of garlic
salt and pepper
1   cup fresh-grated Parmesan cheese

Wash your eggplant and, without peeling it, slice it about ¾-inch thick. Dip these slices first in flour, then into the egg, then into the breadcrumbs so they are well coated. Sauté them in a little olive oil, a few at a time, until they are nicely browned on both sides; tend them carefully and add oil if it is needed.

When they are crisp and brown, arrange them in a baking dish and put a slice or two of Swiss cheese or Mozarella on each one. Make a thick tomato sauce by diluting the tomato paste with wine. Mix the tomato sauce with the oregano, salt, pepper, and crushed garlic clove, and spread 2 to 3 tablespoons on each slice. Finally, sprinkle the grated Parmesan on top of it all. Bake at 400 degrees for about 15 minutes and serve steaming hot.

This hearty dish will serve 4 to 6 people, and is a great favorite of all my friends.

sesame eggplant

1 large eggplant
1 mashed clove garlic
¾ tsp. salt
3 Tbs. sour cream
1 tsp. lemon juice
pinch of cayenne
lots of fresh-ground black pepper
2½ Tbs. sesame seeds

Stab the eggplant in a couple of places with a fork and put it in a medium-hot oven to bake for at least 1 hour—it will be very soft. Let it cool a little and scoop out all the pulp. Discard the skin and mash the pulp well. Add all other ingredients except the sesame seeds.

Roast the sesame seeds in a small pan, either in a hot oven (400 degrees) or over a flame; stir constantly if you are roasting them on top of the range. When they are light brown in color, remove and let them cool a little. Stir half of them into the eggplant mixture. Turn the mixture into an attractive serving dish and sprinkle the remaining sesame seeds over it.

This dish may be served as an appetizer with little crackers or breadsticks. It is also a great condiment for Baked Polenta squares (page 249), and goes very well with an antipasto platter.

The recipe, using a large eggplant, should yield slightly less than 2 cups.

giant stuffed mushrooms

10 to 12 huge fresh mushrooms (1½ to 2 lb.)
6 Tbs. butter
2 cloves garlic, pressed
¼ tsp. thyme
1 medium onion, chopped
3 stalks celery, chopped
1 tart green apple—cored, peeled, and chopped
1 Tbs. parsley
⅛ tsp. marjoram
⅛ tsp. oregano
salt and fresh-ground pepper
1 qt. cubed bread
1 cup vegetable broth

Wash the mushrooms very carefully and remove the stems. If the stems don't leave a fairly large cavity to stuff, hollow the mushrooms out just a bit with a spoon. Melt 2 tablespoons butter in a large skillet, add to it 1 crushed clove of garlic and the thyme, and stir around for a minute or two. Then add the whole mushroom caps and sauté them for a few minutes, moving them around occasionally so that they brown evenly. Remove the mushrooms and set them aside.

Add the remaining butter to the skillet, along with the second clove of garlic, the herbs, the chopped onion, celery, and apple. Chop up the mushroom stems and add them to the skillet. Stirring often, sauté the mixture until the onions are quite transparent. Add the bread cubes, and toss well with the other ingredients. Salt, and pepper liberally.

Continue cooking the mixture until the bread cubes have absorbed the butter. If it seems too dry, moisten with a little vegetable broth.

Stuff the mushroom caps, pressing several spoons of the mixture into each one and forming a small mound on top. Butter a large baking dish (with a tight-fitting lid) and arrange the stuffed mushrooms in it in a single layer. Pour the remaining vegetable broth into the dish and cover it tightly. Bake the mushrooms at 350 degrees for about 45 to 50 minutes, checking occasionally to make sure they are not drying out. Serve hot.

Serves 4 to 5 as a first course or 8 to 10 as hors d'oeuvres.

mushrooms berkeley

1   lb. fresh mushrooms
2   medium bell peppers
1   onion
½   cup butter

Sauce:
2   Tbs. Dijon mustard
2   Tbs. Worcestershire sauce
½   cup brown sugar
¾   cup mellow red table wine
fresh-ground black pepper
seasoned salt

Wash the mushrooms and, unless they are quite small, cut each one in half. Wash and seed the bell peppers and cut them into approximately 1-inch squares. Peel and chop the onion. Melt the butter in a large saucepan and sauté the onion in it until transparent.

Prepare the sauce: Mix together the mustard, brown sugar, and Worcestershire sauce until you have a perfectly smooth paste. Add the wine, season with lots of fresh-ground black pepper, and a little seasoned salt, and stir well.

When the onion is clear, add the mushrooms and peppers to the pan and sauté a few minutes, stirring often. As the mushrooms begin to brown and reduce in size, add the wine sauce.

Simmer the mixture over a medium flame for about 45 minutes, or until the sauce is much reduced and thickened. The mushrooms and peppers will be very dark and evil looking, but irresistible in flavor and aroma.

4 to 6 servings.

marinated mushrooms oriental

1   lb. mushrooms, sliced in half
3   Tbs. butter or Ghee (page 254)
2 to 3 bay leaves
pinch of crushed thyme
1   onion, finely chopped
1   cup strong vegetable broth or vege-
      table **and** Potato Peel Broth (see
      page 50)
1   cup dry red wine
2   Tbs. thick tomato paste
1   Tbs. chopped parsley
salt and pepper

Melt the butter in a large saucepan. Add to it the bay leaves and crushed thyme, and let them sauté lightly for about 5 minutes. Now add the onion, and a few minutes later the mushrooms. Continue to sauté the mixture for a few minutes, then add the broth, wine, tomato paste, and parsley. Grind in lots of black pepper, add salt. Let the mixture simmer slowly for about ½ hour or longer, until the liquid is reduced to a very thick sauce. Remove the bay leaves and serve very hot from a deep, covered bowl. 6 servings.

hot stuffed mushrooms

16 to 20 large fresh mushrooms
2   dozen pitted ripe olives
8 to 10 pickled cocktail onions
1   cup strong vegetable broth
breadcrumbs, as needed
salt and pepper
butter

Wash the mushrooms, remove their stems, and scoop out a little of the insides. Chop the stems well and sauté lightly in a little butter. Mince the olives and onions and add them to the chopped mushrooms, along with a few tablespoons of the broth. Now add some breadcrumbs until the mixture is thick and stiff enough to handle. Season it with salt and pepper.

Stuff the mushroom caps with this mixture, arrange them in a baking dish, and pour the rest of the stock over them. Put a dab of butter here and there among them and bake in a 350-degree oven for about 15 minutes. Serve piping hot.

These mushrooms make a very nice first course, served with some cold, marinated vegetables. 6 to 8 servings.

mushrooms newburg

1½ lbs. medium mushrooms
¼ cup butter
3 Tbs. chopped onion
3 Tbs. sherry

Sauce:

2 Tbs. butter
2 Tbs. flour
2 cups light cream or 1 cup cream and
      1 cup milk, heated
2 egg yolks
2 Tbs. water
salt
cayenne pepper
nutmeg
toast

In a skillet, melt the ¼ cup butter until it bubbles, add the whole mushrooms (carefully washed) and onion, and sauté until almost tender, while you prepare the sauce. Add the sherry and simmer a minute or two.

To prepare the sauce: In another, smaller skillet, heat 2 tablespoons butter and combine it with the flour to make a roux. Add the heated cream and stir with a whisk until it thickens. Beat the egg yolks with the 2 tablespoons water and blend into the white sauce. Pour the sauce over the mushrooms in the pan and stir it all well, seasoning with a little salt, some grated nutmeg, and just a touch of cayenne pepper. Serve immediately, very hot, over toast.

Makes 4 to 6 servings.

italian mushroom casserole

1½ lbs. fresh mushrooms
2   Tbs. butter
¼   tsp. basil
¼   tsp. thyme
¼   tsp. oregano
1   clove garlic, crushed
¼   tsp. paprika
¼   tsp. rosemary
salt and fresh-ground black pepper to
      taste
3 to 4 oz. Parmesan cheese, grated
1   qt. Eggplant Pasta Sauce (page
      246)

Wash the mushrooms carefully. Melt the butter in a large skillet and add the herbs. Sauté the whole mushrooms in it for about 10 minutes, or until they are tender. Stir occasionally so that the herbs may be evenly distributed over the mushrooms, and add salt and pepper to taste.

Butter or oil a medium-size baking dish and arrange the mushrooms in it, making an even layer. Over the mushrooms, sprinkle the grated Parmesan cheese. Carefully pour the pasta sauce over the cheese, spreading it evenly over the top.

Cover and bake in a 350-degree oven for 15 minutes, or just until it is all heated through.

Serves 4.

onions monégasque

60 to 65 tiny boiling onions
1½ cups white wine
½ cup olive oil
⅓ cup wine vinegar
1 tsp. thyme seeds
1 bay leaf
2 to 3 cloves garlic
1 tsp. salt
3 to 4 Tbs. tomato paste
¼ tsp. saffron
¾ cup white sultana raisins

Peel the onions, being careful not to cut too much off from the root end. Put them in a saucepan with the wine, olive oil, vinegar, thyme, bay leaf, garlic, and salt. If necessary, add a little water to cover.

Bring the onions to a boil, turn down the heat, and simmer gently until they just begin to get tender. Stir in the tomato paste, the saffron, and the raisins, and continue simmering until the onions are barely tender, not yet really soft. Chill very well before serving.

Enough for 10 to 12 people when served with other hors d'oeuvres or vegetables. They keep very well in the refrigerator.

potatoes romanoff

6 large potatoes—peeled, boiled, and cubed
2 cups large-curd cottage cheese
1 cup sour cream
1 to 2 cloves garlic, put through a press
1 tsp. salt
2 to 3 scallions, finely chopped
1 cup grated Cheddar cheese
paprika

The potatoes should be boiled until they are just barely tender, not yet soft. Cut them up into rather small cubes and combine them with the cottage cheese, sour cream, garlic, salt, and scallions. Turn the mixture into a buttered casserole and sprinkle the grated Cheddar cheese over the top. Add a little paprika and bake at 350 degrees for about ½ hour. Serve hot.

6 to 8 servings.

onion tarte lyonnaise

1 recipe of Pastry Brisée, without
      sugar (page 286)
2 onions
3 to 4 Tbs. butter
4 eggs
¾ cup cream
¾ cup milk
3½ oz. grated Gruyère cheese
grated nutmeg
salt and pepper

Press the pastry brisée into a 9- or 10-inch quiche or pie dish, chill it for about ½ hour; prick the bottom with a fork and bake at 425 degrees for about 10 minutes.

Peel the onions and chop them roughly, then sauté them in butter until they are just softened, not yet transparent. Let them cool slightly. Beat the eggs in a bowl, add the milk and cream, the grated cheese, some nutmeg, salt and pepper, and mix very well.

Spread the onions on the bottom of the partly baked tart shell, pour the egg and cream mixture over them, sprinkle a little more nutmeg on top, and bake in a preheated oven at 350 degrees for about 30 minutes. When a knife inserted into the tart comes out clean it is ready to serve.

This may be eaten hot or cold and serves 6 to 8 people.

potatoes gruyère en casserole

I often have the unlikely-sounding problem of wondering what to do with all the potatoes I have left when I use the peels for a broth. Here is the problem-solving recipe:

4 to 5 potatoes, peeled and thinly sliced
1   cup sour cream
4 to 6 oz. grated Gruyère (or other mild
      cheese)
1   small onion, finely chopped
2   Tbs. chopped chives
salt and pepper
butter
wheat germ or breadcrumbs

Mix together the sour cream, the grated cheese, the onion, and the chopped chives. Butter a casserole and arrange in it a layer of the potatoes; salt and pepper them well. Follow this with a layer of half the sour cream mixture, and so on, finishing with the rest of the sour cream on top. Sprinkle on some wheat germ, dot with butter, and cover with a buttered lid. Bake at 350 degrees for 2 hours. Serve steaming hot. 4 large servings.

potatoes in wine

4   large russet (mealy) potatoes
3   Tbs. butter
8   tiny white onions
bay leaf
salt and pepper
dry white wine (at least half a bottle)

Floury, brown-skinned potatoes are essential; waxy potatoes will ruin the dish.

Melt the butter in a large skillet. Peel the onions and slice into thirds, sauté them a few minutes in the butter. Peel the potatoes and cut them into $\frac{1}{4}$-inch thick slices. Put them in the skillet with some salt and pepper and a small bay leaf. Pour dry white wine over until they are just covered.

Cover the pan and let it cook gently at least 1 hour. Check that the wine is still covering the potatoes; add some if it is needed, and carefully move them around a little so that they cook evenly.

When they are done, remove the potatoes and onions into a serving dish, bring the sauce to a quick boil and pour it over. Serve very hot. Beware only of eating too much, for it is easy to do. Serves 4 to 6.

ragout of potatoes

6   very large russet potatoes (about 3 lbs.)
2   large onions
¼   cup butter
1   tsp. Bakon yeast
2 to 3 cloves garlic; minced or pressed
1   cup strong vegetable broth
1   Tbs. fresh tarragon or ½ tsp. dried tarragon
salt and pepper
olive oil
wine vinegar
chopped parsley

Peel the potatoes and dice them. Peel and coarsely chop the onions. Heat the butter in a large skillet and stir in the Bakon yeast. Sauté the onion and garlic in it until the onion is transparent. Add the potato cubes and stir around for a few minutes.

When the potatoes are all evenly coated and warmed, add the vegetable broth, the tarragon, some salt and pepper, and just enough water to barely reach the top of the potatoes; it should not be more than a cup. Let this mixture simmer gently for about 45 minutes, stirring often. The potatoes should be tender and most of the liquid gone. A thick sauce will form from the pieces of potato which fall apart.

Pour over the potatoes about 2 tablespoons of olive oil and a little wine vinegar, and mix well. Sprinkle with some fresh chopped parsley and serve steaming hot.

Serves 6 to 8.

baked sauerkraut with peas

1 qt. sauerkraut, rinsed
1 cup whole dried peas, yellow or
  green
1 oz. dried black mushrooms
1 cup sour cream
salt and pepper

Soak peas overnight in water, then cook in the same water (adding more if necessary), for 1 hour at least, until tender.

Cook the mushrooms in 3 cups salted water for nearly 1 hour. Drain, and strain the broth through cheesecloth until absolutely clear. Wash the mushrooms *very* thoroughly, for they are probably still full of sand, and then chop them coarsely. Add the liquid, mushrooms, salt and pepper to taste, and sour cream to the sauerkraut, and simmer in a deep, open pot for another hour, stirring often. The liquid should be much reduced. Butter a fairly deep, attractive casserole or baking dish. Put a layer of the sauerkraut mixture in the bottom, then a layer of peas, and so on, ending with just a sprinkle of peas on the last layer of sauerkraut. Pour the rest of the sauerkraut-mushroom liquid over the layers; it should come almost to the top. Bake for ½ hour at 350 degrees.

Makes 8 to 10 servings.

spinach provençale

2 lb. fresh spinach
1 large onion
1 clove garlic
olive oil
butter
2 eggs, beaten
1 cup fresh-grated Parmesan cheese
salt and fresh-ground black pepper

Wash the spinach leaves carefully and the hard work is over. Chop the onion and mince the garlic. Heat the olive oil in a very large kettle and sauté the onion and garlic in it for a few minutes. When the onion is transparent, add the spinach and cover tightly. In about 2 minutes the spinach leaves will be reduced to a fraction of their former bulk, and you can stir them in with the oil and onions. Cook a few minutes longer and remove from the heat.

Butter a medium-size baking dish. When the spinach has cooled slightly, stir in 2 beaten eggs and ½ cup of the grated Parmesan. Season with salt and pepper to taste, and pour the mixture into the baking dish. Sprinkle the remaining Parmesan over the top and dot with butter.

Bake the spinach in a 375-degree oven for about 10 to 15 minutes and serve steaming hot.

Serves 4.

spanakopita

Spinach was never like this when I was little, but would that it had been! This puffy, golden-brown pastry is worth the effort of going to a special store for *filo* (a Greek kind of strudel dough) and Feta cheese.

2   lb. fresh spinach
1   lb. *filo*
7   eggs
½   lb. Feta cheese
1   onion
olive oil
salt and pepper
oregano
butter

To prepare the filling: Wash all the spinach well and put the leaves into a large bowl. Sprinkle them heavily with salt and then rub it into the leaves with your hands as you tear them into small pieces. After a few minutes of this, the spinach will be reduced to a quarter of its former bulk. Rinse the salt off thoroughly and drain.

Beat the eggs, crumble the Feta cheese, and mix together. Add to the spinach. Chop the onion, sauté it in some olive oil until it begins to brown, and add that to the spinach also. Season the mixture with lots of fresh-ground black pepper and a little oregano.

Now choose a large, oblong casserole or baking dish (about 9-inch x 13-inch should do it) and butter it. Melt about 3 to 4 tablespoons of butter in a little pot and stack the pound of *filo* on a flat surface. Brush the top sheet with melted butter and fit it into the baking pan, with the edges hanging over the sides. The pastry sheets are very large and should extend quite a bit over the edges, even after being fitted against the sides of the pan. Continue in this fashion brushing each sheet with butter and fitting it into the pan on top of the others. Turn each sheet slightly so that the corners fan out around the pan rather than being stacked on top of each other. Do this until you only have two or three pastry sheets left.

Now pour the filling in and then fold over

the ends of the pastry sheets to cover it, brushing with a little more butter. You should have sort of a strange-looking, wrinkled crust on top when you finish. Butter the remaining sheets and place them on top of the whole thing, folding them down to the size of the pan. With a sharp knife cut through the top layers to the filling in about three places. Brush the top with butter and bake at 375 degrees for 50 minutes. Cut into squares and serve very hot. Serves 8 generously.

hot tomatoes à la provençale

6   large, firm tomatoes
1½ Tbs. dried basil or 3 to 4 Tbs. fresh
     basil
1   small bunch fresh parsley
2 to 3 Tbs. chopped scallion
2 to 3 garlic cloves, minced
¼   tsp. dried thyme
salt and pepper
½ to 1 cup dark breadcrumbs
olive oil
lemon wedges

Cut a small round out of the top of each tomato and scoop out the pulp. Drain all the pulp slightly and turn the tomato shells over for a few minutes to drain.

Combine the tomato pulp with the chopped herbs, season with salt and pepper, and add enough fresh, dark breadcrumbs to make a thick paste. Fill the drained tomato shells with this mixture.

Lightly oil a casserole or baking dish and its lid. Arrange the tomatoes in it, cover, and bake for ½ hour at 350 degrees. Then remove the lid and bake 5 minutes more at 400 degrees. Serve hot and pass lemon wedges separately. Serves 6.

kolokithya dolmades *(Grapevine Leaves Stuffed with Squash)*

½ cup (uncooked) long-grain brown rice
1 lb. crookneck squash
2 onions
1 can peeled tomatoes or 4 to 5 fresh tomatoes
2 tsp. oregano
⅓ cup olive oil
1 Tbs. lemon juice
salt and pepper
1 15-oz. jar grapevine leaves or 30 to 40 tender young leaves fresh from a vine

Steam the rice according to directions. While it steams, wash the squash carefully and chop fine, without peeling. Also chop the onions and tomatoes. If you are using canned tomatoes, reserve the liquid. Heat the olive oil in a large skillet and throw in the chopped onion and squash. Sauté them until tender, then add the chopped tomatoes, the lemon juice, oregano, some salt, and lots of fresh-ground black pepper. Mix this together with the cooked rice and your dolma (filling) is ready.

Separate the vine leaves, handling them gently, and put a spoonful of filling in each one. Roll them tightly around the filling, starting from the stem end and folding in the sides so the filling can't come out. When all the filling is used up, line a baking dish with the rest of the vine leaves, arrange the rolled dolmades in it, very close together, and pour the liquid from the tomatoes, or some water, over them. Cover tightly and bake for about 20 minutes in a moderate oven. Serve very hot.

This recipe makes about 25 to 30 dolmades, enough for 6 to 8 servings.

oriental citrus squash

3 small acorn squashes
butter
½ cup orange marmalade
1 Tbs. candied ginger, cut into very
      small pieces
1 Tbs. lemon juice
pinch of nutmeg

Cut the squashes in half lengthwise, remove the seeds, brush them with butter, place them cut-side down on a greased pan, and bake about 40 minutes at 350 degrees. Fill the cavities with a mixture of the marmalade, the minced ginger, lemon juice, and nutmeg, and bake 15 minutes more. Serve very hot.

6 servings.

tomatoes dal and dill

6 large, firm tomatoes
about 2½ cups Spiced Dal (page 263)
fresh chopped dill or dried dill
salt and pepper

Cut the tops off the tomatoes and scoop out the pulp and seeds inside, leaving about ½ inch of meat inside the skin. Sprinkle a little salt on the inside of each tomato, and a fairly generous amount of chopped dill.

If the dal is freshly prepared, so much the better, and if it is left over from another meal, heat it up before stuffing. Into each tomato, stuff carefully as much dal as it will take, patting it down on top and sprinkling with some pepper and a little more dill.

Butter a casserole or baking dish and arrange the tomatoes in it. Cover and bake at 375 degrees for 15 to 20 minutes—no more. The tomatoes should be hot and tender, but not mushy. Serve immediately.

6 servings.

zucchini quiche

1 recipe Basic Shortcut Pastry
    (page 285)
¼ cup grated Parmesan
¼ cup grated Cheddar
½ cup dry breadcrumbs
1½ to 2 lb. fresh zucchini
2 eggs, separated
1½ cups sour cream
2 Tbs. chopped chives
2 Tbs. flour
⅛ tsp. cream of tartar
salt and fresh-ground black pepper
butter

This is a recipe for people who consider food a visual art. First it is constructed, then it is baked—and it's a lovely thing. When you bring it to the table, steaming hot out of the oven, it looks like a fabulous, double-crust, deep-dish pie. When you slice it into wedges, each one looks like a stone or brick wall. The first time I served this dish somebody told me I should have been a mason. (It's very good to eat, too: delicate and light, not at all like a wall.)

Prepare the pie-crust dough, combine the two grated cheeses, and add ½ cup of the mixture to the dough. Chill it, press into a 10-inch pie dish, and put it away to chill again. Mix the rest of the cheese with the breadcrumbs and set it aside.

Wash the zucchini and cut them into ¼-inch slices, trying to make the slices as even in width as possible. Drop them into a kettle of boiling, salted water for 5 minutes and drain.

Beat together the egg yolks and the sour cream; add the chives, flour, salt, and pepper. Beat the egg whites with the cream of tartar until they are stiff but not dry, and fold them into the sour cream mixture.

Arrange a layer of zucchini slices on the bottom of the pie crust, placing them edge to edge, and cover with a small amount of the sour cream mixture. Continue these layers, making two or three more, until it it all used up, and cover the top with the sour cream mixture. Sprinkle over it the cheese and breadcrumb mixture, dot with little slivers of butter; bake for 10 minutes in a 450-degree oven, then turn it down to 325 degrees and bake for 40 minutes more. 6 to 8 servings.

ratatouille

1   onion (or 1 cup of tiny boiling
      onions)
1   smallish eggplant
2   small bell peppers
3   medium zucchini
1   small cucumber
2 to 3 cloves garlic
1   small, hot red pepper
4   Tbs. olive oil
1   cup vegetable broth
1   cup Potato Peel Broth (page 50)
¾   cup tomato paste
3   tomatoes
⅔   cup Simple Vinaigrette Sauce (page
      97)

The onion should be coarsley chopped
(or, if you are using boiling onions, simply peeled), the eggplant diced into
1-inch cubes, the bell peppers quartered
and sliced, the zucchinis cut into ¼-inch
slices, the cucumber peeled, seeded and
diced, the hot red pepper finely minced,
and the cloves of garlic peeled and put
through a press.

Heat the olive oil in a very large skillet
and add to it the minced red pepper and

the garlic. After 2 to 3 minutes add the
onion. Stir for a few minutes more, and
then throw in the zucchini, the eggplant,
and the bell peppers; toss and stir with
two spoons until everything seems to be
as evenly coated in oil as possible. Mix
together in a bowl: the hot vegetable
broth, the strong potato peel broth, and
the tomato paste. Pour this over the vegetables in the skillet and add the cucumbers.

Cook the vegetables slowly in this liquid,
stirring occasionally, until the sauce is
almost gone—about 1 hour. The vegetables should be very tender, but not falling
apart. While cooking, cut the tomatoes
into eighths and a minute or two before
taking the ratatouille off the fire, stir in
the tomatoes. Cool the mixture well, then
pour over it ⅔ cup vinaigrette sauce and
toss lightly. Serve it chilled with hot rolls
or fresh bread.

This dish may also be served hot off the
fire, in which case the vinaigrette is omit-
ted.

This recipe makes about 8 servings.

marinated vegetables à la grecque

There are a good number of variations on the style of cooking vegetables known as "à la Grecque," and here is a good, basic one that can be adapted to a number of vegetables. It did, incidentally, originate in Greece, though it is now well established in French cuisine.

2   cups white wine
⅔ cup olive oil
1   tsp. salt
10 to 12 peppercorns
1   bay leaf
1   tsp. dried thyme
pinch of tarragon
2 or 3 garlic cloves
optional: onion, lemon juice, vinegar
              (for a sharper marinade)

Combine the oil and wine with the seasonings for the poaching liquid in a large skillet. Add just enough water to cover whatever vegetable is being cooked. Simmer the vegetable until it is just barely tender, then drain, blot the oil off, and chill before serving.

My favorite vegetables for this manner of preparation are tender small zucchini, sliced lengthwise into quarters; slender carrot sticks or whole baby carrots; whole green beans; halved fresh mushrooms; green onions; and leeks.

If you intend to cook several kinds of vegetables in the same marinade, cook the more delicately flavored first. For bland vegetables, especially, add some wine vinegar or lemon juice to the poaching liquid, or both.

Serve the vegetables on flat, elegant serving dishes or trays, arranged nicely and sprinkled with a little chopped parsley.

little vegetable tarts

Basic Shortcrust Pastry (enough for a double-crust pie—page 285)
2   medium carrots
12 little boiling onions
⅓ to ½ head cauliflower
1   cup fresh shelled peas
6   large, fresh button mushrooms
butter
Aurore, Béchamel, or Hollandaise Sauce (see pages 86, 84, 90)

Prepare the pastry and line 6 individual ovenproof dishes 4 inches deep. Prick the shells with a fork, put little circles of greaseproof paper or foil in them, and bake at 425 degrees for about 10 minutes.

Scrape and thickly slice the carrots, peel the onions, and break the cauliflower into 12 tiny flowerettes. Drop the peas, carrots, and onions into boiling water for about 4 minutes, add the cauliflower and, after 4 to 5 minutes more, drain the vegetables quickly. After they cool a bit, divide them equally among the 6 tart shells.

Wash the mushrooms and sauté them in butter for about 10 minutes, turning often. Place 1 mushroom in the center of each tart. Pour enough Sauce Aurore into each tart to just cover the vegetables. Grate a little fresh pepper on each one and bake for 15 to 20 minutes in a 375-degree oven. Serve immediately.

I think the Sauce Aurore works wonderfully, and the happy noises of my guests as they ate these seemed to substantiate my feeling. Either Hollandaise or Béchamel would make an interesting variation, however. Hollandaise, of course, would have to be added a little later, for fear of curdling from excess heat.

Serves 6

russian vegetable pie

Pastry:

1¼ cups flour
1   tsp. sugar
1   tsp. salt
4   oz. softened cream cheese
3   Tbs. butter

Filling:

1   small head cabbage (about 3 cups
       shredded)
½   lb. mushrooms
1   yellow onion
to taste: basil
          marjoram
          tarragon
          salt and fresh-ground pepper
3   Tbs. butter
4   oz. softened cream cheese
4 to 5 hard-cooked eggs
dill

Make a pastry by sifting together the dry ingredients, cutting in the butter, and working it together with the cream cheese. Roll out ⅔ of the pastry and line a 9-inch pie dish. Roll out the remaining pastry and make a circle large enough to cover the dish. Put it away to chill.

Shred a small head of cabbage coarsely. Wash the mushrooms and slice them. Peel and chop the onion.

In a large skillet, melt about 2 table-spoons butter. Add the onion and cab-bage, and sauté for several minutes, stir-ring constantly. Add at least ⅛ teaspoon each of marjoram, tarragon, and basil (all crushed), and some salt and fresh-ground pepper. Stirring often, allow the mixture to cook until the cabbage is wilted and the onions soft. Remove from the pan and set aside.

Add another tablespoon of butter to the pan and sauté the mushrooms lightly for about 5 or 6 minutes, stirring constantly.

Spread the softened cream cheese in the bottom of the pie shell. Slice the eggs and arrange the slices in a layer over the cheese. Sprinkle them with a little chopped dill, then cover them with the cabbage. Make a final layer of the sautéed mushrooms and cover with the circle of pastry.

Press the pastry together tightly at the edges, and flute them. With a sharp knife, cut a few short slashes through the top crust.

Bake in a 400-degree oven for 15 minutes, then turn the temperature down to 350 degrees and continue baking for another 20 to 25 minutes, or until the crust is light brown.

Serves 4 to 6.

stuffed pumpkin

1   medium-size pumpkin (6 to 8 lbs., 14-inch in diameter, approx.)
Risotto Doug Edwards (page 228)
soy or Worcestershire sauce
salt and pepper

Cut a circle, about 7 inches to 8 inches in diameter out of the top of the pumpkin. Carefully scrape out all the seeds and the thready pulp. When the pumpkin is thoroughly cleaned, sprinkle the inside liberally with Worcestershire or soy sauce, and with salt and pepper. Set it aside to "marinate" in these seasonings as you prepare the risotto.

When the risotto is ready, stuff it into the pumpkin. Replace the lid, fitting it exactly as it was cut out, and put the pumpkin in a shallow baking dish. Bake it in a preheated, 425-degree oven for about 1 hour, or until it is soft to the touch and the skin begins to char and blister.

Serve it very hot, scooping out generous servings of the filling and scraping some of the soft pumpkin from the inside with each helping. Serves 6 to 8.

eggs, omelets, and soufflés

EGGS

The humble egg astonishes us with its versatility. It binds together, puffs, lifts up, thickens, enriches, makes smooth, and makes strong—all this when its simple beauty would alone earn our admiration.

In its endless supporting roles it enhances breads and baked goods of all kinds, improves upon fine sauces, gives delicate support to many soups, blends subtly with cheeses and vegetables, and so on, through almost every category of food. To some great dishes, it is soul and substance: custards would not exist without it, nor would crêpes, or mousse . . . a serious thought.

Here, however, I am offering recipes in which the egg itself is the star performer. It takes splendidly to a fantastic range of seasonings, changing like a chameleon with herbs and spices of all types. The same egg that is the unassuming staple of your breakfast table is a sophisticated, airy soufflé at dinner, or impressively dressed on the half-shell at a buffet.

parsleyed eggs on the half-shell

6   eggs
1   bunch fresh parsley
7   Tbs. butter
salt and pepper

I have known this elegant and simple dish ever since early childhood and, as a consequence, when I first was exposed to American-style deviled eggs, I found them painfully plebeian by comparison.

For 6 eggs you will need a good-sized bunch of fresh parsley, a little less than 1 stick of butter, and salt and pepper to your taste.

Cook the eggs in water until they are hard, at least 10 to 15 minutes, but do it ever so slowly and gently—the better to protect their shells. When they are cool enough to handle, take a very sharp knife, preferably one with a serrated edge and, cupping an egg carefully in one hand, chip around it lengthwise, and then slice through the egg. Remove any little loose pieces of shell, scoop out the egg—white and yolk both—and dump it in a bowl.

Proceed in this fashion until all the eggs are in the bowl, and you have 12 perfect half-shells before you (maybe 10 or 11, because it *is* hard). Now the real work is finished and the fun begins.

Wash and chop the parsley. Chop up the eggs with a pastry cutter and mash them with about 3 or 4 tablespoons of softened butter, the chopped parsley, and salt and pepper according to your discretion. Mix this all up well into a manageable paste and stuff the eggshells with it, smoothing down the tops so they are nearly flat. This much can be done ahead if you wish. When you want to serve them, melt some butter in a large pan and turn the eggs upside-down in it. Leave them over a low flame for about 10 minutes, or until they are light brown and crisp on top and heated through. Then turn them back over on a platter and serve. If your guests seem at a loss for proper eating etiquette, guide them thusly: pick one up with your fingers and gently lift a portion of the stuffing out of the shell with your fork.

dill-deviled eggs

6   hard-cooked eggs
4 to 5 Tbs. sour cream
4 to 5 Tbs. chopped fresh dill
salt and pepper

If you do not have the time and/or the patience for the half-shell routine, here is a nice idea for deviled eggs which still manages to avoid that mayonnaise-mustard business that I find so tiresome.

Peel the eggs, slice them in half, and empty the yolks into a bowl. Mash the yolks with the sour cream and dill, adding salt and pepper to your taste. Put this mixture back into the egg whites and sprinkle a little more dill on top. Serve chilled.

eggs florentine

2   lb. fresh tender spinach
3   Tbs. olive oil
4   eggs
salt and pepper
butter
3 to 4 Tbs. grated sharp Italian cheese
Sauce Béchamel (see page 84)

Wash the spinach carefully and use only the leaves. Heat the olive oil in a fairly large saucepan and add the washed spinach leaves. Cover tightly for about 5 minutes, then remove the cover and stir, so that all the leaves are wilted and evenly coated with oil. Cook another few minutes and season with salt and pepper.

Lightly oil or butter a 2-inch deep baking dish. Arrange the hot spinach in it, a little higher at the edges than in the middle, and press in 4 hollows with the back of a spoon. Pour a little melted butter in each indentation and carefully break in the 4 eggs. Over them sprinkle the grated cheese, and then pour on just under 1 cup of Béchamel sauce.

Put it in the oven 10–15 minutes at 350 degrees, and serve hot. 4 servings.

curried stuffed eggs

6   hard-cooked eggs
2   Tbs. sour cream
2   Tbs. dried dill weed, or 3 to 4 Tbs.
       fresh dill weed
1   cup chopped, sautéed mushrooms
salt and pepper

Sauce:

3   Tbs. butter
3   Tbs. flour
2   tsp. curry powder
2   cups milk, heated
salt and pepper
paprika

Slice the eggs in half, scooping out the yolks into a bowl. Mash them with the sour cream, dill, some salt, and a generous amount of freshly ground black pepper. Now add the mushrooms, sautéed very lightly and quickly in a little butter. Mix it all up well and stuff the eggs, forming nice mounds on top. Arrange the eggs in a shallow, lightly buttered baking dish.

In a small skillet or the top of a double boiler, make a roux of the butter and flour; add the curry powder and slowly add the heated milk, stirring all the while until you have a smooth sauce. Season also with some salt and pepper and pour it over the eggs. Sprinkle a little paprika on top and put it into the oven at about 375 degrees for 10 or 15 minutes. Serve immediately, very hot.

baked eggs in zucchini

4 lb. zucchini
2 to 3 scallions, chopped
2 Tbs. butter
2 Tbs. olive oil
6 eggs
salt and pepper
Hollandaise Sauce (page 90)

Wash the zucchini carefully, scrubbing lightly under water, but don't peel them. Grate all the zucchini coarsely. In a large bowl, toss with 2 teaspoons salt, and let it rest this way for about 5 minutes. Take out the zucchini by handfuls, squeezing it gently to remove all excess water, and pile it on paper towels to drain. Zucchini prepared this way does not become a soft, stewy affair when it is cooked. (Meanwhile take 6 eggs from the refrigerator so they reach room temperature before using and preheat oven to 350°.)

Now heat the butter and olive oil in a large skillet, and add to it the chopped scallion. After a few minutes, add the zucchini and some fresh-ground black pepper, and sauté it over a medium-hot flame for about 8 to 10 minutes, stirring almost constantly.

Butter 6 small, individual casseroles. Divide the zucchini between them and make a shallow hollow in the center of each one.

About 15 to 20 minutes before you want to serve this dish, break one egg carefully into each little casserole of zucchini: it should just fit into the hollow place. Sprinkle the eggs with a little salt and a grate of black pepper. Bake them for about 15 minutes (350 degrees). The white should be completely set and the yolk still a little soft inside.

Spoon some hot Hollandaise sauce over each egg when you take them out of the oven and serve immediately.

Prepared this way, the Baked Eggs in Zucchini makes a very nice first course. If it is meant to carry the meal, double the recipe—using slightly larger oval dishes—and put 2 eggs in each serving.

OMELETS

The omelet, somehow, is quite easy to make perfectly and just as easy to spoil completely. Properly prepared it is a light and golden pleasure, tender and moist inside, smoothly veiled in butter outside. It is served hot from the pan, either by itself, splendidly simple, or gently concealing a savory or sweet filling. It is not the overcooked or greasy travesty passed off as an omelet by so many restaurants (the same ones that use canned fruit in their salads—villains!).

To be easily right, rather than easily wrong, acquaint yourself with the character of the omelet and learn the simple attentions it requires. Delicious omelets will always be only moments away.

Take care that your eggs are fresh, and the butter of fine quality. Cook the omelet quickly, in a proper pan, appropriate in size. Prepare the filling first so the omelet can be served at once when ready. As with soufflés, it is better that the guest waits a moment for the omelet than vice-versa, for the omelet doesn't wait gracefully—it gets tough and cold.

The omelet pan should be made of fairly heavy metal, and have rounded, gently slanting-out sides. The shape of a good omelet pan permits easy handling of the omelet while it cooks and easy transfer to the plate when done. Many a stylish omelet left a straight-edged pan only to find itself scrambled eggs by the time it reached the plate. If you use an omelet pan exclusively for eggs, you need only rub it clean with a cloth when finished, and properly made omelets will not stick to it.

For a basic omelet, enough for two people, use a pan about 8 inches across. Larger omelets can be made, of course, but it is preferable to make several small omelets than one huge, unwieldy one. For several people, individual omelets of two or three eggs are a good idea. When you have the filling and all ingredients ready, you can turn one out in about a minute and a half.

simple omelet for two

5   eggs
1   Tbs. water
2   Tbs. butter
2   tsp. grated Parmesan
salt and pepper

Break 4 whole eggs into a bowl; add the yolk of the fifth, putting its white in a separate small bowl. Beat the solitary egg white until just fluffy, and whisk together the other ingredients—egg, water, salt and pepper, grated cheese—until just mixed. The cheese, in modest quantity, does not assert its own flavor at all, but rather intensifies the flavor of the eggs.

Heat the pan and add butter. When it sizzles, combine the fluffy white with the rest of the eggs, pour them into the pan, and give it one quick swirl with the whisk. As it begins to set, gently lift the edges with a spatula so the liquid on top can run underneath. Do this until the liquid no longer runs, and while the eggs are still a little moist on top, slide the omelet toward the handle of the pan and

fold it either in half or in thirds. If you have a filling for the omelet, spread it on the instant before you fold the omelet. Serve immediately.

individual omelets

For each omelet:

2   eggs
1   tsp. water
salt
1   Tbs. grated Parmesan
optional: 2 Tbs. whipped egg whites
butter

Multiply the ingredients by the number of people you want to serve and have them ready: eggs beaten lightly with water, salt and Parmesan, whipped egg whites separately if you want them, and a hot pan with butter nearby.

To make each omelet, sizzle the butter in the pan, pour in the proper amount of egg mixture, and swirl in with the whisk a little whipped egg white. Now lift the edges a little with a spatula, and when the eggs are barely set, spoon on some filling or cheese, fold over, and serve.

simple mushroom omelet

4 to 5 eggs
12 to 15 fresh mushrooms
2   shallots
1   Tbs. cream if desired
butter
salt and pepper
sour cream or sauce, if desired

Wash the mushrooms carefully and slice them. Slice also the peeled shallots and, in a deep skillet, sauté them in a few tablespoons of butter. Whisk the eggs in a bowl (with cream, if you like). Add salt and pepper. Heat the omelet pan and put in some butter. Just before pouring the eggs into the pan, add the raw, sliced mushrooms to the shallots over a medium heat.

As you tend to your omelet, frequently stir the mushrooms; both should reach the peak of perfection at just the same moment. Put the mushrooms on one side of the omelet, fold it over, and serve immediately. You may want to put sour cream on top, or a delicate sauce, previously prepared, but this omelet does very well just as it is. 2 servings.

cheese and pepper omelet

5   eggs
salt and fresh-ground black pepper
butter
½   cup fresh-grated Parmesan cheese
4   oz. grated Gruyère cheese
½   green bell pepper, seeded and thinly
       sliced

Beat the eggs lightly with the salt and pepper, and stir in the Parmesan cheese. Melt some butter in an omelet pan and pour the beaten eggs in, giving them another stir with the whisk when they are in the pan.

When the omelet is nearly set, but still moist on top, sprinkle the Gruyère cheese over it, and over that the sliced bell peppers. Put the omelet under the broiler for about 2 to 3 minutes, or until the cheese is bubbly.

Fold the omelet over, slide it out on a serving plate, and serve immediately.

Serves 2.

apple and roquefort omelet

5   eggs
2 to 3 Tbs. grated Parmesan cheese
salt and fresh-ground black pepper
1   tart green apple
2   Tbs. butter
2   oz. Roquefort cheese, crumbled

Beat the eggs with the salt, pepper, and Parmesan cheese. Quarter the apple, peel and seed it, and cut into slices. Melt a tablespoon of the butter in the omelet pan and sauté the apple slices in it for about a minute, just long enough to heat them through. Remove the apple slices and add the remaining tablespoon of butter. When it is sizzling pour in the beaten eggs.

As soon as the omelet is set, and before it can dry out, spread the warm apple slices and the crumbled Roquefort on it, fold over, and serve immediately.

Serves 2.

spanish omelet

6 individual omelets or 3 large ones
1 long green chili pepper (about
    2 Tbs. diced)
1 medium green bell pepper (about
    ¾ cup diced)
½ onion (about ¾ cup diced)
2 cloves garlic
3 Tbs. olive oil
1 lb. peeled tomatoes, chopped
¼ cup sliced green olives
2 Tbs. capers
1 bay leaf
generous pinch of thyme
pinch of crushed tarragon
fresh-ground black pepper and salt
grated sharp Cheddar cheese

Roast the chili pepper under the broiler, turning it as often as necessary, until the skin is charred and crisp. Split it open, discard the seeds, and strip the pepper out of the skin. Chop it up.

Seed and dice the green pepper and chop up the onion. Put the garlic through a press. Heat the olive oil in a large skillet and add the onion, garlic, and peppers.

When the onion and garlic are quite transparent, add the tomatoes, olives, capers, and herbs. Season to taste with salt and pepper, and leave to simmer gently for at least ½ hour, longer if possible, stirring occasionally.

Prepare the omelet (or omelets) as usual, and when it is nearly set, pour on some of the hot sauce, sprinkle with grated, sharp Cheddar cheese, and put under the broiler just until the cheese is melted and bubbly. Serve immediately.

This recipe makes enough sauce for 6 individual Spanish omelets or 3 large omelets.

SOUFFLÉS

A soufflé is always a very special compliment to your guests. It is its ephemeral nature that is responsible for the mystique of the soufflé. Brought to the table straight from a hot oven in the full glory of its lofty architecture, it lasts only for a choice moment of drama and acclaim. Then, it must be eaten at once or it will disappear of its own accord. Thus a sweet excitement climaxes the dinner, and not lasting long enough for reconsideration or ennui, the airy soufflé leaves a more intriguing memory than sturdier fare.

To make a proper soufflé, you must carefully follow certain procedures. If you do this, and your oven is reliable, the results are almost guaranteed, so don't be frightened off.

The basic ingredients of most soufflés are: butter, flour, a liquid, a flavoring, eggs, and perhaps a spirit or sweetener for dessert soufflés. This is the way it is done: First, the butter should be melted in a heavy saucepan, and when it is foamy, the flour stirred in to make a paste. This roux, as it is called, should be heated a few moments before the liquid is added, bit by bit, as you whisk to make a smooth sauce. Remove the pan from the heat and, still whisking, add the egg yolks, one at a time. Now you have the basic sauce to which you add the cheese, vegetables, herbs, or whatever flavoring you will use. This much can be done in advance if you wish to be free of bother at dinner time. If you do prepare a day ahead, be sure to keep the sauce *refrigerated* in a tightly closed container and to reheat it *slightly* before proceeding.

Now comes a crucial moment in the making of a soufflé. The beating of the egg whites and their handling thereafter is the yes-or-no to your subsequent success. The egg whites should be at room temperature before they are beaten. Do not let a drop of water mix into the whites, and if a bit of yolk has slipped in when separating the eggs, scoop it out carefully with one of the broken shells. If you forgot to take them out in time, let them stand in some warm water for a few minutes. Add a pinch of salt and, unless you are using an unlined copper bowl, add also a pinch of cream of tartar.

The copper bowl is recommended for the chemical reaction which takes place between its very slight acidity and the egg whites. From this (or the cream of tartar), the egg whites are stabilized and will not separate or deflate. As to the instrument of beating, nothing is superior to the wire whisk. Be sure that both the bowl and whisk are very clean and dry. Beat the egg whites until they are stiff, but still smooth and moist. If they are so peaky and dry that they form clumps, you have gone too far and must begin anew.

Take about a cupful of these perfectly beaten egg whites and mix them very gently into your sauce. Then pour the sauce over the rest of the beaten egg whites and, using a spatula, fold it in with the utmost care, and stop a bit short of a homogeneous mixture. Every extra fold deflates. Pile this mixture into a buttered soufflé dish, place it in the center of a preheated oven, and softly close the door.

After the prescribed amount of time, check your masterpiece. If it has risen high above the dish, if it is deep gold in color, and it does not wobble when touched, it is ready and should be served at once. If not, give it another 5 minutes.

As to the soufflé dish: it should be straight-edged and proportionate in size to the number of eggs used. For large soufflés especially, tie around it a "collar" of folded, greased paper which should extend an inch or two over the top. Remove just before serving.

asparagus soufflé

3 Tbs. butter
4 Tbs. flour
1½ cups milk
6 egg yolks
1 Tbs. chopped fresh parsley
1 Tbs. chopped chives
salt and pepper
4 to 5 Tbs. grated Parmesan cheese
1 cup cooked asparagus, cut into
      small pieces
pinch of cream of tartar
8 egg whites

Butter a 6-cup soufflé dish and tie a collar around it (see preceding page).

Melt the butter and add the flour, stirring until smooth. Whisk in the milk slowly, until you have a smooth, thick sauce. Remove the pan from the heat and, whisking carefully, add 1 egg yolk at a time until they are all in the sauce. Add the seasonings, the cheese, and the pieces of asparagus. Be certain that none of the asparagus pieces are from the tough ends of the stalks.

Add a pinch of cream of tartar and a little salt to the egg whites (which should be at room temperature), and beat them with a whisk until they are stiff but not dry. Mix a few heaping spoonfuls of the egg whites into the sauce to make it somewhat lighter, then fold in the rest with great care. Pile it all gently into the prepared soufflé dish and place it carefully in the center of a preheated 350-degree oven. It should bake about 35 to 40 minutes, or until it has risen high above the dish and does not wobble when tapped.

This will feed 6 people if you are also serving other courses, or 4 if it is to be the feature attraction and you are all very hungry. Serve the soufflé immediately out of the oven, and with a hot Dill Sauce (page 92) for a truly fantastic combination.

chestnut soufflé

With very minor changes, this soufflé can play two distinct roles: the savory soufflé, to stop all conversation in the course of a dinner, or the sweet soufflé, for a lovely breakfast or dessert. Not many palates have met this taste, but precious few can resist it when they do. Although chestnuts are a seasonal delicacy here, they can be found in cans and jars, either puréed or whole, in many delicatessens and specialty stores.

3   Tbs. butter
4   Tbs. flour
1   cup light cream or milk
6   egg yolks
7   egg whites
2 to 3 Tbs. grated Parmesan cheese
1   cup chestnut purée
tiny pinch of nutmeg
salt and pepper
cream of tartar

Melt the butter and add the flour to make a roux. Gradually stir in the cream or milk with a whisk until you have a smooth, thick sauce. Remove the pan from the heat and whisk in 1 egg yolk at a time until they are all in. Stir in the cheese, the chestnut purée, and the seasoning. Add the cream of tartar and some salt to the egg whites, which should be at room temperature, and beat them with a whisk until they are stiff but not dry. Stir in a few spoonfuls of the whites into the sauce, then very carefully fold in the rest. Pile it all into a prepared 6-cup soufflé dish and bake in a preheated, 350-degree oven for about 35 to 40 minutes, or until it tests done. Serve immediately to 4 to 6 people.

For a sweet soufflé, simply add 2 to 3 tablespoons of sugar and a few drops of vanilla to the chestnut purée, and eliminate the grated Parmesan. If you like, you may also thin the purée with about a tablespoon of cognac. A Sunday morning breakfast of sweet chestnut soufflé and hot cornbread, along with fresh coffee and the fruit of the season, was one of the most appreciated meals I ever prepared.

cheese soufflé

6 oz. grated Swiss or Gruyère cheese
2 Tbs. grated Parmesan cheese
6 egg yolks ⎫ brought to room
8 egg whites ⎭ temperature
3½ Tbs. butter
4 Tbs. flour
1½ cups milk
salt
⅛ tsp. cream of tartar
1½ tsp. prepared Dijon mustard
¼ tsp. powdered garlic
¼ tsp. powdered lemon peel
pinch of cayenne
pinch of nutmeg
grated black pepper

Melt the butter in a saucepan and stir in the flour. Cook this roux for a few minutes, then add the milk, stirring with a whisk until you have a smooth, thick sauce. Remove the sauce from the heat, and stir in the cheese and seasonings. When the sauce has cooled considerably, stir the egg yolks in with a whisk.

Add a little salt and cream of tartar to the egg whites, and whip with a wire whisk until they are stiff.

Prepare a soufflé dish by buttering it and tying a "collar" of buttered greaseproof paper or tin foil around it. Stir about a cup of the whipped egg whites into the cheese sauce. This will lighten the texture of the sauce and allow you to fold in the remaining whites without losing too much air. When the whites are folded in, pile the mixture carefully into the soufflé dish.

Place the dish in a preheated, 400-degree oven and turn the heat down to 375 degrees. Bake for 40 to 45 minutes and serve immediately with White Wine Sauce or Herb and Wine Sauce (see pages 91 and 88).

Serves 6.

spoonbread: a corn-meal soufflé

Spoonbread is only a bit less light than most soufflés, owing to the rather coarse texture of the corn meal. All in all, it's a delightful difference. Serve it for breakfast, with cream cheese and preserves, or—for a classic down-home dinner—pair it with your greatest baked beans.

1½ Tbs. butter
2 cups milk
½ cup white corn meal
3 eggs, separated
¾ tsp. salt
pinch of cream of tartar

Butter a soufflé dish with a little of the butter and preheat the oven to 400 degrees. Scald the milk and stir into it the remaining tablespoon of butter and the corn meal. Continue simmering and stirring until the mixture is thick, then let it cool to lukewarm.

Beat in the egg yolks. Whip the egg whites separately with the salt and cream of tartar until they form stiff peaks, and carefully fold them into the mixture.

Pile it into the prepared soufflé dish and bake at 400 degrees for about 40 minutes. Serve at once.

Serves 3 to 4.

eggplant soufflé

1 medium eggplant (about 1 lb.)
1 tsp. salt
2 Tbs. butter
1 small clove garlic, put through a
   press
2 Tbs. flour
1 cup milk
2 to 3 oz. fresh-grated Parmesan
   cheese
½ tsp. fresh-ground black pepper
3 egg yolks
4 egg whites
⅛ tsp. cream of tartar

Bake the eggplant in a pie dish in a 400-degree oven for about 45 minutes or until the pulp is soft. Cool it under running water so that you can handle it, then split it in half and let the excess water drain out. Scrape out all the pulp and mash it well. Season it with a teaspoon of salt.

Melt the butter in a small saucepan and add the garlic to it. Stir in the flour and let the roux cook for a few minutes. Heat the milk slightly and beat it into the roux with a whisk. When the sauce thickens, remove it from the heat and stir in the grated cheese and the eggplant pulp. Season with black pepper. Finally, add the egg yolks, lightly beaten.

Add a pinch of cream of tartar to the egg whites and beat them with a whisk until they are quite stiff but not yet dry. Stir about a third of the egg whites into the eggplant mixture thoroughly. Gently fold in the remaining whites.

Pile the mixture into a buttered 6-cup soufflé dish and place it gently into a preheated, 350-degree oven. Bake the soufflé about 45 to 50 minutes and serve at once.

Serves 4.

three-cheese ramequins

Ramequins are nothing more mysterious than tiny soufflés. There is some small difference in preparation, but the principle is the same. Being individual portions, they are perhaps even more delightful to serve.

5   eggs, separated
2   Tbs. brandy
¼   tsp. dry mustard
pinch of crushed thyme
pinch of grated nutmeg
pinch of cayenne pepper
salt and fresh-ground black pepper
½   cup Ricotta cheese
¾   cup grated Romano cheese
¾   cup grated Swiss cheese

Separate the egg whites from the yolks. Beat the yolks together with the brandy and seasonings, and stir in the three cheeses.

Beat the whites with a whisk until they hold a stiff peak. Add a quarter of the whites to the egg-yolk mixture and stir in thoroughly. Fold in the remaining whites gently.

Empty this mixture into 4 buttered ramequins or tiny baking dishes. Place them in a preheated, 425-degree oven for about 15 to 20 minutes, or until they are puffed and nicely browned on top. Serve at once.

Serves 4.

ramequins with artichoke purée

1 lb. artichoke hearts (drained weight)
4 Tbs. olive oil
1 Tbs. white wine vinegar
pinch of tarragon
1 clove garlic, crushed
salt and black pepper
8 eggs
6 Tbs. sour cream
1½ cups finely grated Parmesan cheese
1 Tbs. brandy
⅛ tsp. nutmeg
⅛ tsp. cayenne pepper
1 cup fresh, light breadcrumbs
⅛ tsp. cream of tartar

Purée the artichoke hearts in a blender together with the olive oil, vinegar, tarragon, garlic, salt, and pepper.

Divide the purée equally among 6 to 8 individual buttered soufflé dishes or ramequin cups, making a smooth layer in the bottom of each.

Separate the yolks from the whites of the eggs. Add all the remaining ingredients, except the cream of tartar, to the yolks and stir well. Beat the whites with the cream of tartar until they are stiff but not dry. Stir about a third of the beaten whites into the egg-yolk mixture. Fold in the remaining whites gently. Divide this mixture evenly among the dishes, spooning it carefully over the artichoke purée. Bake the ramequins for about 25 minutes at 350 degrees, or until they are lightly browned on top and puffy.

Serves 6 to 8.

walnut and cheese soufflé

2 Tbs. butter
1 clove garlic, put through a press
½ medium onion, minced
pinch of thyme
3 Tbs. flour
1 cup tomato purée
½ cup cream
¾ cup finely ground walnuts
1 cup grated mild Cheddar cheese
¼ tsp. dry mustard
salt and fresh-ground black pepper
4 egg yolks
6 egg whites
⅛ tsp. cream of tartar

Melt the butter in a heavy-bottomed saucepan and sauté the onion and garlic in it until transparent. Add a pinch of thyme and stir in the flour. Let the roux cook for a few minutes, then stir in the cream and the tomato purée, beating with a wire whisk to make a smooth sauce. When it is all heated through and thick, beat again with the whisk, and add the walnuts and cheese. Remove the sauce from the heat and beat in the mustard, egg yolks, and some salt and pepper.

Beat the egg whites with the cream of tartar and some salt until they are stiff but not dry. Stir a third of the egg whites into the sauce. Fold the remaining whites in gently. Pile the soufflé into a 6-cup, buttered soufflé dish and place in a preheated 400-degree oven. Turn the oven down immediately to 375. Bake the soufflé for 35 to 40 minutes.

Serves 4 to 6.

potato soufflé

2   cups hot mashed potatoes (about 2
      large russet potatoes)
½   cup sour cream
3   oz. grated sharp Cheddar cheese
      (about ¾ to 1 cup)
4   eggs, separated
salt and pepper
3   Tbs. chopped chives or scallions
cream of tartar

Beat the mashed potatoes with the sour
cream, the shredded cheese, salt and
pepper, and the egg yolks. A blender does
the best job of this in about 2 minutes.
Stir in the chopped chives or scallions.

Beat the egg whites with a little salt and
a pinch of cream of tartar until stiff. Fold
them carefully into the potato mixture
and pile it into a buttered soufflé dish.
Bake in a preheated, 350-degree oven for
about 45 minutes and serve at once.

Serves 4.

crêpes and pancakes

The simple crêpe has such a purity of flavor that it has been paired successfully with every conceivable kind of filling and sauce—sweet, tart, savory, and spicy. The simplest crêpes remain my favorites, though. They are a joy *au naturel,* or with just a dusting of sugar! And the most wonderful breakfast I ever ate consisted of simply a platter of hot, feathery-light crêpes accompanied by a bowl of sour cream and assorted, fresh, summer fruit—strawberries, sliced peaches and nectarines, and juicy plums. Such a breakfast will convert you to crêpery at once, especially if served outdoors, under the full, summer trees.

The making of crêpes is not a difficult process, even in the beginning, and two or three crêpes should make you a master. Invest in a crêpe pan—a heavy, shallow frying pan with gently sloping edges—or use a good omelet pan. Be sure it is well buttered at the start, and swirl a piece of butter around in it between crêpes. The first one will not be perfect, but as soon as you regulate the heat of the pan, you will also regulate your crêpes. Pour in about 2 or 3 tablespoons of batter and then quickly tilt the pan around in one smooth motion to spread the batter evenly. Cook the crêpe about a minute on each side, or just until it is golden and firm enough to be easily turned.

One of the glories of crêpes is that, unlike pancakes, they can be prepared ahead of time and reheated later. Because they consist almost completely of milk and eggs, with only a bit of flour to bind them, they are thin and soft to begin with, and thin and soft they remain.

Part of the charm of pancakes, I suppose, is eating them in the kitchen, hot off the griddle. But if something less casual is desired, a German baked pancake can be served (it's ready all at once, not a serving at a time) with great elegance and very little trouble. Serve it for breakfast, lunch, or for an unusual, light supper. All the batter is baked in one skillet, then the huge, puffy pancake is smothered with spicy, buttery, hot apple slices and folded over before being served. Wedges of sharp, aged Cheddar cheese perfect the meal.

french crêpes

⅔ cup white flour
½ tsp. salt
3 eggs
2 cups milk, scalded and cooled
2 Tbs. melted butter
butter for the pan
cognac (optional)

Sift together the flour and the salt. Beat the eggs and mix them into the flour. Add the milk and, stirring with a whisk, carefully add the melted butter. If you like, you may also add 1 or 2 tablespoons cognac. Strain the batter through a sieve and set it aside for an hour or two.

Heat a crêpe pan and brush it with butter. For a 6-inch pan, use about 2 to 2½ tablespoons batter. Take the pan from the heat when it is almost smoking, pour in just enough batter to cover it, swirling it lightly to distribute the batter evenly. Cook over a medium heat about a minute, loosening the edges gently with a spatula; turn over and cook another minute on the other side. The crêpes may be used immediately or stacked on a plate for later use. After the first crêpe, if you are using a proper pan, you will need very little butter.

Crêpes may be kept in the refrigerator for a day or two. The stack should be wrapped neatly in a clean, dry cloth for storage.

I keep a crêpe pan for crêpes only, and it is a good habit. Never use your crêpe pan for anything else, and you will never have to wash it. Just wipe it clean with a dry cloth after use. Taken care of this way, your pan will yield lovely crêpes with no problem of sticking and tearing.

About 20 crêpes.

parmesan crêpes

1 cup flour
1 tsp. salt
6 eggs
3 cups milk
3 Tbs. melted butter
½ cup grated Parmesan cheese
butter for the pan

Sift the flour and salt into a bowl and stir in the beaten eggs. Add the milk slowly, beating with a whisk, then the melted butter and the finely grated Parmesan. The batter should be very smooth and have the consistency of cream. Let it stand at least an hour or two before making the crêpes.

To make the crêpes, heat your crêpe pan and melt some butter in it. When the pan is almost smoking pour in about 2 to 3 tablespoons of the batter at a time, swirling it around to the edges immediately. The crêpe should cook about a minute or so on each side. Butter the pan slightly between each crêpe, for the cheese would like to stick and make things difficult. Stack the crêpes on a plate, and when you have finished, roll them up and arrange them on a buttered baking dish. Cover the dish with one or two damp tea towels and heat the crêpes for about 10 minutes in a moderate oven. Serve them very hot with Creamed Black Mushroom Sauce (see page 87), also hot.

This recipe makes about 20 to 24 crêpes, enough to feed 6 hungry gourmets.

simple breakfast pancakes

1¼ to 1½ cups unbleached white flour
1 Tbs. sugar
¼ tsp. salt
1 Tbs. baking powder
3 eggs, separated
2 cups milk
¼ cup melted butter

Sift the dry ingredients into a mixing bowl. Beat the egg yolks with the milk and melted butter, and stir into the flour. Beat the egg whites until they are fluffy, but not dry, and fold them into the batter.

Heat a large skillet or griddle and oil it lightly. Drop the pancake batter on by large spoonfuls and brown nicely on both sides. Serve immediately with butter, syrup or honey, jelly, yogurt, or whatever. Fresh fruit and yogurt are especially recommended for a festive and satisfying breakfast.

This recipe serves 3 to 4.

blini *(Russian Yeast Pancakes)*

2 pkgs. dry yeast
4 cups warm milk
2 tsp. melted butter
2 tsp. sugar
4 eggs
2½ cups white flour
1½ tsp. (approximately) salt
½ cup cream
salt

Dissolve the yeast in a little of the warm milk, then add the rest of the milk, the melted butter, sugar, egg yolks, and flour. Stir this mixture with a whisk until it is absolutely smooth, then add about 1½ teaspoons salt, and put it aside while you whip the egg whites. When the whites are quite stiff, fold them into the mixture, as well as the cream. Now put the bowl in a warm place and don't disturb it for at least 20 minutes, maybe a little longer.

Fry the *blini* in butter on a large griddle or pan, browning them lightly on both sides. Serve them hot with sour cream and chopped, hard-cooked eggs.

Serves 4 to 6.

vegetable crêpes

3   Tbs. olive oil
¾   cup onion, chopped
¾   cup scallions, chopped
2   cloves garlic, put through a press
1½ cups green pepper, diced
2   cups peeled and diced tomatoes
1   tsp. crushed basil
2   tsp. crushed parsley
salt and fresh-ground black pepper
⅓   cup milk
⅓   cup flour
2   eggs
1   Tbs. melted butter
3   oz. grated Swiss or Gruyère cheese
2   oz. grated Parmesan cheese

Heat the olive oil in a large skillet and sauté the onion, scallions, garlic, and green pepper in it until the onion is transparent. Add the tomatoes and increase the heat. Stir in the herbs, season liberally with salt and pepper, and continue cooking and stirring until the water from the tomatoes is nearly all evaporated. Correct the seasoning and remove from the heat.

Blend together all ingredients for the batter: the milk, flour, eggs, melted butter, and a little salt. Put the batter aside for about ½ hour.

When the vegetable mixture has cooled, stir in the batter. Melt some butter in a heavy-bottomed skillet and pour out a little less than ¼ cup of batter for each crêpe. Fry them to a golden brown on both sides.

Arrange the crêpes on cookie sheets and sprinkle a heaping tablespoon of the mixed grated cheeses on each one. If the crêpes are still warm, pop them under the broiler for a few minutes. If they have been allowed to cool, place them in a 350-degree oven for about 7 or 8 minutes.

Serves 4 to 5.

crêpes au fromage *(Cheese-stuffed Crêpes)*

1   recipe French Crêpes (page 184)
6   Tbs. butter
8   Tbs. flour
2   cups milk
3   oz. grated Swiss or Gruyère cheese
1   oz. grated Sapsago (Romano or Parmesan may be substituted—with quite different results, of course)
3   egg yolks
fresh-ground black pepper
nutmeg
White Wine Sauce (page 91)

Prepare the crêpe batter according to directions on page 184.

Melt the butter in a heavy-bottomed saucepan and stir in the flour. When this roux has cooked a few minutes, heat the milk and pour it in gradually, beating all the while with a wire whisk. When a perfectly smooth and thick sauce has been attained, stir in the grated cheeses. Remove the sauce from the heat and beat in the egg yolks. Season with black pepper and nutmeg.

Oil a square baking pan and spread the thick sauce evenly in it. Chill for several hours or until stiff enough to cut.

Make the crêpes as directed. Cut the stiff cheese sauce into about 20 narrow oblongs, each about 1-inch wide and 3 inches long. Wrap a crêpe around each oblong, tucking under the sides as you wrap.

Arrange these crêpes in a lightly buttered baking dish and put them into a preheated, 400-degree oven for about 20 minutes. They should be soft inside and bubbling hot. Serve them immediately with a delicate White Wine Sauce and a fruit salad.

Serves 6.

almond crêpes

1   recipe French Crêpes (page 184)
2   eggs
1   cup sieved or whipped cottage
    cheese
8   oz. almonds, blanched and ground
½   cup toasted wheat germ
1   Tbs. butter
½   onion, minced
1   small clove garlic, put through a press
2   Tbs. sesame seeds
nutmeg
salt

Garnish:

White Wine Sauce (page 91) or Cranberry-Cumberland Sauce (page 89)

Prepare crêpe batter according to directions on page 184.

Beat the eggs, then beat in the cottage
cheese. Add the ground almonds and the
wheat germ. Sautè the onion and garlic
in the butter until it is transparent, then
add the sesame seeds and sautè a few
minutes longer. Stir the onions, garlic, and
sesame seeds into the almond mixture.
Season lightly with salt and nutmeg, and
stir well.

Make the crêpes as directed. Place 2 or
3 tablespoons of this filling on a crêpe and
roll it up as you would a blintz, folding
the sides in as you roll to make a very neat
little package. Fill all the crêpes this way.

If you like your crêpes crisp, fry them in
a little butter on both sides until they are
golden brown and heated through. An
alternate method of heating the crêpes is
to arrange them in a lightly buttered baking dish and to bake them for about 20
minutes in a preheated, 350-degree oven.
Serve hot with White Wine Sauce or
Cranberry-Cumberland Sauce.

Serves 5 or 6.

potato pancakes

2½ cups grated raw potatoes
4   Tbs. finely chopped onion
1   tsp. salt
2   large eggs
3   Tbs. cracker meal or fine, dry
        breadcrumbs
fresh-ground black pepper to taste
oil and butter

Garnish:

Sour cream
applesauce

Peel and grate 3 large potatoes and press the excess water out thoroughly. Measure out 2½ cups of grated potatoes. Stir in the finely chopped or shredded onion, the salt, 2 lightly beaten eggs, and the cracker meal or breadcrumbs. If the batter is still too moist, you may add a little more cracker meal. Grate in black pepper to taste.

Heat a large, heavy skillet and melt some butter in it. Add an equal amount of salad oil. There should be almost ¼ inch of melted fat in the skillet. Drop the pancake batter in by heaping spoonfuls and flatten slightly with the back of the spoon. Fry the pancakes until crisp and brown on both sides. Serve very hot with cold sour cream and applesauce.

Serves 3 to 4.

cottage cheese pancakes

6   eggs, separated
2   cups small-curd cottage cheese
⅔ cup flour
2   Tbs. sugar
1   tsp. salt
dash of cinnamon
⅛ tsp. cream of tartar
oil or butter for frying

Garnish:

Sour cream, preserves, honey, apple butter, or powdered sugar

Beat together the egg yolks, cottage cheese, flour, sugar, salt, and a sprinkle of cinnamon.

In another bowl beat the egg whites with the cream of tartar until they are stiff but not dry. Fold the beaten whites gently into the cheese mixture.

Drop the batter by large spoonfuls onto an oiled griddle or skillet. Fry the pancakes until golden brown on both sides and puffy. Serve at once with sour cream, preserves, honey, apple butter, or powdered sugar.

This is the perfect protein breakfast for the morning sweet-tooth.

Serves 4 generously.

orange whole wheat pancakes

2   eggs
¼   cup oil
2   cups whole wheat flour
½   tsp. soda
½   tsp. salt
orange juice (about 1½ to 2 cups)

Beat the eggs and the oil together. Sift together the dry ingredients and add them to the eggs. Gradually add orange juice until you have a batter of the consistency you like. You probably will use about 1½ to 2 cups. Fry the pancakes on a medium-hot griddle and serve immediately.

This is a fine, delicately flavored pancake, best served with sour cream or yogurt and honey. For an interesting variation in taste and texture, add a few spoons of ground or chopped walnuts to the batter.

Serves 3 to 4.

german apple pancake

This is a pancake—just one—you bake, and it's ready all at once for everyone, instead of a serving at a time. It can be a special-day breakfast for two or three people, a light, late supper, or a beautiful, warm dessert for four to six people. In that last category, I personally much prefer it to apple pie.

Pancake:

3   large eggs
¾   cup milk
¾   cup white flour
½   tsp. salt
1½   Tbs. butter (unsalted preferred)
½   cup thin-sliced apples (optional)

Filling:

1   lb. tart, fresh apples (Pippin are great)
¼   cup melted butter
¼   cup sugar
powdered cinnamon and nutmeg

Topping:

2   Tbs. melted butter (optional)
powdered sugar

Preheat the oven to 450 degrees. Beat together the eggs, milk, flour, and salt until very smooth. Add some very thinly sliced apples if desired. In a heavy 12-inch skillet, melt about 1½ tablespoons butter. As soon as it is quite hot, pour in the batter and put the skillet in the oven. After 15 minutes, lower the oven temperature to 350 degrees and continue baking for another 10 minutes. The pancake should be light brown and crisp.

During the first 10 or 15 minutes of baking, the pancake may puff up in large bubbles. If it does, pierce it thoroughly with a fork or skewer.

While the pancake is baking, prepare the apple filling. Peel and thinly slice a pound of apples. Sauté them lightly in ¼ cup butter and add ¼ cup sugar. Season to taste with cinnamon and nutmeg. The apples should be just tender, not too soft. About 8 to 10 minutes of cooking over a medium flame should be plenty. (The filling can be prepared ahead and reheated just before serving.)

When the pancake is ready, slide it onto an oval platter, pour the apple filling over one side, and fold the other side over. A little melted butter can be poured on if you choose, and the whole thing carefully sprinkled with powdered sugar through a sieve. Serve it at once, slicing pieces off crosswise.

cheese

Cheese is as noble as bread and as brilliant as wine, and may the three remain always the greatest tradition in gastronomy.

Regard cheese with all the reverence it deserves. At the same time, try to know more about it, for there's a good chance, if you grew up in the average American household, that you have barely made its acquaintance. The noble name of cheese, like bread, has been assaulted by unbridled commercialism. It is attached to horrifying assortments of "spreads," "processed cheeses," and "cheese foods." Politely but firmly ignore them. Walk out of the supermarket where they commonly cohabit with poor imitations of aristocratic lineages, and search out a cheese shop, a good delicatessen, or one of the many ethnic groceries or specialty shops that stock a selection of cheeses.

There admire the lordly cylinder of English Stilton, and the wheels of true Roquefort. If it is autumn or winter you might take home a small round of Normandy Camembert, pressing it gently first to establish its ripeness (it should give just a little). Admire the honest American Cheddars—pale orange and flaky. One that is properly aged (a year is a fair time) will crumble in your fingers and melt in your mouth. Admire the Italian Gorgonzola and smooth Provolone, but never fall prey to an imitation of the latter, for the original is made from water buffalo's milk and can't even be attempted here. For cooking, carry away a good-sized wedge of hard, old Parmesan. Grate it fresh when you need it, and discover it at last: that gritty business in the plastic cannisters is hardly more than the thief of its name.

While most cheeses have their preferred stations either on the menus or in the kitchens of gourmets, almost all of the "eating cheeses" have at one time or another been used to advantage in some cooked, baked, stewed, or steamed preparation. Likewise, the cheese cannot be found that isn't eaten fresh somewhere.

The list of local cheeses the world over is beyond my calculation and the scope of this book, but I do think it worth introducing—or reviewing—a few of the most popular and readily available kinds of cheeses, domestic and imported.*

*See also *The Cheese Book* by Vivienne Marquis and Patricia Haskell, and *The Complete Book of Cheese* by Bob Brown.

We begin properly with the great blues, which are indisputably English Stilton, French Roquefort, and Italian Gorgonzola. Danish Blue, Blue Cheshire, Minnesota Blue, and many regional variations humbly follow them. They range well in sharpness and in creaminess of texture, but all the cheeses of this type are distinguished by the thin branching veins of greenish-blue mold which permeate them. In picking a Roquefort or Stilton, look for a rich ivory color, rather than chalky white, and for veins which reach evenly through all parts of the cheese. Above all, taste! Taste Roquefort with its steady companions, the fine red wines of France, or Stilton with a piece of ripe fruit for one of the most perfect endings a fine meal could find.

Universally popular as dessert cheeses are Camembert and Brie, the two greatest, soft-ripened French cheeses. Both have fairly thick crusts, powdery with mold, and are best when soft and just a bit runny: Ripe Camembert or Brie will give very easily under a slight pressure from your fingers. These are not cheeses for all seasons, however; buy them from September to March. Other soft-ripened dessert cheeses worth noting are Boursin, the mild Italian Bel Paese and American Liederkranz, both fairly new as cheeses go, and well received. Serve all these cheeses at room temperature, preferably with ripe pears or crisp, chilled apples. Or, be unconventional and find a place for them in some inspired cookery.

Always in demand for sandwiching, melting, puffing, grating, and eating are the two most available Swiss cheeses: Emmenthal and Gruyère. They are often combined in fondues, and both take beautifully to Parmesan. Emmenthal is the large-holed Swiss, copied in abundance everywhere, and Gruyère its tiny-eyed or "blind" brother. Even holes, a gentle shine, and a reassuring firmness to the touch give away a good Swiss.

As to Parmesan, that is a cheese for the ages, quite literally, for when mature and sharp it keeps for untold years. It is eaten fresh when extremely young. Grated old Parmesan, on the other hand, has found its way into some of the most tempting gastronomical inventions of France and its native Italy. From there, of course, it has conquered the world. Pecorino and Romano, also Italians, offer variety in this family of pungent and hard grating cheeses.

Cottage cheese, also known as pot cheese and, in fact, by a variety of names, is often disdained as the plague of dieters. Try it in crisply browned hotcakes or steaming Russian *pilmeni,* and your respect for it will grow. Its Italian cousin, Ricotta, performs brilliantly in baked and boiled pastas of many description, as well as in rich tortes and confections. With both cheeses, absolute freshness is of prime importance.

Great American and Canadian Cheddars abound. Once known as "store cheese," Cheddar ranges from mild to very sharp in flavor, from ivory to bright orange in color. It is firm, sometimes even brittle in texture, and marries superbly with good crackers or water biscuits. Also esteemed in supporting roles with this cheese are mustard, pretzels, and beer. In Cheddar, let age be your guide: the older the cheese, the fuller and sharper will its flavor be. A well-aged Cheddar melts divinely—most often in a sizzling Welsh Rabbit.

Cream cheese is made well almost anywhere and it is not only used for cheesecake (though where would we be without that?). It is the basis for an infinite variety of spreads, and is used in the stuffings for lucky cavities in pastries and sweetmeats. Try it *au naturel* on homemade herb bread, or spike it with another cheese. As with pot cheese, freshness is essential.

For hearty and simple fare, Dutch Edam and Gouda can be depended upon. The familiar, bright red cannonballs and flattish rounds are mild in flavor and firm (but not too firm) in texture. Along with a special friendship with peasant black bread, they take extraordinarily well to creaming with various spices and spirits.

A few words about buying cheese: For the untrained shopper, the first and extremely important choice is that of merchant. Find a trustworthy, reputable supplier (ask around, search) and the complications will be minimized. He or she can advise you on the origin, age, and quality of the cheese, and, if you strike a proper rapport, the possibility of a little sampling is good. Aside from that, the one generally reliable rule in the selection of any cheese is to find the original. Whatever country or region made a cheese first almost surely makes it best. Imitations often turn out to be rather nice cheeses in their own right—but different.

Take care in the choosing, study the subject well, and you will have some superb meals with no cooking at all. Above all, take your cheeses out of the refrigerator at least an hour before serving so that they are at room temperature. What could be finer on a summer evening than a good bread, a platter of ripe cheeses, a crisp salad, and a lightly chilled wine? In wintertime, round out the menu with a hot and hearty soup.

Such meals remind me of the old nursery rhyme refrain:

"Hi-ho the dairy—oh,
The cheese stands alone."

baked walnut and cheddar balls béchamel

1½ cups ground walnuts
4   oz. grated, mild Cheddar
½   cup breadcrumbs
½   cup wheat germ
½   onion, minced or grated
¾   cup milk
2   Tbs. parsley
fresh-ground pepper
salt
3   cups Sauce Béchamel (page 84)
2   eggs

In a large bowl, mix together the ground walnuts, the finely grated cheese, the breadcrumbs, the wheat germ, the minced onion, and the milk. Season the mixture with chopped parsley, a lot of fresh-ground black pepper, and some salt. Finally, add the well-beaten eggs.

Roll the mixture into balls, slightly smaller than eggs in size, and arrange them in a buttered baking dish. Make 3 cups of Béchamel sauce, well seasoned with thyme and onions, and pour it over the walnut balls in the baking dish. Bake in a hot oven (375 to 400 degrees) for about 35 to 40 minutes. Serve very hot from the baking dish.

This recipe makes about 20 savory walnut balls, light in texture and peculiarly delicious in taste.

roquefort mousse

2 envelopes gelatin
1 cup light cream
3 eggs, separated
9 to 10 oz. Roquefort cheese
½ cup heavy whipping cream
pinch of cream of tartar

Sprinkle the gelatin over the light cream in a small pot and, when it has softened, begin heating it gently, stirring often until the gelatin is completely dissolved and the cream is hot. Beat the egg yolks until they are fluffy and lemon-colored. Keep beating while you add half of the hot cream, a little at a time. When you have added half of it, stir it all back into the cream in the pot and—stirring carefully with a wooden spoon—continue heating until it just begins to thicken.

Mash the Roquefort well with a fork, being careful not to leave any large lumps. Now mix in some of the cream and egg yolk mixture and work the cheese into as smooth a paste as possible—then add the rest of the mixture and stir it all up. Put this away to cool for a few minutes while you beat the whipping cream just until peaks form and the egg whites until they are stiff but not dry. Adding a pinch of cream of tartar to the egg whites helps.

Very carefully fold in the whipped cream and then the beaten egg whites. If you perform this operation with a heavy hand, the air will escape from the egg whites and your elegant mousse will more resemble an opaque aspic, so be careful. Transfer the mixture into a well-oiled mold of about 5-cup capacity, and chill for several hours or until set. When you are ready to serve it, turn it out on a platter—perhaps on some salad greens—and garnish it with the vegetables of your choice. I prefer tomato halves Provençale and radish roses. Artichoke hearts are nice with this, as are grilled mushrooms.

Your mousse should be light in texture and not rubbery. The flavor is piquant, but delicate enough that ample portions can be eaten. This recipe will serve about 6 at supper or 8 to 10 if several other courses are offered.

cheese fondue neufchâteloise

8 oz. aged Swiss cheese
8 oz. Gruyère cheese
2½ Tbs. flour
1½ cups dry white wine (preferably a
Swiss Fondant or a Johannisberg-
Riesling)
1 large clove of garlic
fresh-ground black pepper
2 to 4 Tbs. kirsch
cubed French or Italian bread

Grate all the cheeses very coarsely, or chop them finely, and toss them together with the flour. Rub the fondue pot or the chafing dish with the clove of garlic and leave it in the pot. Heat the dish and pour in the wine. As soon as the wine starts to bubble, turn the heat down and begin adding the cheese, bit by bit, as you stir with a wooden spoon. Within very few minutes you should have a fine sauce, smooth and bubbling. Grind in some black pepper and add a little kirsch; taste it and, if you like the taste, add a little more kirsch. I usually like 4 tablespoons.

Serve the fondue immediately, with large cubes of French bread to be speared with forks and dipped into the sauce. Be sure to regulate the heat under the chafing dish so that the fondue continues to simmer slowly but does not come to a boil. Whoever loses his bread in the fondue pays a forfeit.

Serves 5 to 6.

swiss and cheddar fondue

8 oz. aged Swiss Gruyère
8 oz. aged Cheddar
1½ cups dry white wine
3 Tbs. flour
2 Tbs. kirsch or rum
1 Tbs. lemon juice
grated nutmeg
1 clove garlic
cubed French bread

Grate the cheeses coarsely and combine them thoroughly with the flour.

Rub a fondue pot well with the garlic. Pour in the wine and heat until it begins to bubble. Gradually add the cheese, stirring all the while with a wooden spoon. When the cheese has melted, add the kirsch or rum, as well as the lemon juice and nutmeg, and continue stirring over low heat for another 5 minutes or until the fondue is velvety smooth.

Regulate the heat under the pot so that the fondue stays piping hot without boiling. Spear cubes of French bread on forks and dip into the fondue.

Serves 4 to 6.

stuffed pierogi (A Cream-

This is one of my favorite dishes and everybody who tries it is delighted. It is adapted from a similar delicacy that my mother makes. It is a time-consuming chore, however, and you are well-advised to prepare the *pierogi* a day ahead and bake them when needed. They are delicious hot and wonderful cold. This recipe makes about 35.

Dough:
1 cup butter
8 oz. cream cheese
¼ cup heavy cream
3 cups flour
1 tsp. salt
1 egg
1 tsp. water

Cream the butter with the cheese and let it soften. Beat in the cream and then add 2¾ cups flour and the salt. Reserve the rest of the flour for use in rolling out. Chill the dough well.

When you are ready to make the *pierogi*, dust a large board or other flat surface with a little flour, dust the rolling pin with

Cheese Dough Stuffed with Mushrooms)

flour, and carefully roll out the dough to about ⅛-inch thickness. Test occasionally to be sure that the dough is not sticking to the board.

Cut the rolled dough into squares about 2½ inches in size. Into each square put a teaspoonful of the filling. Moisten the edges with a little egg beaten with the water, and bring the four corners up to the center. Seal the edges very carefully, as they have a tendency to come apart in baking if they are sloppy. When you are finished and ready to bake, brush the tops of the pierogi with a little more of the beaten egg.

Bake them in a preheated 375-degree oven for about 15 to 20 minutes, or until they are golden brown.

This filling is so delicious that I tend to run short after some overzealous tasting. Beware of this dangerous pitfall.

Filling:
5   oz. dried black mushrooms
1   large onion, finely chopped
3   Tbs. butter
2   slices black bread
2   tsp. dill
2   hard-cooked eggs
salt and pepper
2 to 3 Tbs. sour cream (optional)

Cook the mushrooms in as little water as possible until they are soft, about ½ hour or more. Drain off the water through cheesecloth and reserve it. Now wash the mushrooms very carefully, one by one if you must, to get rid of every bit of dirt. Put them through the food chopper on a coarse grind and sauté them with the chopped onion in the butter.

Soak the pieces of dry bread in the mushroom water and put them through the food chopper also before adding to the mushrooms and onion. Add the dill and season well with salt and pepper. Mash or sieve 2 hard-cooked eggs and stir them into the sautéing mixture. Taste and correct seasoning. At this point, if you would like a milder-flavored filling, add the sour cream. Otherwise, sauté about 10 minutes more, cool, and fill into the prepared dough.

leniwe pierogi *(Cottage Cheese Dumplings)*

The literal translation from the Polish is "lazy dumplings"—presumably as opposed to the sort you stuff and bake. These take only about 20 minutes to make and are a delicious change from potato dumplings. An added attraction is their high protein content.

1   lb. small-curd cottage cheese, partially creamed
1   Tbs. soft butter
1   tsp. salt
4   eggs, 3 of them separated
1½ cups flour (approximately)
4 to 5 Tbs. melted butter
½   cup breadcrumbs

Put the cottage cheese through a sieve and combine it with the soft butter, salt, 1 whole egg, 3 egg yolks, and 1 cup of flour in a mixing bowl. Blend it well, beat the remaining egg whites until they are stiff, and fold them into the cheese mixture. Now add as much of the remaining flour as is needed to make the dough manageable. It should still be very soft.

Fill a very large kettle with water (about ⅔ full) and salt it, then bring it to a rolling boil. Now, back to the dough: it is still rather soft and sticky. Traditionally, it is now rolled out on a floured board and cut into nifty parallelograms, but they always become messy lumps in the end. So do this: Just take a spoonful of the dough at a time and drop it into the boiling water. Cook several at once. They will rise to the top soon after you drop them in. After they rise, let them cook a few minutes on top, then remove them carefully with a slotted spoon and keep warm.

Serve them hot, garnishing them with the breadcrumbs heated in the melted butter. This last is essential, for it provides a very intriguing contrast in texture.

Serves 4 to 6.

fromage romanesque

16 oz. cream cheese
¾ cup sour cream
3 tsp. honey
salt
3 eggs, separated

Beat together the cheese and the sour cream, then blend in the honey, salt, and egg yolks. I suggest that this be done in the blender, for this mixture should be completely smooth and cream cheese likes to lump a little. When it is well beaten, separately beat the egg whites until they are stiff and fold them into the other mixture. Pour it all into a buttered baking dish, preferably a rather shallow, round one, and bake at 350 degrees for ½ hour. Serve hot. With it I recommend a delicate Mornay sauce, made from Béchamel (see page 85).

This is a peculiar dish: light, but very filling—delicate, but with a very definite character. It may be served as a separate course, with Mornay or another mild sauce, or it may be accompanied by some appropriate garden-fresh vegetable and slices of rich, dark bread to make a complete, light meal. Try it with young asparagus spears—*there* is a perfect pair. On the other hand, with the addition of a little more honey, it becomes a hot dessert, which can be accompanied well by fruit and a custard sauce.

This recipe makes 5 to 6 servings.

cheese and scallion quiche

Here is a delicious spin-off from the classic Quiche Lorraine. It is just as wonderful served steaming hot out of the oven or well-chilled, perhaps as a picnic dish.

Basic Shortcrust Pastry for 1 crust (page 285)
½ cup scallions, chopped
butter
Bakon yeast (not a meat product)
6 to 8 oz. Swiss or Gruyère cheese,
    cubed
3 eggs, beaten
1½ cups cream
nutmeg
salt and pepper

Line a pie dish or quiche form with the pastry and bake it 5 minutes only in a preheated 450-degree oven. Be sure you prick the crust first with a fork, or you will have a giant, shortcrust balloon as I once did.

Sauté the scallions in about 1 tablespoon of butter with a pinch of Bakon yeast. Sprinkle them on the bottom of the crust. On top of them, spread the cheese cubes.

Now combine the eggs with the cream, add a little nutmeg, some salt and pepper, and blend it all well. Pour this mixture over the cheese and bake the quiche for 15 minutes at 450 degrees, then turn the oven down to 350 degrees and bake about another 10 to 15 minutes or until a knife comes out clean. Serve either very hot or well chilled.

6 servings.

tiropites

Greek *filo* makes the flakiest pastry in the world. These cheese turnovers become wonderfully puffy and crisp and, when several people are eating them at once, their crackling makes a bizarre and charming noise.

1 lb. Greek *filo* (strudel dough)
melted butter
1 lb. Feta cheese
¼ cup grated Parmesan
2 eggs
lots of fresh-ground black pepper
chopped oregano
olive oil

Take ½ lb. of the *filo* and place the sheets carefully one on top of the other, brushing each with melted butter. Cut this layered sheet into 9 even squares—they should be about 4½ inches across. Repeat the procedure with the remaining *filo*.

Crumble the Feta and combine it with the Parmesan, eggs, a little oregano, and about 1 teaspoon of olive oil. Grind in a lot of fresh black pepper—but add no salt, as the Feta is very salty. Mix well. Place a spoonful of this mixture in the center of each square, moisten the edges of the square with water, and fold it over so that the corners meet to form a triangle. Press the edges very firmly together to seal.

Brush the turnovers with more butter and bake at 350 degrees for about ½ hour, or until nicely browned. Serve them very hot. They are accompanied well by cold, marinated vegetables or a large Greek Salad (see page 105).

Serves 6 to 8.

liptauer cheese: a variation

1   lb. full-cream Ricotta cheese (or
        cottage cheese, or softened cream
        cheese)
4   Tbs. softened butter
2   tsp. French mustard
1½ tsp. caraway seeds
1   Tbs. currants or chopped dates
1 to 2 Tbs. capers
salt and a lot of fresh-ground black
        pepper
1 to 2 Tbs. chopped black olives
paprika
Garnish: 2 to 3 hard-cooked eggs
            pimiento peppers

Work the softened butter into the cheese until a smooth mixture is obtained. Stir in the mustard, add everything except the paprika. Mix well and form it into an even mound on a small platter. Sprinkle with some paprika. Garnish the cheese with thin strips of raw pimiento and slices of hard-cooked eggs. Chill and serve with a coarse-textured black bread. This cheese can make a good accompaniment to certain soups, and is also perfect as a first course, with bread and raw or pickled vegetables.

cheese blintzes

Crêpe batter for blintzes:

3   eggs
1   cup milk
½   tsp. salt
2   Tbs. butter or oil
¾   cup flour
butter for frying

Filling:

1   lb. (2 cups) Hoop cheese (a soft,
        baker's cheese)
2   eggs
1   Tbs. lemon juice
¼   tsp. salt
2   Tbs. sugar
¼   tsp. powdered cinnamon
seeds from 4 cardamom pods, pounded
        in a mortar

First make all the crêpes, using the recipe given above, or the basic French Crêpes recipe (page 184) if you prefer. The difference is that the recipe given here makes slightly heavier crêpes.

Whip all the ingredients for the batter in

a blender and put it aside for an hour. Heat a 6-inch crêpe pan, let butter sizzle in it, and pour in about 2 or 3 tablespoons of the batter. Tilt it quickly around to spread the batter evenly, and fry the crêpe over a medium flame, about a minute on each side or just until it's golden. Continue in this manner until all the crêpes are ready, stacking them on a plate.

Now, prepare the filling. Beat all the ingredients together thoroughly with a fork, and that's all there is to it.

Place a good-sized spoonful of this filling in the center of a crêpe, then carefully wrap one side over the filling and begin to roll it. Fold the edges in and finish rolling the blintze. You should have a short, plump cylinder with neatly tucked-in ends. Continue this way until all the blintzes are ready.

Now, either fry them lightly in butter, several minutes on either side so that they are crisp and light brown, or bake them. To bake the blintzes, arrange them in one layer in a shallow, buttered baking dish and brush the tops with melted butter. Bake them in a preheated, 425-degree oven for 15 to 20 minutes. Whether baking or frying, be sure to serve them at once, piping hot.

Blintzes are traditionally accompanied by sour cream and various preserves. Yogurt and honey are also delicious condiments.

This recipe makes about 12 to 15 blintzes, enough for 4 to 5 hungry people.

savory cheese and onion pie

Basic Shortcrust Pastry for one 10-inch
    pie (page 285)
10 oz. cheese: half Swiss and half
    Switzerland Gruyère, or in
    proportion desired
2 Tbs. flour
2 large onions
4 Tbs. butter
1 tsp. chopped basil
2 large, firm tomatoes, sliced
2 large eggs
¾ cup cream

Prepare the shortcrust pastry as directed, line a 10-inch pie dish, and chill it.

Grate all the cheese and toss it with the flour.

Melt the butter in a large skillet, slice the onions and sauté them very gently in the butter until they begin to turn golden, about ½ hour. Spread about ⅓ of the cheese over the bottom of the pie dish, then spread the onions over it. In the butter that is left in the pan, heat the tomato slices with the chopped basil for a minute or two. Arrange the tomato slices over the onions, then cover with the remaining cheese.

Beat the eggs with the cream and pour it over the cheese. If you like nutmeg, sprinkle a little on top. Bake in a pre-heated, 350-degree oven for about 35 to 40 minutes, or until the top browns nicely. Serve hot, in wedges.

Serves 6.

pizza rustica

This is not a pizza you're likely to find in this country: it is a hearty, 2-crust pie—an *Italian* pizza.

Basic Shortcrust Pastry for double-crust
    pie (page 285)
5   eggs
1   lb. Ricotta cheese
2   Tbs. chopped onion
1   cup grated Parmesan
chopped parsley, about 1 Tbs.
salt and fresh-ground black pepper
2   Tbs. olive oil
2   cloves garlic
10 oz. tomato purée
4   oz. tomato paste
¼   tsp. dried marjoram
½   tsp. dried oregano
⅔   cup sliced ripe olives
½   lb. thinly sliced Mozzarella cheese
1   very large bell pepper

Prepare the shortcrust pastry as directed. It is especially good (for this pie) if you use only lemon juice and Marsala instead of water, to moisten it. Line a 10-inch pie dish and roll out a top crust.

Beat the eggs, stir in the Ricotta cheese, onion, parsley, Parmesan cheese, and season liberally with salt and pepper. Set aside.

Heat the olive oil in a small saucepan. Crush the cloves of garlic into it and add the herbs. When the garlic is clear and begins to turn gold, stir in the tomato purée, tomato paste, olives and, once again, season well with salt and black pepper.

Slice the Mozzarella thinly. Seed the green pepper and slice it into matchsticks.

Now you are ready to assemble: Spread half (or a little more) of the Ricotta mixture in the prepared pie shell. Arrange over it half the Mozzarella slices. Cover with half the tomato sauce, and spread half the green pepper over it. Repeat all the layers and cover with the top crust. Pinch the edges securely together and flute. With a very sharp knife, make 3 long, parallel slashes through the top crust.

Bake the pie in a preheated, 425-degree oven for about 35 to 40 minutes or until it is well-browned. Let it stand for ½ hour before serving. Serves 6 to 8 generously.

cheese enchiladas

8 tortillas

Sauce:

3 Tbs. olive oil
½ large onion, chopped
3 to 4 cloves garlic, crushed
2 oz. (or more if you like a hotter sauce) diced green chilis—Ortega canned chilis are quite good.
1 lb. cooked, peeled, and chopped tomatoes
1 cup tomato juice or thinned purée
¼ tsp. powdered oregano
¼ tsp. basil
1 cup strong vegetable broth
1½ Tbs. cornstarch, dissolved in water

Filling:

8 to 10 oz. grated sharp Cheddar cheese
½ cup sliced black olives
2 to 3 scallions, chopped
a little chopped parsley

Begin by preparing the sauce. Heat the olive oil in a skillet and sauté in it the chopped onion and finely minced garlic. When the onion is quite transparent, add the diced chili, the tomatoes, tomato juice, and the herbs. Simmer for a while, then add a cup of very strong vegetable broth. This can be made from a vegetable concentrate and spiked with some Kitchen Bouquet or with a similar vegetable seasoning. Dissolve the cornstarch in a little water and stir it into the sauce. Let it cook very slowly for another 10 minutes at least. If the sauce seems too thick, stir in a little water.

Prepare the filling: Have—on separate plates—the grated cheese, sliced olives, chopped scallions, and chopped parsley.

Oil lightly an oblong baking dish. Take one tortilla at a time and place it gently on the heated sauce. When it starts to get warm, draw it carefully off. On the saucy side of the tortilla, arrange the filling: a few tablespoons of cheese, some olives, scallions, and a sprinkle of parsley—all in a fat line, slightly off-center. Now roll the tortilla tightly around this filling and place it in the baking dish. When all eight are in, side by side, pour the sauce over them.

Bake the enchiladas for 15 to 20 minutes only in a preheated 350-degree oven. They should be thoroughly heated but not overcooked. Serves 4.

classic welsh rabbit (also known as Welsh Rarebit)

2   Tbs. butter
½   cup light beer or ale at room
      temperature
2   egg yolks
½   tsp. dry mustard
pinch of cayenne
1   tsp. Worcestershire Sauce
3   cups coarsely grated aged Cheddar
      (This is about ½ lb. by my meas-
      ure. The cheese should be flaky
      and sharp, a sign of its maturity.)
buttered toast or English muffins

Use a double boiler, a chafing dish, or a very heavy, enameled, cast-iron skillet over an easily regulated small flame.

First melt the butter. Beat together the ale, egg yolks, and seasonings. Have this, along with the grated cheese, at your side, and a wooden or enamel spoon in your hand. You are ready to begin.

Add the cheese a little at a time to the butter, stirring constantly and in one di-rection only. When the melting cheese forms a thick mass, add a little of the ale mixture. Never stop stirring! When all the cheese is in and melted, and sufficient ale has been added to make a smooth velvety sauce, continue the stirring, over very low heat, for another 10 minutes or so. Never let the Rabbit boil, but keep it steaming hot. It will thicken a little, and you should add more of the ale mixture, to your taste, as you stir.

When it finally is as smooth as thick cream and heavily coats the spoon, serve it at once over toasted bread or muffins, on hot plates. Broiled or sautéed slices of tomato on the toast make a delicious variation.

A suggestion: If the plates and toast are in the warm oven while you are stirring, you have no hassle when ready to serve.

Serves 2 to 3.

tomato rabbit

¾ lb. sharp Cheddar cheese
3 to 4 Tbs. brandy
6 oz. tomato paste
pinch of soda
2 Tbs. butter
2 Tbs. flour
1 cup milk
¼ tsp. cayenne (less if you want a mild
     Rabbit)
¼ tsp. dry mustard
salt and fresh-ground black pepper
4 toasted English muffins

Grate the cheese. Stir the brandy into the tomato paste and sprinkle a little soda over it.

Melt the butter in a heavy saucepan on a low flame and add the flour. Cook this roux for a few minutes, then stir in the milk. When this sauce begins to thicken, add the tomato paste mixture. Stirring gently with a wooden spoon—in one direction only for the greatest smoothness—gradually add the cheese and seasoning. When all the cheese is melted, continue stirring for another 8 to 10 minutes, over a tiny flame, until the Rabbit is absolutely slick. If it seems a bit too thick, a little more milk or brandy may be stirred in, as you wish.

Serve the Rabbit piping hot, over toasted English muffins.

Serves 4.

mexican cheese pudding

4 whole eggs
4 egg yolks
1 cup milk or light cream
1 cup sour cream
2 cups grated Swiss cheese
2 cups grated fresh Parmesan cheese
pinch of nutmeg
¼ tsp. crushed oregano
¼ tsp. crushed thyme
¼ tsp. chopped dill
salt and fresh-ground black pepper
Saltine crackers
snipped chives
paprika

Garnish:

Tomato and Chili Sauce (page 85)

Beat together the eggs, milk or cream, and sour cream with a whisk or an electric beater until very light and foamy. Add the grated cheeses, the nutmeg, oregano, thyme, dill, and some salt and pepper.

Butter a 9-inch square baking dish generously. Line the bottom with Saltine crackers. Pour half the egg-cheese mixture over the crackers and spread it evenly. Cover with another layer of Saltines. Pour the remaining mixture over the crackers and spread evenly. Sprinkle a little paprika and chopped chives over the top.

Bake at 350 degrees for 50 to 60 minutes or until puffy and browned on top. Cut into squares and serve with Tomato and Chili Sauce.

Serves 6.

cheese and potato pudding

4   medium potatoes
½ lb. cheese—half Swiss, half Fontina
½ onion
4   eggs
2   cups milk
4   Tbs. flour
salt and fresh-ground black pepper
pinch of thyme
nutmeg
grated Parmesan cheese
breadcrumbs
butter

Peel and thickly slice the potatoes and boil them for 10 minutes only. Butter a large casserole liberally. Grate the cheeses and chop the onion.

Now, arrange a layer of the potatoes in the baking dish, salt and pepper them, sprinkle over a little onion, and cover with a light layer of grated cheese. Continue in this fashion until all these ingredients are used.

Beat together the eggs and milk with the flour, some salt and pepper, and a little nutmeg. Add a pinch of crushed thyme. Pour this over the layers of potatoes and cheese. It should come just to the top. Sprinkle some grated Parmesan and breadcrumbs over it and dot with butter.

Bake for 45 to 55 minutes at 350 degrees. It should be well-browned and slightly puffed.

Serves 4 to 6.

camembert (or brie) à la vierge

Here is a straightforward and simple cheese preparation to delight the connoisseur. You must love the cheese, for there is very little else.

For two:
1   round of Camembert or Brie
2 to 3 Tbs. flour
1   egg beaten with 1 Tbs. milk
salt
1   cup (or more) dry breadcrumbs
butter

Take a wheel of Brie or Camembert that is just ripe, not yet very runny, and slice it in half through the full circle. Take each of the thin rounds and dredge them—first in flour, then in the beaten egg, then in the fine breadcrumbs and salt. Now, quickly, once more in the egg and once more in the crumbs. The crust should be rather thick.
Now simply melt some butter in a skillet and sauté the cheeses until nicely browned and crisp on either side. Serve at once, accompanied by a fresh fruit salad, a crisp tossed salad, or both, and a good bread.

potted edam

1   round Edam cheese (2 lbs.)
1½ cups Port wine
1½ Tbs. caraway seeds
¾ tsp. dry mustard
¼ tsp. cayenne pepper
1½ tsp. ground cumin seeds

Slice off the top of a round Edam cheese and scoop out all the cheese, leaving the shell intact. Grate the cheese and combine it with the remaining ingredients. Mash the cheese with the wine and spices until it is a fairly smooth paste. Fill the cheese back into the shell, cover with tight-sealing plastic wrap, and put away in the refrigerator for a week or two. The cheese can be eaten right away, but it won't be the same—it really requires a certain amount of time to marry flavors and mellow properly. Allow the cheese to reach room temperature before eating. Serve with water biscuits or plain wheat wafers.

The prepared cheese may also be packed into a crock.

rice and other grains

The food that sustains more than half the world is one of the classic cooking problems for most of the other half. Approach it with respect and treat it with care to create delicate and exotic dishes. *You will be rewarded. Be careless, even casual about it, and you will likely be disappointed too.*

There is no foolproof way to cook every kind of rice, simply because there are so many varieties. This shouldn't discourage you. Most packaged rices indicate cooking time, and when you learn the basics of boiling and steaming white and brown rice, you will soon learn to deal with small differences.

In any case, unless you are using processed, packaged rice, *always* wash rice very carefully before cooking it. Rinse it in clear, cold water, pick out the pieces of grit and dirt, then drain it and dry between clean tea towels. Never soak rice before cooking it. Try to plan your schedule so that the rice is just ready at the moment that it is to be eaten—this is usually not much trouble, for once you put the rice in the water, the most work you do is watch the time. And *do* watch the time carefully. Overcooked rice—worse luck—is as common as it is awful.

As to choosing between brown and white rice—be guided by your personal preference, of course, but don't disregard the question of good nutrition. In that category, brown rice is indisputably superior to white, or polished, rice. It has twice as much protein and is much higher in vitamin and mineral content.

boiled white rice

To boil white rice, put a good quantity of water in a large pot—a quart or more to each cup of rice—salt it, add a few drops of lemon juice and a pat of butter, and bring the water to a boil. Then dribble in the clean grains gradually as you stir gently with a wooden spoon. After 15 minutes, fish out a few grains and try them. They should be tender but not mushy—*al dente,* as the Italians say. If they are still gritty and hard, another two or three minutes should do it. The instant your rice reaches the proper point of tenderness, drain it thoroughly. Don't run cold water over it now, or stir it with a spoon, for cooked rice mashes all too easily. If you like, toss it gently with two forks to fluff it and separate the grains.

Preferably the rice should be served as soon as it is ready. If it must wait a few minutes, put it into the pot (drained) and cover. The natural steam will keep it hot for a while. If it must wait longer than a few minutes (not recommended, you understand), keep it hot in a colander over boiling water.

steamed brown rice

Brown rice is usually steamed, and takes considerably longer to reach tenderness than does white rice.

Begin with careful washing. Then put the rice in a pot with 2½ cups of water to each cup of rice, and a little salt. Boil it, uncovered, for 5 minutes, then lower the heat as much as you can, cover the pot tightly, and let it steam for 45 minutes. Don't lift the lid to snatch a quick look and see how it's coming!

After 45 minutes, turn off the heat and let it stand, still covered, for another 10 minutes. At that time, when you lift the lid, you have every right to expect to find perfectly cooked rice, tender but not mushy, with all the water absorbed. Separate the grains with a fork and serve.

1 cup of uncooked brown rice makes about 3 cups of cooked rice—enough for 4 servings.

saffron brown rice

For each cup of uncooked rice:
2½ cups water
1   Tbs. lemon juice
¼   tsp. saffron
½   tsp. salt
¼   cup currants (optional)

Prepare the rice as directed in the pre-ceding recipe for Steamed Brown Rice, adding the saffron, salt, lemon juice, and currants to the water when it begins to boil. This is a superb rice to serve with curries.

saffron white rice

3   cups cooked rice
1½ Tbs. lemon juice
¼   tsp. saffron
currants (optional)

Prepare the rice as directed in the recipe for Boiled White Rice (page 220). While it cooks, dissolve the saffron carefully in the lemon juice. When the rice is ready, toss it lightly with the saffron mixture. If you wish to add currants, boil them with the rice or steam them separately: this will puff them up and make them tender and plump, rather than the dry little strangers they are to begin with.

5 to 6 servings.

stuffed peppers

8 or 9 long green chili peppers, or 6
    medium bell peppers
4½ cups cooked brown rice
1 cup cooked green peas
2 tsp. dried dill
1 to 2 tsp. olive oil
salt and pepper
4 to 5 tomatoes, peeled and cut
chopped basil and oregano

If you like fairly hot peppers, use the long chili peppers. If hot peppers are a little too much for you, stay with the mild, green bell peppers.

In any case, blanch the peppers for a few minutes in boiling water, cut the tops off, and scoop out the seeds. Combine the rice with the peas, olive oil, dill, and some salt and pepper. Stuff this mixture into the peppers and arrange them in an oiled baking dish. Sprinkle them with a little chopped basil and oregano, arrange pieces of tomato around them, and add water just to the top of the peppers. Cover and simmer, either on a burner or in a medium oven, for about ½ hour. Serves 6.

rice parmigiana

2 cups cooked white or brown rice
    (see page 220)
1 cup coarsely chopped *fresh* parsley
¼ cup chopped scallions
1 cup grated Parmesan cheese
2 eggs, beaten
¼ cup milk
salt and pepper

Toss the rice with the chopped parsley, scallions, and cheese. Beat the eggs thoroughly with the milk, and add ample salt and pepper. Combine the two mixtures and pour into a well-buttered baking dish. Place the dish in a pan of hot water and bake at 350 degrees for 30 to 35 minutes, or until it seems firm.

Serves 4 as a side dish.

risotto alla milanese

5 Tbs. butter
1 onion, chopped
2 cups pearly white rice, preferably
    from the Lombardy region of Italy
½ cup Marsala wine
5 to 6 cups Garlic Broth (page 51)
¼ to ½ tsp. saffron
salt and pepper

In a large, heavy-bottomed skillet melt the butter and sauté the chopped onion until quite transparent. Add the rice, and stir it around until all the grains are coated with butter. Stir in the Marsala, then add 5 cups of hot broth, salt and pepper, and the saffron; stir well. Cover the skillet tightly and lower the heat.

After 20 minutes have passed, taste the rice to see if it is done. It may need to steam a few minutes longer, and it's possible that a little more broth may be needed. This all depends on the particular rice you are using. The rice is ready to serve when it is tender (not mushy) and all the broth is absorbed. Serve it with butter and grated Parmesan cheese passed separately. Serves 6.

kasha (Buckwheat Groats)

1 cup dry buckwheat groats
1 egg, lightly beaten
2 cups boiling water
2 Tbs. butter
salt and fresh-ground black pepper

Stir together the buckwheat groats and the egg. Transfer the mixture to a hot skillet and stir over a high flame until the grains are separate and dry. Add the boiling water, butter, salt and pepper to taste, and stir once more. Cover tightly, lower the flame to a tiny one, and leave to steam for ½ hour.

Serves 3 to 4.

kasha knishes

Filling:

4 to 6 Tbs. butter
1½ onions, chopped
½ lb. mushrooms
¼ tsp. crushed thyme
¼ tsp. dill
salt and pepper
2 cups cooked kasha (see preceding
    page)

Dough:

2½ cups unbleached white flour
1 tsp. baking powder
½ tsp. salt
2 eggs
½ cup salad oil
2 Tbs. water

To prepare the filling, melt the butter in a large saucepan and sauté the chopped onion in it. Wash the mushrooms carefully and chop them coarsely. Add the mushrooms and the herbs to the onions and stir well. Season with salt and plenty of fresh-ground black pepper. Continue to sauté for another 7 to 10 minutes after adding the mushrooms, then stir in the kasha, let it all heat through, and the filling is ready. There should be enough for 18 knishes.

Now prepare the dough. Sift all the dry ingredients into a bowl. Add the eggs, oil, and water, and work the dough thoroughly with your hands, kneading until it is smooth.

Divide the dough into 2 even pieces. Roll it out as thinly as possible, without tearing holes in it. Cut out circles approximately 3 inches across. Place a heaping tablespoon of filling in the center of each circle and draw the edges together over it, pinching firmly to seal.

Place the knishes on an oiled baking sheet, pinched side up. Bake them at 375 degrees for about 35 to 45 minutes. They should be lightly browned.

18 knishes.

dolmades (*Stuffed Grapevine Leaves*)

1   medium eggplant
⅓   cup olive oil
1   medium onion, chopped
2   Tbs. lemon juice
1½ tsp. oregano
1   tsp. dill
1   clove garlic, crushed
1   tsp. salt (more to taste)
fresh-ground black pepper
4   cups cooked long-grain rice
1   jar grapevine leaves
1   lb. peeled tomatoes
¼   tsp. basil

Peel the eggplant and chop it finely. Heat the olive oil in a large skillet and add to it the onion and eggplant, the lemon juice, oregano, dill, and garlic. Stir until the oil is evenly distributed over the eggplant. Season with salt and pepper and add about 1½ cups of hot water. Allow this mixture to simmer for an hour or so, or until the eggplant is very tender and the water nearly all evaporated. More water can be added if it cooks away before the eggplant is ready. When the mixture is thick and very soft, turn off the heat and stir in the rice. Correct seasoning to taste.

Rinse the grapevine leaves carefully. Place a spoonful of the filling in the center of each one and wrap the leaf around it, folding in the sides.

Chop up the tomatoes into a thick sauce, seasoning with a little basil, some salt, and pepper. Arrange the dolmades in an oiled baking dish and pour the tomato sauce over them. Cover and bake for about ½ hour in a 350-degree oven. Serve with Greek Salad (page 105), Sesame Ring (page 37), and Retsina. Eat outdoors, under a grape arbor.

Serves 6.

german rice ring

3 large, firm cucumbers
3 Tbs. butter
½ cup milk
6 oz. grated sharp Cheddar cheese
2 Tbs. flour
salt and fresh-ground black pepper
1½ cups long-grain white rice
1 large onion, chopped
2 Tbs. butter
½ tsp. crushed basil
1 Tbs. cumin seeds, pounded lightly
   in a mortar
3 firm, ripe tomatoes, diced
½ cup chopped fresh parsley

Peel the cucumbers, quarter them lengthwise, and scrape out the seeds. Slice the cucumbers thickly, cutting on a slant, so as to obtain flat little disks. Melt the 3 tablespoons butter in a large skillet and sauté the cucumbers in it for 7 to 10 minutes. Add the milk and allow it to heat for several minutes. Toss the grated cheese with the flour and stir it into the milk and cucumbers slowly.

Season with salt and a large amount of fresh-ground black pepper. Keep the mixture simmering over a tiny flame, stirring it often, as you prepare the rice.

Boil the rice in a large quantity of salted water. As it boils, sauté the chopped onion in the 2 tablespoons butter, adding to it the basil and the partly crushed cumin seeds. As soon as the rice is tender (about 15 minutes) drain it and add it to the butter and onions. Stir in the diced tomatoes and, when they are hot, the parsley, as well as a little salt and pepper to taste.

Transfer the cucumbers to a large platter and surround them with the rice. Serve immediately.

Serves 4 to 6.

rice pilaf

1   oz. dried dark mushrooms
2   Tbs. olive oil
2   Tbs. butter
¾   cup diced bell pepper
¾   cup diced pimiento pepper
1   chopped onion
¾   cup chopped scallions
salt
½   tsp. crushed thyme
½   tsp. fresh-ground black pepper
      (more to taste)
1   cup long-grain white rice
½   cup dry white wine
1½ cups light vegetable broth, hot
2   firm, ripe tomatoes, diced
3 to 4 Tbs. fresh chopped parsley

Garnish:

ripe olives

Soak the dried mushrooms in warm water for an hour or two (longer if possible) and wash them thoroughly. Chop them up into small pieces.

Heat the olive oil and the butter in a large saucepan. When it is quite hot, add the peppers, scallions, and onion and sauté over a high flame for 8 to 10 minutes only. Stir almost constantly and season with thyme, salt, and pepper. Be generous with the salt and pepper, keeping in mind the rice to be added.

Stir in the rice and sauté a minute longer. Pour in the wine and the broth, stir once, cover tightly, and leave on a very low flame for 25 minutes. Do not lift the lid during this time.

At the end of 25 minutes, open the saucepan and quickly stir in the tomatoes and parsley. Taste, and add more salt and pepper if needed. As soon as the tomatoes are hot, pile the rice into a deep, heated serving dish and garnish with whole or sliced ripe olives and serve.

Serves 6.

risotto doug edwards

I will say this, though it may brand me anti-American in some circles: The sad truth is that America has never really developed a cuisine of her own. So, small wonder that gourmet cooking here is inevitably associated with "foreign" cooking.

Of course there are certain regional specialties which are unique to this country but, even taken together, they hardly comprise a cuisine. There is happening now, however, a gastronomical movement which may turn out in time to be just that. It begins with this desire: to abandon the often foul and always tedious world of "convenience" preparations and return to the enjoyment of natural foods. It is rooted in creativity. It may go on to become a delicious and varied gastronomy.

My friend Doug is a real vegetarian's vegetarian. He abandoned not only meat, but also all dairy products. Within this discipline he experiments enthusiastically, adding his own taste and temperament to a growing movement. This recipe is a collaboration—basically Doug's, with a little help from me. It is a very agreeable example of this new move to more natural food.

½ recipe Risotto alla Milanese (see page 223)
1   large eggplant (1 lb. at least)
salt
butter and olive oil
6   scallions
salt and pepper
Worcestershire sauce
3 to 4 fresh carrots
1⅓ cups cooked kidney beans (canned are all right)
½   cup roasted pumpkin seeds
⅓   cup roasted, large sunflower seeds (shelled)

Prepare half a recipe of Risotto alla Milanese and set it aside.

Wash the eggplant and slice it, without peeling. Sprinkle the slices with salt on both sides and allow them to rest for 20 to 30 minutes as the excess water seeps out. Rinse very lightly, drain, and press dry. Eggplant treated this way will not absorb too much oil and has a wonderful, light flavor.

Cube the eggplant slices. Heat a little olive oil and butter in a large skillet. Chop the scallions and sauté them lightly for a few minutes. Add the eggplant and continue sautéing for about 10 more minutes, stirring almost constantly. Season the eggplant with some salt, plenty of fresh-grated black pepper, and a little Worcestershire sauce.

Scrape and thickly slice 3 or 4 carrots. Steam them until they are about half tender—a few minutes only.

Now combine the rice, pumpkin seeds, sunflower seeds, eggplant, carrots, and beans. Toss together lightly and check the seasoning. Add more salt and pepper if necessary.

Pile the mixture into a lightly oiled baking dish, cover *tightly*, and place in a pre-heated, 475-degree oven, for about 45 minutes. Serve steaming hot.

6 to 8 servings.

pasta

"Every individual who is not perfectly imbecile and void of understanding, is an epicure in his way; the epicures in boiling potatoes are innumerable." Dr. Kitchener, quoted in *The Greedy Book*.

The epicures in preparing pasta are just as plentiful, and it is worth a little effort to join their ranks. This country is blessed with a large Italian population. It is well represented in restaurants, but most Italians, understanding the delicate nature of the art, wisely partake of their pasta at home. Follow their example. Remember how wonderful is the privacy of home, even when shared with friends, for such a voluptuous activity as the eating of pasta.

Pasta is quite manageable if you only recognize the few nonnegotiable demands it makes. If you start with the best materials you can anticipate the best results—again, look to the Italians. Good pasta can be obtained from the bins of an Italian grocery, and there is probably one near you if you only look around. Otherwise, good pasta can be magically created from the simplest ingredients in your own kitchen. (It is not found in supermarkets where visually convincing imitations nestle against envelopes of vile "sauce" mixes.) Having secured your pasta, get some ripe Italian plum tomatoes, fresh if you are lucky, or else in cans. Herbs from your herb garden are preferred, but dried ones—well cared for—are fine. Virgin, pure olive oil is worth the extra pennies it costs, and should be purchased at the same Italian grocery where your favorite pasta waits in the barrel. Finally, the cheeses must be chosen. Pregrated cheese is an insult to pasta and to cheese. The Italian grocer will slice off a wedge of pungent Romano or Parmesan for you, which you can take home whole or have grated there. Delicatessen Mozzarella is reliable, but Ricotta should be purchased really fresh, sliced from a block rather than prepackaged.

When you have procured the finest ingredients, handle them respectfully. The sauces take some time to prepare. You have heard that spaghetti sauce must be simmered very slowly for hours to blend and marry the flavors. That is quite true—with a notable exception. If you are using fresh tomatoes and fresh herbs, only sufficient time to achieve the desired consistency is needed to have a sauce of very lively flavor. But long or short, the sauce must be absolutely piping hot when served, for pasta cools faster than anything and tastes good only when steaming. Give it all the help you can by keeping not only the sauce but also the serving plates properly hot, and wasting not a moment between kettle and table.

It is precisely this matter of proper timing, both in cooking and in serving, that is so ill-suited to most restaurants but easily managed at home. To boil pasta properly, you need an enormous kettle, preferably enameled. A pound of pasta, which can feed four, requires a full gallon of well-salted and hysterically boiling water. Put the pasta in slowly—never breaking long spaghetti, but letting it curl round as it softens. Pasta varies in thickness, so boiling time will vary also. At the end of six or seven minutes, you should pull a strand to taste it, and repeat this fail-safe test about once each minute thereafter until your tooth tells you the pasta is *al dente,* tender but just firm enough to allow a bite. It may take seven minutes, it may take twelve, or even fifteen. Since your sauce is bubbling, your fresh cheese grated, your plates heated, and your guests waiting eagerly, all that remains to be done is to drain the pasta for a mere instant in a hot colander and pile it onto the plates. A tiny nub of butter may be added to each serving at this time. You will have a feast.

I have included here several sauce recipes for pasta, some simple and some elaborate, as well as boiled pasta, baked pasta, stuffed, and layered pasta. There is pasta from many lands and each is different from the others, save in this one respect: pasta by any name needs salad—crisp and hearty and green—with the piquant bite of good wine vinegar. The two are Yin and Yang to each other, and together will reward you at table.

antipasto

An antipasto platter, traditionally served as the first course of a pasta dinner, is as infinitely variable as the condiment tray which accompanies curry. This appetizer can be served either in place of or in addition to a salad. The selection of vegetables and other appetizers can be arranged on one large platter or, for a more elaborate affair, small samplings can be served on individual plates.

A very light dressing of olive oil and vinegar is customarily poured over the antipasto when it is already arranged on the plate—but sparingly.

Suggested ingredients for an antipasto plate include: crisp lettuce; finochio celery; sliced tomatoes; quartered or sliced hard-cooked eggs; whole radishes; green olives; black olives; pimiento peppers, fresh or in oil; green bell peppers; marinated artichoke hearts; marinated mushrooms; pickled peppers and mixed pickled vegetables; pickled beets; raw cauliflower broken into flowerettes; sweet pickles; dill pickles; raw carrot sticks; and whole green onions.

Be as plain or fancy as you wish, however, using your imagination and your appetite as a guide. Just remember that antipasto, as the name implies, acts as a foil for pasta. The richer the pasta dish, the lighter the antipasto should be.

A typical platter might include several raw vegetables, olives, and marinated artichoke hearts, all arranged on crisp leaves of Romaine or Boston lettuce.

fresh pasta

4 cups white flour, approximately
2 tsp. salt
3 eggs, lightly beaten
¼ to ⅓ cup water

Put the flour and salt in a large mixing bowl and make a well in the center. Pour in the eggs, as well as ¼ cup water. Mix the dough with your hands, adding a little more water if necessary. When all the flour has been absorbed into the dough, begin kneading it on a lightly floured board. Pasta dough is tougher than bread dough, so be prepared to work.

Knead with vigor and determination for 10 to 15 minutes (this is how the Italians keep fit while eating all that pasta) until the dough is smooth and elastic.

Cut the dough into 4 equal parts and cover 3 of them to prevent drying out while you roll out the first. Form the dough into a square or rectangle, as nearly even as possible. Roll it out with a rolling pin, turning it regularly to keep the shape even, until it is thin enough to be transluscent when held up to the light. A well-kneaded, elastic pasta dough, if it is evenly rolled, will not tear easily and can be made very thin—but it does take time and energy.

When it is rolled out to the desired thinness, simply cut it into the sort of noodles you want and lay them out on a tea towel to dry for an hour or more. Roll and cut all the portions of dough in this manner. You will have enough pasta for 4 enormous portions or 6 more reasonable ones.

To cut out fettucine, cut each large, thin square of pasta dough in two. Place one half on the other and, with a very sharp knife, cut into ¼-inch strips. Separate and lay out to dry.

To cut out lasagne noodles, cut the large squares of dough into 2-inch strips, separate, and lay out to dry.

Boil the pasta in a large quantity of salted water, testing for doneness as usual. Depending on thickness, it should take from 15 to 20 minutes.

stuffed manicotti

1   qt. Tomato and Wine Sauce (page 244)
¼   cup chopped fresh parsley or 2
        Tbs. dried parsley
2   beaten eggs
3   cups Ricotta cheese
½   tsp. salt
4 to 5 Tbs. finely chopped onion
½   cup grated Parmesan
1   tsp. caraway seeds
About 16 manicotti shells
2 to 3 Tbs. grated Parmesan

Make a good quart of Tomato and Wine Sauce.

Stir the chopped parsley into the beaten eggs. Combine the eggs with the Ricotta cheese, salt, onion, and grated Parmesan. Heat the caraway seeds in a dry pan for a few minutes over a medium flame. This heat releases their flavor—otherwise they will taste like bits of sawdust. Stir them into the cheese mixture, hot out of the pan.

Stuff the uncooked manicotti with this mixture; it should fill about 16 shells. Pour about half the sauce into a baking dish.

Arrange the manicotti in the dish on top of the sauce, then pour the rest of the sauce over them and bake in a hot oven (400 degrees) for 20 minutes.

Before serving, take off the cover, sprinkle with a little grated Parmesan, and bake uncovered for a few minutes.

6 to 8 servings.

trenette con pesto

Sauce:

5   oz. fresh basil leaves or 3 Tbs.
       crushed dry basil
½   cup pine nuts
½   cup grated Parmesan
2   small cloves garlic
5   Tbs. olive oil
salt and pepper

3   medium potatoes
½   lb. very tender, young green beans
¾   lb. trenette (thin noodles)

Traditionally, this sauce is made by crushing the ingredients in a mortar until a creamy paste is attained, then mixing in some oil. If you care to follow this procedure, by all means do. A handier procedure however, which yields just as tasty a sauce and smoother, as well as eliminating the period of convalescence necessary after using the strenuous first method, is this: Put all the ingredients except the oil into a blender. Follow blender instructions for pulverizing solid ingredients, then slowly add the oil and blend on a high speed until you have a smooth, homogeneous sauce. Season it with salt and pepper.

Have the sauce ready first, in any case. Peel the potatoes; if they are very large, cut them in half lengthwise, then slice very thinly (about ⅛ inch). In a large spaghetti pot, put a gallon of cold water, some salt, and the potato slices. Bring it to a boil and, as soon as it is boiling, add the green beans which have been washed and cut into 1-inch pieces, and the noodles.

Cook only about 12 to 13 minutes: the beans and the pasta should be *al dente*. Drain in a colander, put it all into a heated bowl or on a platter, and pour the sauce over it. Now, quickly but gently, mix the sauce in by lifting the pasta with two forks until all is smoothly coated. Serve very hot.

Serves 6 to 8 generously.

pasta con funghi *(Pasta with Mushrooms)*

1   quart Simple Tomato Sauce
      (page 245)
1½ lbs. fresh mushrooms
3   Tbs. butter
¼   tsp. each of:
      basil
      thyme
      oregano
      paprika
      rosemary
1   clove garlic, put through a press
salt and fresh-grated black pepper, to
      taste
1 to 1½ lb. fettucine
2   cups fresh grated Parmesan or
      Romano cheese

Prepare the tomato sauce according to directions on page 245.

Wash the mushrooms and cut them into thick slices. Melt the butter in a large skillet and stir into it all the herbs. Add the sliced mushrooms and toss them around until all are uniformly coated with butter and herbs. Season with salt and pepper and continue sautéing, with an occasional stir, while preparing the pasta and heating the sauce.

Boil the pasta in a large quantity of salted water until it is just *al dente*, 15 to 20 minutes depending on thickness; fresh pasta will take considerably less time, however. Drain immediately and transfer to heated plates. Spoon some hot tomato sauce over each serving, then pile some of the sautéed mushrooms on top of the sauce. Finish off each serving with a sprinkle of grated cheese and serve at once, passing the remaining cheese separately.

Serves 4 to 6.

pasta with four cheeses

5   oz. finely cubed Gruyère cheese
5   oz. finely cubed Fontina cheese
1¾ cups finely grated Parmesan cheese
5   oz. coarsely grated Mozzarella cheese
1½ Tbs. flour
¼   cup butter
1   cup milk or light cream
1   lb. shell macaroni

First prepare all the cheeses, grating and cubing as specified, and then toss the Gruyère, Fontina, and Parmesan with the flour, leaving the Mozzarella separate.

Heat the butter and milk or cream in a large, heavy-bottomed saucepan until the butter is melted. Stir in the three combined cheeses, bit by bit, and continue stirring gently with a wooden spoon until you have a smooth sauce. Keep it hot over a very low flame, and give it an occasional stir while you boil the pasta.

Cook the pasta in a large quantity of boiling water until it is *al dente*, 15 to 20 minutes. Drain it and immediately transfer to a large serving bowl which has been warmed in the oven. Pour the cheese sauce over the macaroni and stir quickly with two spoons. At the last instant, just before serving, stir in the Mozzarella quickly—do not overdo the stirring, for pasta cools quickly. Now serve at once onto heated plates.

Serves 4.

lasagne

1½ qt. Tomato and Wine Sauce (page 244)
about 1½ lbs. spinach (2 cups when
    chopped and packed)
1 onion
1 to 2 Tbs. olive oil
1 to 2 cloves garlic, minced
2 lbs. Ricotta cheese
¼ lb. grated Romano or Parmesan
    cheese
3 eggs, beaten
salt and pepper
2 to 3 Tbs. chopped fresh parsley
½ lb. Mozzarella cheese
1 lb. lasagne noodles

Prepare a good 1½ quarts of Tomato and Wine Sauce.

Wash spinach carefully and chop coarsely. You should have about 2 well-packed cups of chopped spinach. Chop the onion and sauté it lightly in the olive oil with the minced garlic. Combine the Ricotta cheese, grated Romano, spinach, sautéed onion, beaten eggs, and mix well. Season the mixture with a little salt, plenty of fresh-ground black pepper, and some chopped parsley.

Grate the Mozzarella coarsely and cook the lasagne noodles until they are just *al dente*. Now you are ready to assemble the lasagne.

Butter a large, oblong baking dish, or two smaller square ones. Arrange a layer of lasagne noodles in the bottom, then spread on a layer of Ricotta cheese mixture, sprinkle that with Mozzarella, and cover it over smoothly with Tomato and Wine Sauce. Repeat these layers once or twice more, until everything is used up. Be sure to end with sauce on top, regardless of whatever is directly beneath it.

Cover the baking pan with aluminum foil, crimping the edges tightly. Bake the lasagne at 350 degrees for 40 minutes, take off the foil cover, and bake it another 10 to 15 minutes uncovered. Serve very hot, with herb bread or garlic toast, and follow it with a very green, very crisp salad.

Serves 10 to 12.

pastitsio

Pastitsio Sauce:

¾ cup dried lentils
1   large eggplant (the size of a
       cantaloupe)
3   Tbs. olive oil
3   Tbs. butter
2   onions, finely chopped
½ tsp. cinnamon
½ tsp. oregano
salt and pepper
1   clove garlic, crushed
8   medium tomatoes, peeled (or 2 lb.
       canned tomatoes)
8   oz. tomato paste
½ to 1 cup grated Parmesan cheese
1   lb. noodles

Custard Sauce:

3   Tbs. butter
3   cups milk
3   eggs
3   Tbs. flour

Wash the lentils, cover them with 3 cups boiling water, and let them soak a few hours. Pour them into a pot, together with the water; add a little salt and olive oil, and cook them until the water is almost gone—about ½ hour or 45 minutes.

Meanwhile, heat the olive oil and butter in a large skillet, and add to it the chopped onions. Wash the eggplant and, without peeling it, chop it into small pieces and add it to the onions, along with the garlic and other seasonings. Cover the pan and let it sauté, stirring now and then. After about 10 minutes, chop the tomatoes and add them and, when the lentils are ready, add them also with the little liquid that is left. Again, let it cook awhile, and stir occasionally until it is very thick. Then stir in the tomato paste, heat it through, correct the seasoning, and the sauce is ready to use.

Boil the noodles in salted water until they are just barely *al dente*—still stiff—about 10 to 12 minutes. Butter a large casserole or oblong baking dish and put half the noodles in an even layer across the bottom. Sprinkle Parmesan over them, then carefully cover them with half the sauce. Now make a layer of the rest of the noodles, again sprinkle with Parmesan, and cover with the rest of the sauce. This much can be done ahead of time, if you like, and refrigerated.

Now make a custard sauce. Heat the butter in a saucepan, stir in the flour, and let the roux cook a few minutes. Then pour in the heated milk, stirring with a whisk. Beat the eggs in a bowl and pour the white sauce over them slowly as you continue beating with the whisk.

Pour this sauce over the entire casserole. It should drain through to the bottom and bind the whole thing together. If it just sits obstinately on top, slide a knife in and out of the four layers in a few places. Sprinkle a little more Parmesan on top and cover. Bake for 1 hour at 400 degrees, and serve very hot.

This recipe feeds 8.

baked macaroni and cheese

This great dish has acquired a very unfortunate reputation here. The reason is that it was "popularized" by commercial packagers of almost-prepared foods, and underwent some serious personality changes in the process. Well, here it is in its simple glory, much the way you may find it served in Rome, for it is indeed an old Roman dish.

3   cups Sauce Béchamel
1   lb. mostaccioli noodles (about
       2½ inches long)
4   oz. Parmesan cheese, fresh-grated
¾   lb. Fontina cheese, coarsely grated
salt and fresh-ground black pepper
1   cup buttered breadcrumbs

Prepare the Béchamel according to the recipe on page 84, but add more thyme and bay leaf than usual. (An interesting variation is to make the Béchamel for this dish with skim milk. It works quite well, as the amount of cheese in the dish ensures its richness.)

Having made the sauce, boil the pasta in a large kettle of salted water until it is just *al dente*. Combine the grated cheeses and set aside. Butter an attractive 2½- or 3-quart baking dish.

As soon as the pasta is ready, drain it and place ⅓ of it in the baking dish. Cover it with ⅓ of the cheese and pour over the cheese ⅓ of the sauce. Grate on plenty of black pepper. Make 2 more layers like this, and sprinkle the buttered breadcrumbs all over the top. Put the dish into a preheated 350-degree oven and bake for 15 to 20 minutes, then serve at once, well browned and bubbly.

I assure you, this dish bears very little resemblance to the macaroni and cheese of American convenience foods. Serve it with a sharply flavored salad and a good Chianti, and you will have a feast.

Serves 4 to 6 generously.

pasta e fagioli

1¼ cups dried navy or pea beans
salt
⅔ cup olive oil
1 bay leaf
2 to 3 cloves garlic
3 carrots
2 small stalks celery
1 large onion
3 Tbs. olive oil
1 to 2 cloves garlic, crushed
1 tsp. dried oregano leaves
½ tsp. dried basil
salt and fresh-ground black pepper
6 to 7 firm, ripe tomatoes, peeled and
    cut into large pieces
½ lb. shell macaroni
chopped fresh parsley
grated Parmesan cheese

Combine the beans with 6 cups of water and soak overnight in the refrigerator. The next day, pour them into a kettle, without draining, and add 1½ teaspoons salt, ⅔ cup olive oil, a large Italian bay leaf, and 2 or 3 peeled whole cloves of garlic. Let the beans simmer until they are tender—2 to 3 hours. When they are ready, drain them and reserve the liquid, discarding the garlic and bay leaf.

Meanwhile, scrape and dice the carrots, slice the celery, and chop the onion. Sauté these vegetables in hot olive oil in a large skillet, adding the crushed garlic, salt and pepper, and herbs. After about ½ hour, add half the tomatoes, cover and let cook another 10 to 15 minutes.

Cook the macaroni in boiling salted water until just barely tender, *al dente*. Combine the beans with the cooked vegetables and pasta in a large kettle, and add about 1½ cups of the reserved bean liquid and the rest of the tomatoes. Cover and simmer another 10 to 15 minutes, stirring occasionally and adding more salt and pepper if necessary. Turn the mixture out onto a large, attractive platter and sprinkle over it chopped fresh parsley. Serve steaming hot and pass grated Parmesan or Romano cheese in a bowl.

Serves 6 to 8.

tomato and wine sauce for pasta

1   oz. dried Italian dark mushrooms
1   cup Potato Peel Broth (page 50) or
      water
½ to 1 onion, chopped
1 to 2 cloves garlic, minced
3   Tbs. olive oil
basil
oregano
parsley
1   bay leaf
salt and fresh-ground black pepper
2½ cups tomato purée, or thinned paste
lemon peel
1   cup red wine
Worcestershire sauce

Simmer the dried mushrooms in the broth or water for about 20 minutes. Strain the broth through a sieve lined with muslin, or something comparable (very important), and wash the mushrooms thoroughly, one by one, until you are certain that not a speck of dirt is left. Chop them coarsely and return to the strained broth.

In a skillet, heat the olive oil and add to it the chopped onion and garlic. After a few minutes, crush some basil, some oregano, and some parsley, adding that also to the pan.

When the garlic is brown and the onion transparent, add the tomato purée, the mushrooms and their broth, a twist of lemon peel, an Italian bay leaf, and season with salt and fresh-ground black pepper. Stir around a little and pour in the wine.

Let it simmer on a very low heat for about 15 to 20 minutes if it is to be baked (with manicotti or lasagne), or an hour if it is intended for spaghetti. Discard the bay leaf and lemon peel before serving, and add a few drops of Worcestershire sauce.

This recipe makes about 1 quart of sauce.

simple tomato sauce for pasta

1 lb. Italian plum tomatoes, peeled
½ onion, chopped
2 cloves garlic, put through a press
2 Tbs. olive oil
¼ green bell pepper
1 small bay leaf
sprig of parsley
pinch of oregano
pinch of basil
salt
fresh-ground black pepper
red wine

If you can find fresh, ripe plum tomatoes, so much the better for you. If not, canned plum tomatoes will do very well.

Heat the olive oil in a skillet and sauté the onion and garlic in it. Put the peeled tomatoes and the bell pepper in the blender and whirl at high speed for about a minute. Pour the resulting liquid into the skillet. Add a bay leaf, a little parsley, some oregano and basil, salt to taste, and lots of fresh-ground black pepper.

Allow the sauce to simmer gently for at least ½ hour, but the longer the better. Stir it occasionally and add water if it cooks down too much. You might also add a few tablespoons of red wine.

Serve hot over freshly cooked pasta, with fresh-grated Parmesan cheese.

2 to 3 generous servings. Double the recipe for about a quart of sauce.

eggplant pasta sauce

½ cup olive oil
2 to 3 garlic cloves
1   medium eggplant (about 1 lb.)
2   green bell peppers
3   cups peeled and chopped tomatoes
½ to ¾ cup sliced black olives
3 to 4 Tbs. capers
1   tsp. crushed oregano
½ tsp. crushed basil
salt to taste
lots of fresh-ground black pepper
12   oz. tomato paste
2   cups dry white wine (more if
      needed)

Heat the olive oil in a large skillet. Mince the garlic or put it through a press, and add it to the olive oil. Let it heat gently while you prepare the eggplant.

Wash the eggplant first, then chop it very thoroughly, without peeling. Seed and dice the green peppers.

Add the peppers, eggplant, tomatoes, olives, and capers to the oil. Stir well until the oil is evenly coating all the vegetables.

Now add the remaining ingredients, stir again, and cover the skillet. Lower the heat to a very small flame and allow the sauce to simmer gently for about 1 hour. Stir occasionally to keep any of it from scorching, and add more wine or some water if it gets too thick.

Makes about 2 quarts of sauce.

mushroom sauce for pasta

1½ oz. dried dark mushrooms
2 to 3 cups water
½ onion, chopped
2 to 3 cloves garlic, minced
butter as needed
olive oil (about 1 Tbs.)
4 oz. tomato paste
1 bay leaf
sweet basil
oregano
salt
fresh-ground black pepper
Worcestershire sauce

Soak the mushrooms in water, then simmer them slowly until they are soft. Drain off the liquid, straining it through muslin to catch any grit. Reserve the liquid.

Wash the mushrooms carefully and chop them coarsely. Sauté them in butter with the onion and garlic. When the onion begins to brown, add a little olive oil, the tomato paste, and the mushroom liquid. Stir well.

Add to this a bay leaf, a little crushed sweet basil, and a pinch of oregano. Salt it to taste and grind in plenty of fresh black pepper. Cover and let it simmer slowly for as long as possible, stirring often and adding water as it is needed to maintain the proper consistency.

Before serving, add a few drops of Worcestershire sauce.

Serve steaming hot over pasta.

polenta

Here is a dish that is staple fare for many Italians, and unheard of for most Americans—perhaps because it is too simple? As with pasta, there are a great many possible variations.

6   cups water
2   cups yellow corn meal
salt
¼   cup butter
½   cup grated Parmesan cheese

Bring the water to a boil in a large pot, and pour the corn meal in slowly, stirring constantly. Add salt and butter. Cook slowly on a low flame for 20 to 30 minutes, and stir often with a wooden spoon. The Polenta should be thick, but smooth and soft. When it is ready, stir in the grated Parmesan and cook a few minutes more.

Serve with tomato or mushroom sauce, or with additional cheese and butter. This dish goes well with sharp-flavored or marinated vegetables.

Serves 6 to 8.

baked polenta

1   recipe Polenta (see preceding recipe)
2   eggs, beaten with 2 Tbs. water
salt and pepper
½ cup wheat germ
½ cup breadcrumbs

Prepare Polenta as directed, then pour it
into a buttered shallow pan. Let it cool
and set. When it is solid, cut it into small
squares or oblongs. Dip each one in
beaten egg, then in a mixture of breadcrumbs and wheat germ. Arrange them on
a buttered baking sheet and bake for
about ½ hour at 350 degrees, or until
nicely browned. Serve hot with sour
cream, Béchamel sauce, tomato sauce, or
sesame eggplant. These make a very nice
first course for an Italian dinner.

Serves 6 to 8.

curries and indian preparations

Thousands of years before the rise of Christianity and the onslaught of Western Civilization, a great culture was already flourishing in India. At its best, it was and remains marked by wisdom approaching universal understanding, and a way of life harmonious with universal laws.

It is small wonder, then, that the art of cooking was held in the highest esteem there and even, in some instances, considered a sacred ceremony, close to religious rite. Food preparations were approached seriously in regard to both nutritive and artistic value. Throughout the many regional cuisines which flourished in this atmosphere, curries of every description remained central. They have been a ritual of Indian life for some six thousand years.

In recent times, curry has become "popularized," undergoing all manner of adjustment for foreign palates. Often, the curry is lost in the translation. Many people suffer from the delusion that a curry is anything to which one adds a bit of curry powder, and more interesting still, that curry powder is the dried and ground root or fruit of some particular plant.

Many foods can be "curried" by the addition of certain spices. The name curry, however, can truthfully be applied only to the spicy Indian soup of a thousand different characters, exotic and masterfully seasoned. The simplest curries are thin soups, eaten from a bowl or poured over rice. More elaborate curries can contain almost any vegetable or fruit, and are often served with great platters of sweet and cooling condiments—but more of that later.

First, a word about curry spices. To dispel all doubts about the mythical curry tree, still growing in many people's minds, curry powder is a combination of many spices. Up to fifty ingredients will possibly be found in a curry powder—but that is rather extreme. Most commercially packaged curry mixtures are a combination of about fifteen to twenty spices. Indian cooks, mixing and grinding their own spices daily, use even fewer ingredients, often about eight or ten for each particular curry. Some of the spices and herbs most likely to be found in curry seasonings include: coriander, cumin seed, chili or cayenne peppers, fenugreek, ginger, mustard seed, white and black pepper, turmeric, allspice, cloves, paprika, poppy seeds, saffron, sage, garlic, nutmeg, anise, and cardamom.

Personally, I rarely use prepared curry powder. Following the advice of an Indian cookery book, I started blending my own spices, adjusting the mixture to suit the dish and rarely using more than eight or nine separate ingredients. I found it more interesting to vary the spices as I came to know them and the time involved is but a minute or two. Although many Indian cooks, and good cooks everywhere, grind special mixtures in a mortar, that certainly is not always necessary. Some of the spices used in the curry recipes given here can very effectively be used whole, others are most commonly available already ground; they are simply heated together in oil or clarified butter—the Indian staple called "ghee."

One essential part of the traditional curry dinner is the condiment tray. A simple meal may be served with two or three condiments, but it is not unusual to have ten or twenty, all set out in a wondrous assortment of little bowls: foods that are mild and sweet, hotly spiced and aromatic, savory and tart.

Chutneys and all varieties of sweet and sour pickled fruits and vegetables, incomparably and often intensely seasoned, are the most frequent escorts of the well-outfitted curry. But the list of possibilities is, as nearly as I can tell, endless. One book of curry cookery lists possible condiments which include various chutneys and pickles, pickled walnuts, pickled mushrooms, preserved ginger, pine nuts, pistachio nuts, peanuts, cashews, shredded coconut, soaked raisins, onion rings or strips, chopped hard-cooked eggs, chopped green peppers, sliced scallions, chopped chives, chopped parsley, chopped orange, lemon, lime, or grapefruit peel, and green or ripe olives. Also listed are some more elaborate small dishes, including apricot halves broiled with anise seasoning, baked grapefruit with sherry and cinnamon, deviled almonds, peach halves stuffed with seasoned cream cheese, stewed gooseberries, and spiced eggs.

Cooling and delicious preparations of yogurt, called "raitas," are also served with curry. A raita may combine yogurt with vegetables or fruits, raw and cooked, and, of course, the perfect seasonings, fragrant and delicate as curries are hot. Raitas, together with platters of sliced fresh fruits, balance the fiery ardor of the hottest curries.

I have found that a true banquet of fine Indian food can be prepared in less time than many a smaller meal of some other cuisine. It is also easier to serve, as courses are not called for. The Indian dinner is commonly served all at once, save only the sweet which follows by itself. To keep all foods at their proper temperatures, I suggest heating plates for the curry and rice, and providing separate cool bowls or small plates for raita or chilled fruit. Give special attention to the arrangement of the table, so that all is accessible to all—then enjoy the feast.

ghee (Clarified Butter)

Melt a pound or more of butter in a heavy-bottomed saucepan. When it is entirely melted, carefully skim off the foam from the top and discard it. Heat the butter again until it foams, and skim once more. Do this once or twice more, until all the foam is gone.

Carefully decant the melted butter into a container, pouring it off until only the fine sediment at the bottom of the pan is left.

This ghee, or clarified butter, will keep well for up to five or six weeks without refrigeration.

orange curry

1   Tbs. Ghee (page 254) or butter
4   whole cloves
1-inch stick of cinnamon
¼   tsp. cumin seeds
pinch of cayenne pepper
¼   tsp. mustard seeds
1   tsp. freshly grated ginger (green)
cardamom seeds from 2 pods
1   qt. fresh-squeezed orange juice

Heat the ghee or butter and add all the spices to it. Heat the spices for a few minutes, then add the orange juice. Cook it slowly for 15 to 20 minutes. Serve hot, in small bowls or cups, with or without spoons. This is a fascinating way to start a dinner, or even to end it.

Serves 6 (small servings are sufficient—this is a very aromatic, potent liquid).

cauliflower curry

2 lb. (2 medium heads) cauliflower
3 Tbs. butter or Ghee (page 254)
½ tsp. ginger
½ tsp. salt
½ tsp. turmeric
½ tsp. cayenne
¼ tsp. cinnamon
½ tsp. coriander
½ tsp. mustard seeds
½ tsp. cumin seeds
1 clove garlic, put through a press
½ cup water
1½ cups fresh peas
2 Tbs. torn cilantro leaves (Chinese parsley)
2 tomatoes, diced

Wash the cauliflower and break it into small flowerettes. Heat the butter or ghee in a large skillet and add to it all the spices. Stir the mixture around, and when the spices are thoroughly warmed, add the cauliflower and the water. Stir again, cover tightly, and let the cauliflower steam until it is almost tender. Add the peas and cilantro and cook another 5 to 7 minutes, stirring gently from time to time with a wooden spoon. At the last moment, add the tomatoes and, as soon as they are hot, the curry is ready to serve.

Serves 4 to 6.

potato curry

6   medium-size russet potatoes
3   Tbs. Ghee (page 254)
1   tsp. salt
1   tsp. cumin seeds
½   tsp. mustard seeds (or ground
       mustard)
1   tsp. turmeric
1   tsp. ground coriander
½   tsp. ground cayenne pepper
2   cups water
1   cup yogurt
⅔   cup cooked (but not mushy) sweet
       peas

Peel the potatoes and dice them as evenly as you can. Heat the ghee or oil and, when it is warm, add the spices. Let them simmer for 2 or 3 minutes, then add the potatoes and immediately stir them around and turn them over until they all seem evenly coated with ghee and spices. Continue this process for about 5 to 10 minutes more, so that some of the potato cubes are a little crisped.

Add 2 cups of water, lower the heat, and simmer slowly for about ½ hour, giving an occasional, gentle stir. The potatoes should be tender by this time. Now add the yogurt and the green peas, and heat it all up together for another 5 minutes or so, and serve.

About 4 to 6 servings.

carrot curry

4 to 5 cups sliced fresh carrots
1 cup fresh orange juice
water
1 tsp. salt
4 Tbs. butter or Ghee (page 254)
1 ripe banana
2 to 3 Tbs. raisins
4 to 5 cardamom pods (seeds only)
1½ tsp. turmeric
1½ tsp. mustard seeds
4 whole cloves
1 Tbs. cumin seeds
¼ tsp. cayenne pepper
1½ Tbs. cornstarch
½ tsp. prepared curry powder
(optional)

Scrape the carrots and slice them on a slant—not too thin. Put them in a pot with the orange juice, salt, and enough water to just cover. Simmer the carrots for about 5 minutes.

In a large skillet, heat the butter or ghee and add to it all the spices. Heat them for a few minutes, then add the carrots in their liquid, the raisins, and the banana, very thinly sliced. Simmer the curry slowly for about ½ hour. If the liquid seems too thin still, take some of it out into a cup and mix it well with a little cornstarch. When you have a smooth, thin paste, return it to the curry and stir in. Heat a few minutes more and the curry is ready to serve.

Serves 4 to 6.

curry of eggplant and peas

1 large eggplant (at least 1 lb.)
salt
1 large russet potato
½ onion
3 Tbs. butter or Ghee (page 254)
½ tsp. cumin seeds
1 tsp. turmeric, powdered
¼ tsp. cayenne pepper
½ tsp. mustard seeds
1 cup water
1½ cups fresh shelled peas
½ cup yogurt

Wash the eggplant and, without peeling it, slice it about ¾-inch thick. Salt the slices heavily and set them aside for at least ½ hour. The excess water will gradually work its way out, and the eggplant will thus absorb much less fat.

Peel and cube the potato and chop the onion. Rinse the eggplant slices very quickly and press out the water. Cut them into large cubes.

Heat the butter or ghee in a large skillet and add ¼ teaspoon salt and the spices.

When they are all hot, stir in the onion and potatoes, toss them around a little, then add the water and cover tightly.

After about 20 minutes, remove the cover, add the eggplant, peas, and yogurt, and stir well. Continue simmering for another 10 to 15 minutes, stirring often.

Serves 4.

curry of eggplant and potatoes

(A Bombay Curry)

2   medium eggplants (about 2 lb.
       together)
3   large russet potatoes
2   bell peppers
½   cup butter
1   tsp. ground ginger
1½ tsp. salt
1   tsp. turmeric
½   tsp. cayenne pepper
½   tsp. ground cinnamon
½   tsp. ground coriander
1   tsp. mustard seeds
1   tsp. cumin seeds
2   cloves garlic
2½ cups water
4 to 5 firm red tomatoes

Wash the eggplants, slice them, and salt them well. After about ½ hour, press out the excess water, and cut the slices into large cubes. Peel and cube the potatoes, and cut up the seeded bell peppers into ½-inch squares.

Melt the butter in a very large skillet, or a large, shallow saucepan. Add to it all the spices, as well as the cloves of garlic, put through a press. Sauté the spices in the butter for several minutes, then add the eggplant, potatoes, and green peppers. Toss the vegetables until they are rather evenly coated with spices. Add the water, cover the pan, and let the vegetables simmer for about 20 to 25 minutes. Stir them around occasionally so that they cook evenly. Remove the cover and cook over a low flame for 15 minutes more, stirring often but gently. Add the tomatoes, cut into small wedges. As soon as the tomatoes are hot through, serve the curry.

This delicate curry should be accompanied by a sweet or delicately flavored rice and various condiments.

Serves 4 to 6.

vegetable curry

2 cups yellow wax beans, cut into
1-inch pieces
2 medium potatoes, peeled and diced
3 medium carrots, scraped and sliced
4 Tbs. peanut oil, Ghee (page 254), or
butter
2 tsp. cumin seeds
1 tsp. salt
2 tsp. mustard seeds (or 1 tsp. ground)
2 tsp. turmeric
1 tsp. coriander seeds (or ½ tsp.
ground coriander)
½ tsp. cayenne pepper
1 cup yogurt
1 cup fresh green peas

Put all the vegetables, except the peas,
into a pot and add enough water to just
cover them. Salt lightly and boil for 5 to
10 minutes only. In another large pot, heat
the peanut oil (or butter or ghee) and add
the spices to it. Stir them around for a few
minutes, then add the vegetables in their
water. Bring it all to a boil, add the yogurt
and the peas, stir well, and reduce the
heat. Let it simmer for about ½ hour or
a little longer, and serve very hot with
rice, preferably saffron rice. Serves 6.

banana raita

1 tsp. butter or Ghee (see page 254)
1½ tsp. cumin seeds
¼ tsp. cardamom seeds
¼ tsp. ground coriander
¼ tsp. cayenne pepper
2 cups mashed ripe bananas
2 cups yogurt

Melt the butter or ghee in a skillet. Pound
the spices together lightly in a mortar—
they should not be completely crushed—
and add them to the butter. Stir the spices
around in the pan for a few minutes and
then quickly stir in the mashed bananas.
Remove from the heat, stir in the yogurt,
transfer to a serving dish, and chill well
in the refrigerator.

Serves 6.

watercress raita

Depending on the yogurt you use, this may be a rather thin raita. If it is, place a very small bowl by each plate and serve with a ladle. The cooling effect of this raita, sipped from a spoon between hot bites of curry, is most appreciated.

1   cup finely minced watercress leaves
1   pt. yogurt
1   clove garlic, crushed
1½ tsp. sugar
½   tsp. salt
pinch of cayenne pepper
½   green bell pepper
½   red bell pepper (optional)

Chop the watercress leaves very finely and add them to the yogurt, along with the crushed garlic, the salt, sugar, and cayenne. Mince the green pepper and stir it into the yogurt, blending everything well. Chopped red pepper may be sprinkled over the top as a garnish.

Serves 4 to 6 as a condiment.

potato raita

3   potatoes
1   tsp. butter or Ghee (page 254)
1½ tsp. cumin seeds
1   tsp. coriander
1   tsp. salt
¼   tsp. cayenne pepper
1   pt. yogurt

Boil the potatoes, peel them, and chop rather coarsely.

Heat the ghee or butter in a small pan and add the spices. After a few minutes, add the yogurt, remove from the heat, and stir well. Pour the yogurt mixture over the potatoes, mix thoroughly, and chill before serving.

4 to 6 servings.

bryani

¼ cup butter or Ghee (page 254)
1½ tsp. cumin seeds
1½ tsp. mustard seeds
¼ tsp. cayenne pepper (more to taste)
½ tsp. salt
1   clove garlic, crushed
¼ tsp. turmeric
¼ tsp. ground ginger
½ tsp. ground cinnamon
½ tsp. ground coriander
3   cups peeled and diced eggplant
1   cup sliced green onions
1   cup cut yellow wax beans
1   cup seeded and diced pimiento
      peppers
1   cup diced tomatoes
3   cups cooked long-grain white rice
3   cups saffron rice
⅓ cup coarsely chopped cashews
⅓ cup pine nuts
⅓ cup raisins

Melt the butter or ghee in a large, heavy skillet and add to it all the spices. Stir the spices in the butter for several minutes and, when they are quite hot, add the prepared vegetables. Turn the vegetables over and over again until they are uniformly coated with the butter and spices, then continue sautéing them, stirring often, until the vegetables are just barely tender.

In a large, glass baking dish, arrange the cooked white rice in an even layer. Spread the vegetables over this rice in another even layer. Make yet a third even layer of the saffron rice on top of the vegetables. Sprinkle the nuts and raisins over the saffron rice, and press them in lightly. Cover the dish *tightly* and bake 35 to 40 minutes at 325 degrees.

Serves 6 to 8.

spiced dal

This is one of the most highly concentrated forms of protein, and a staple food of India—a country largely vegetarian for many reasons. If you cannot get the Indian split-grain dal, then split peas can be substituted. It is simple to prepare, ridiculously inexpensive, and delicious. Enjoy!

1½ cups moong or urhad dal (or yellow
     split peas—see note above)
4   cups water
1½ tsp. salt
3   Tbs. butter or Ghee (page 254)
1   tsp. cumin seeds
1   tsp. ground turmeric
½-inch stick cinnamon
¼ tsp. cayenne pepper
¼ tsp. ground ginger
¼ tsp. ground coriander
½ tsp. mustard seeds
6   whole cloves

Wash the dal or split peas and boil in the salted water until it is all very soft and most of the water absorbed. Stir often.

Heat the ghee or butter in a saucepan, and add the spices to it. Stir them around for a few minutes, then remove from the heat. Pour the dal into the butter and spices, being careful to protect yourself from the spattering which is likely to occur. Return to the heat, stirring often, and let it simmer until it has the consistency of a fairly thick sauce. Serve very hot.

6 servings.

sweets

However careful we vegetarians might be, it does happen sometimes that we prepare a wonderful meal which is balanced in all respects except as regards protein. A great Italian pasta dinner often lacks sufficient protein, as might a certain Indian curry, or other delicacy. The tasty solution to such a problem is, of course, a protein-rich dessert.

With that thought in mind I planned this section on sweets. Some recipes I included simply because they were too special or delicious to leave out; others, because certain hearty dinners demand light and fruity desserts. A good number of them, however, are based on eggs, milk, cheese, or nuts, making them the perfect finale for a meal that had not quite enough protein. A light dinner ending with Rice Pudding, Torta di Ricotta, or Ginger Cheesecake, for example, will supply large portions of protein. Keep in mind also sweet soufflés and crêpes—both distinguished ways to complete an elegant supper.

There are dinners, certainly, which do not lend themselves to an overly filling dessert. These meals usually supply adequate protein in themselves, and should be finished with a light touch, such as an ice or a fruit dessert. If it should happen, though, that such a meal does need protein, serve fresh fruit for dessert and bring the Yogurt Pie or the custard out two hours later! You will be a sure success, and the shape of your meal will not be distorted or overdone.

chocolate custard

4   large eggs
¼   tsp. salt
¾   cup sugar
1   tsp. vanilla extract
½   tsp. almond extract
1¼ cups evaporated milk
1   cup cream
3½ oz. unsweetened chocolate
butter

Beat the eggs with the salt, half the sugar, the vanilla, and the almond extract. Heat together the milk, cream, chocolate, and the remaining sugar until the chocolate has completely melted. Stir with a whisk to blend.

Combine the two mixtures and pour into a well-buttered baking dish. Place the dish in a pan of hot water and bake at 325 degrees for 1 hour: a knife inserted in the center should come out clean.

Cool in the baking dish, then unmold and chill in the refrigerator. Serve this amazing concentration of chocolate with great quantities of sweetened whipped cream.

Serves 8.

zabaglione

6   egg yolks
4   Tbs. sugar
¾   cup Marsala

Beat the egg yolks and sugar in the top of a double boiler until they are lemon-colored. Add the Marsala and continue beating.

Pour boiling water into the bottom of the double boiler and set it over low heat. Continue beating the mixture gently with a whisk until it thickens.

Let the custard cool for a few minutes, then smooth it out once more with the whisk and fill 6 very small dessert dishes or parfait glasses. Chill for 1 hour or so before serving.

This is a beautiful custard with a very intriguing texture, but potent! The servings really should be small, and some delicate cookies or wafers would go well alongside.

Serves 6.

ginger sherbet

1 Tbs. gelatin
3 Tbs. cold water
1½ cups milk
1½ cups light cream
¾ cup sugar
1 tsp. vanilla
3 Tbs. finely chopped candied ginger
2 egg whites, stiffly beaten (optional)

Soften the gelatin in the cold water, then heat it very gently until it dissolves. Combine the milk, cream, sugar, vanilla, and ginger. If you have a blender, blend at high speed for a few moments to shred the ginger and combine it with the milk. Stir in the dissolved gelatin and pour it all into a large ice-cube tray.

Freeze firm (it won't get as hard as ice cubes), then break it into pieces and beat with an egg beater until it is smooth. If you like, you can fold in two stiffly beaten egg whites at this point. Put it into a serving dish, or individual dishes, and freeze again until firm.

Serves 6.

yogurt pie

1 baked pie shell
some kind of fresh fruit: peaches, nectarines, strawberries, raspberries, bananas, etc.
1 cup yogurt
1 cup small-curd, uncreamed cottage cheese
3 Tbs. honey
½ tsp. vanilla extract

Bake your favorite sweet pastry crust (or the one on page 286) and let it cool.

Line the bottom with the fresh fruit you have chosen and sprinkle a little sugar on it. Beat together the yogurt, cottage cheese, honey, and vanilla, then press it through a fine sieve. Stir it again and pour into the pie shell. Decorate the top with more bright fruit, like strawberries or thin slices of peach. Chill the pie in the refrigerator for several hours before serving.

Serves 6.

apple pudding

4 to 5 tart green apples
3   Tbs. butter
⅛   tsp. cinnamon
⅛   tsp. nutmeg

Custard:

1   cup butter
¾   cup sugar
6   eggs
1   cup milk, heated
1   Tbs. vanilla extract
2   Tbs. cognac
dash of salt

Topping:

⅔   cup flour
¼   cup sugar
½   cup brown sugar
½   tsp. cinnamon
½   tsp. nutmeg
¼   tsp. salt
4   Tbs. butter

Peel and core the apples and slice them rather thickly. Sauté the slices in the 3 tablespoons butter with the cinnamon and nutmeg for about 10 minutes.

Cream together the butter and sugar, then beat in the eggs and the hot milk, as well as the vanilla, cognac, and a bit of salt. Heat the custard lightly, beating with a whisk, until it is perfectly smooth and beginning to thicken.

Arrange the apple slices in a large, buttered baking dish, preferably glass. Pour the custard over the apples. Mix together all the dry ingredients for the topping and cut in the butter until you have a coarse-textured meal. Sprinkle this over the custard.

Bake at 350 degrees for about 40 to 45 minutes. Serve hot or cold, plain or with cream.

Serves 8.

rice pudding

½ cup rice, no more
salt
⅔ cup water
3½ cups milk
finely grated rind of 1 lemon
finely grated rind of 1 orange
1 tsp. ground nutmeg
pinch of ground cloves
2 eggs, separated
⅔ cup heavy cream
3½ Tbs. sugar
½ tsp. vanilla extract
½ cup seedless raisins

Wash the rice. In a large enameled saucepan, cook it in the salted water until the water is absorbed. Add the milk, the grated lemon and orange rinds, half the nutmeg, and a pinch of ground cloves. Let it simmer about 15 to 20 minutes, or until the rice is quite tender, stirring occasionally with a wooden spoon.

Remove from the heat and let it cool slightly. Stir in the egg yolks, cream, sugar, vanilla, and raisins. Whisk the egg whites until fluffy and fold them into the mixture. Pour it into a well-buttered, shallow baking dish, sprinkle the top with some sugar and the rest of the nutmeg, and bake in a slow oven (about 300 to 325 degrees) for 2 to 3 hours, or until it is nicely browned on top.

Serve hot or cold, with cream or custard sauce.

This is a great dish for ending a meal that is otherwise low in protein, and a delicious experience anytime. You will find it more flavorful and interesting than most rice puddings.

Serves 6.

baked cup custard

4   egg yolks
2   egg whites
⅓   cup sugar
pinch of salt
2   Tbs. cognac
½   tsp. vanilla extract
pinch of nutmeg
1   cup evaporated milk
1   cup light cream
½   cup water

Beat the egg yolks and whites in a bowl with the sugar, salt, cognac, vanilla, and nutmeg. Heat the evaporated milk, cream, and water together, but do not let it boil. Pour the warmed milk into the egg mixture, stirring with a whisk to blend. Divide the custard among 4 to 5 buttered custard cups and place them in a baking dish about halfway filled with hot water. The water should not reach too high around the cups lest it splash into the custard.

Bake the custards at 350 degrees for about 50 to 60 minutes, until a knife inserted into a custard comes out clean. Serve the custards chilled. Serves 4 to 5.

cream cheese tart

Here is a delicately flavored cheesecake, light as a mousse.

1   recipe Pastry Sucrée (page 287)
8   oz. cream cheese
3   eggs, separated
3   oz. milk or light cream
4   Tbs. sugar
1   tsp. grated orange peel
1   tsp. grated lemon peel
½   tsp. pure almond extract

Prepare the pastry, line a 10-inch pie dish, and partially bake (see page 287) for 10 minutes in a hot oven.

Cream together the cheese, cream, egg yolks, sugar, and flavoring. An electric blender does it quickly and smoothly.

Whip the egg whites with a wire whisk until they are stiff. Fold them carefully into the cheese mixture and pile it into the partly baked pastry shell.

Bake at 350 degrees for about 20 minutes. The filling will puff up and form a smooth brown crust. It is very natural for it to gently settle from its heights as it cools, so don't be disappointed: the texture remains light and fine. Serves 6 to 8.

galub jamun

—is a very special sort of Indian sweet-meat, with an impossible fragrance: roses and saffron. Ordinarily it takes days to make, but here is a simplified version, using American convenience foods. Don't be fazed by this—it is still an astonishing and exotic creation. It will always be greeted with a chorus of: "What is it?"!

1   cup sugar
3   cups water
seeds from 1 cardamom pod
2   cups instant nonfat dry milk
½   cup Bisquick
½   cup melted (not hot) Ghee
      (page 254)
¼   cup milk
¼   tsp. saffron
2   tsp. rose water, or ½ tsp. pure rose
      extract

In a deep pot, combine the sugar, water, and cardamom seeds to make a syrup. Bring it to a boil, then lower the heat and simmer very slowly.

In a mixing bowl, sift together the dry milk and Bisquick. Add the ghee and rub it all together with your fingers until you have a mixture that resembles coarse sand. Add the milk and work it in well with your hands. Carefully form the dough into small, compact balls, about the size of walnuts. Arrange them on a greased baking sheet, not too close together, and bake at 375 degrees for 10 minutes. They should be golden brown—be careful that the bottoms don't get burnt.

The syrup should be very slightly reduced, but still very thin. Add the saffron, remove the syrup from the heat, and add the rose water or rose extract. Arrange the jamuns in a beautiful, shallow serving dish or bowl, and pour the slightly cooled syrup gently over them. They may be served warm or cool, and small servings suffice (1 or 2 per person, for they are very rich and concentrated). Inhale deeply before tasting, and sip some hot, fragrant tea with them.

This recipe makes about 18 to 20 jamuns—or 10 servings.

ginger cheesecake

1 recipe Pastry Brisée Sweet (page 286)
14 oz. Neufchâtel cheese (or cream cheese)
½ cup sugar
2 eggs
2 tsp. lemon juice
1 Tbs. freshly grated ginger
1½ cups sour cream
5 Tbs. sugar
2 Tbs. slivered, crystallized ginger

Butter a 9-inch pie pan and press the pastry dough into it. Flute the edges, keeping them inside the pan. Prebake the pastry as directed (page 286).

In a mixing bowl, blend the cheese, sugar, eggs, lemon juice, and grated ginger. Beat until the mixture is very smooth and pour into the pie shell. Bake in a preheated 350-degree oven for 20 to 25 minutes.

Mix the sour cream with the 5 table-spoons sugar and the slivered ginger. Spread over the cheese filling while still hot from the oven. Turn the oven off, and return the pastry to it for a few minutes, then remove and chill well in the refrigerator. 6 to 8 servings.

spicy sweet potato pie

1 recipe Pastry Brisée Sweet, unbaked (page 286)
1½ cups mashed cooked yams (about 3 yams)
3 eggs, beaten
¾ cup dark brown sugar
1 tsp. cinnamon
½ tsp. ginger
½ tsp. cloves
¼ tsp. nutmeg
¾ tsp. salt
1⅔ cups undiluted evaporated milk

Garnish:
whipped cream

Prepare the pastry and line a 9-inch pie pan. In a large bowl, combine the mashed yams, beaten eggs, sugar, spices, and milk. Beat until well blended, preferably in an electric blender or with an electric mixer. Pour this mixture into the pie shell and bake in a preheated 375-degree oven, for 55 minutes. Cool before serving, and garnish with whipped cream.

6 to 8 servings.

torta di ricotta

2 cups white flour
1 tsp. baking powder
¼ tsp. salt
¾ cup butter
2 Tbs. cognac or brandy

Filling:

5 Tbs. chopped almonds or 5 Tbs.
    chopped pine nuts and almonds
2 to 3 Tbs. chopped citron
1 Tbs. flour
2 cups (1 lb.) ricotta cheese
4 eggs
1 cup sugar
½ tsp. pure vanilla extract or 1 tsp.
    almond extract

confectioner's sugar
cherries and whole almonds for
    decoration

Sift together the flour, baking powder, and salt. Cut in the butter with a pastry cutter until you have a fine meal, then sprinkle over the cognac and work the dough with your hands until it is smooth. Put it away to chill.

Combine the chopped nuts, citron, and the flour, then add the cheese. Beat the eggs until pale and fluffy, slowly adding the sugar and flavorings. Stir the eggs into the cheese mixture and beat thoroughly with a wooden spoon.

When the pastry is well chilled, roll out ⅔ of it and line a buttered, 10-inch pie dish. Pour the cheese filling into it. Roll out the remaining pastry and cut it into very thin strips. Arrange these in a lattice pattern on top of the filling, pressing the ends to the edge of the crust. Bake for about 40 to 45 minutes at 375 degrees. Cool and sprinkle with confectioner's sugar (through a sieve), then decorate with the cherries and almonds.

Serves 10 to 12.

cottage pudding (A Cake)

2½ cups sifted white flour
2 tsp. baking powder
½ tsp. salt
½ cup butter
1 tsp. vanilla extract
½ tsp. powdered lemon peel
¾ cup sugar
2 eggs, separated
1 cup milk
3 to 4 green apples (Pippin)
powdered cloves, nutmeg, and allspice

Sift together the flour, baking powder, and salt. Cream the butter together with the vanilla, lemon peel, and ⅔ cup sugar. When this mixture is creamy, beat in the egg yolks. Then, little by little, stir in the flour and milk alternately, beating thoroughly with a wooden spoon. Beat the egg whites until stiff and fold into the batter.

Butter a 10-inch pie or quiche dish. Peel and core the apples and cut them into quarters. Cover the bottom of the dish with these apples. Carefully pour the batter over the apples and smooth it with a spoon. Sprinkle the top with the remaining sugar and the spices. Bake for 40 to 45 minutes in a preheated 375-degree oven.

Let the cake cool slightly and dust it with confectioner's sugar (it sprinkles very nicely through a fine sieve). Serve as is or with a sweet sauce.

Serves 6 to 8.

summer fruit tart

1   recipe Pastry Sucrée (page 287)
8   oz. cream cheese
⅓   cup sugar
1   Tbs. grated lemon rind
2   Tbs. lemon juice
2   peaches
6 to 7 small purple plums
fresh strawberries
½   cup strawberry or blackberry jelly
additional fresh fruit

Prepare the pastry, as directed, then chill it well for an hour or two. Then, on a lightly floured board, roll it out carefully into an oblong—about 9 inches x 14 inches. Either fit it into a buttered, oblong baking pan, or make your own from aluminum foil, folded twice for sufficient thickness. The crust should have a raised edge about ¾ inches high on all sides. Prick with a fork in several places and chill in the freezer for an hour or so before baking at 375 degrees for about 20 minutes. Let it cool in the pan, then take it out and place it on a large, elegant serving platter.

Beat together the softened cream cheese, the sugar, lemon juice, and grated rind until smooth and creamy. Spread this mixture evenly over the pastry crust.

Peel the peaches and slice them rather thinly. Wash the strawberries. Cut the plums in half, without peeling, and take out the stones. Arrange these fruits in rows across the pastry, making as fine a show of it as you can. Finally, melt the jelly and brush it over the fruit to give it all a jewel-like glaze.

Chill very well before serving. If you have room on the serving tray, arrange a few small pieces of fresh fruit at the ends of the pastry—strawberries with their stems and leaves, a few polished plums, an apricot or two, or some additional peach slices are all lovely.

This pastry should serve about 10 people, but it is so seductively beautiful and so delicious that you should expect everyone to want a double portion.

linzertorte

1   cup butter
1   cup sugar
1   Tbs. grated orange peel
1   tsp. grated lemon peel
2   egg yolks
1½ cups sifted white flour
1   tsp. baking powder
2   tsp. cinnamon
½   tsp. cloves
¼   tsp. salt
1   cup ground, blanched almonds
      (filberts, walnuts, or a combination
      may be substituted)
1   cup tart fruit preserves (I
      recommend currant, plum, or wild
      blackberry preserves)

Optional Garnish:

whipped cream.

Cream the butter with the sugar, then add the grated peel and egg yolks, and beat well. Sift together the dry ingredients, except the nuts, and add to creamed mixture. Stir in the nuts last and work the dough with your hands until smooth.

Chill well.

Butter a spring-form cake pan, preferably an 8-inch one with high sides. Take ⅔ of the dough and press it into the pan, making a 1-inch edge around it. Spread most of the preserves over the top. They should not reach the top of the edge. With the remaining dough, form long strips, about ½ inch across, and place them on the cake in a lattice pattern. Fill the squares with more preserves and bake in a preheated 350-degree oven for 50 to 60 minutes. Cool before cutting.

This torte is delicious as it is, also lovely with whipped cream. Cut it into small pieces, for it is very rich.

tarte aux poires

1   recipe Pastry Brisée Sweet (page 286)
1   cup sugar
5 to 6 pears (Anjou)
1½ cups milk
2   egg yolks
2   Tbs. flour
1½ cups water

Make a crust and fill a 9- or 10-inch pie pan. Bake it in a hot oven (400 degrees) for 5 minutes only, then set aside.

Peel and core the pears and slice them in half lengthwise. Arrange them carefully in a large saucepan and add the water. Simmer them gently and, after about 15 to 20 minutes, add ⅓ cup sugar. Continue to simmer for another 5 to 10 minutes. Very carefully remove the pears to a plate and let them cool. The syrup in the saucepan should continue to simmer until it is greatly reduced and very thick. Warm the milk in another saucepan with the remaining sugar. Beat the egg yolks well with the flour and whisk in the warm milk. Arrange the pear halves in the pie crust—the most attractive way is to form a circle—and pour the custard over it.

Bake at 400 degrees for about 40 minutes. The custard will have brown patches on top. Let it cool slightly, then pour the syrup over the top. Cool to room temperature before serving.

This is a more complicated pie than most, but if you put it together carefully you will have a true aristocrat of pastries. Its life is extremely short, but very sweet.

Serves 6 to 8.

cold lemon soufflé

5   eggs, separated
1¼ cups sugar
3   large lemons
2   envelopes unflavored gelatin
2   cups whipping cream
⅛   tsp. cream of tartar
2   cups fresh blackberries
sweetened whipped cream (optional)

Beat together the egg yolks and sugar. Grate the rinds of all 3 lemons and squeeze out the juice, measuring out ⅔ cup of it. Add the rind to the egg yolks, then gradually add the ⅔ cup lemon juice, beating all the while.

Soften the gelatin in ½ cup water and heat until it is liquid. Allow it to cool slightly.

Whip the cream lightly and stir it into the lemon mixture, then stir in the gelatin and continue stirring until the mixture begins to thicken.

Beat the egg whites with the cream of tartar until they are stiff but not dry; fold into the lemon mixture. Spoon the soufflé carefully into a prepared soufflé dish and chill in the refrigerator for several hours, or until completely set.

To serve, spoon the soufflé into individual dessert dishes and top each serving with a generous portion of ripe berries and, if desired, sweetened whipped cream.

Serves 10 to 12.

mazurek

2 cups white pastry flour
1 cup sugar
¼ tsp. salt
½ cup butter
1 egg
¼ tsp. almond extract
3 Tbs. cream

Sift together the flour, sugar, and salt. Cut in the butter as you would for a pie crust, until the mixture resembles coarse sand. Beat together the egg, cream, and almond extract, and add it to the flour. Mix lightly and spread in an oblong, buttered baking pan. Bake at 350 degrees for ½ hour, remove from the oven, and quickly cover with topping. Return to the oven for 20 minutes. Cool and decorate with lucre (see below), candied cherries, whole almonds, orange peel, etc.

(This is a very rich pastry; cut it into small squares to serve.)

Fruit Topping:

1 cup sugar
2 eggs
8 oz. dried apricots, finely diced
½ cup candied lemon peel
½ cup chopped almonds
1 cup chopped figs
juice of 1 lemon
juice of 1 orange

Separate eggs and beat the whites until they thicken. Add the sugar and beat until smooth and thick, but not too stiff or dry. Fold in the other ingredients. Spread this mixture on the Mazurek after ½ hour baking and return to oven for 20 minutes.

Lucre:

Mix confectioner's sugar with warm water, drop by drop, until it is smooth and just thin enough to run off the spoon in a heavy thread. Flavor with a few drops of vanilla or almond extract.

apple crisp

2   lbs. tart green apples (about 5 to 5½
        cups sliced)
¼   cup water
½   cup sugar
½   cup brown sugar
½   tsp. nutmeg
½   tsp. cinnamon
¼   tsp. salt
¾   cup flour
½   cup butter

Peel the apples and slice them thinly. Put them in a rather shallow 1-quart casserole and sprinkle them with the water. Put them aside while you prepare the crust.

Sift together the dry ingredients and cut in the butter until all is well combined. Sprinkle this mixture thickly and evenly over the apples. Don't mix the two together.

Cover the casserole and bake at 350 degrees for ½ hour, then uncover and bake another ½ hour. The crust will be crisp on top, and will have partly seeped down through the apples, flavoring them and binding them slightly together.

Serve hot or cold, alone or with Crème Anglaise (page 284).

fresh fruit compote

Start with a large bunch of seedless grapes—peeled; a medium pineapple—cored, peeled, and cut into large chunks; one or two tart, crisp apples—peeled and sliced; and a cupful of pitted and halved fresh cherries.

Combine them all in a clear glass bowl with enough brandy and kirsch to moisten all the fruit well, a sprinkle of sugar if you like, and let it marinate in the refrigerator for a few hours before serving.

Especially nice accompanied by Vanilla Sand Cookies (page 282).

preserved fruit compote

This elegant and refreshing dessert is especially recommended by the fact that it is not seasonal: all the ingredients are available dried or in jars.

10 to 12 dried prunes
10 to 12 small dried figs
spice tea
1   pkg. frozen raspberries (or an equal amount of fresh, if they are in season)
1   lb. canned peach or apricot halves
1   lb. canned greengage plums
½   lb. canned loganberries
cognac
syrups from cans

Soak the prunes and figs in hot spice tea, such as Constant Comment or Spice Bouquet, for several hours. Defrost the raspberries, drain carefully and set them aside: they are to be added last. Drain the peaches or apricots, the plums, and the loganberries, reserving a little of the syrup from each. Combine a few spoons of each syrup, then add cognac (or Armagnac) to double the amount, or more. Combine all the fruits in a deep glass or crystal bowl, rinsing the prunes and figs first, and pour over them the syrup. Last, add the raspberries and give it a gentle stir, so that all is mixed but nothing is crushed. Chill several hours.

Serves 8 to 10.

fruit ambrosia

2   cups fresh pineapple, diced in large
      chunks
2   oranges, peeled, sectioned, and cut
1 to 2 bananas, sliced
2   peaches or nectarines, peeled and
      sliced
fresh strawberries, as many as you like
3 to 4 pieces of candied ginger, very
      thinly sliced
½   cup coarsely grated coconut
¼   cup honey
¼   cup cognac or fruit-flavored liqueur
¼   cup lemon juice

Peel the fruit, cut it up, and toss very
lightly in a bowl, together with the ginger
and coconut. Cover and put aside to chill.
Mix a dressing of equal parts of honey,
brandy or liqueur, and lemon juice. Then,
if it is either too sweet or too tart for your
taste, add slightly more lemon juice or
honey. Just before serving, toss again with
the dressing.

It is a lovely dessert on a hot day or after
a heavy meal. This recipe makes enough
for 6 to 8 people.

vanilla sand cookies

3   sticks of butter (¾ lb.)
3   cups flour
¾   cup sugar
1   tsp. vanilla extract
⅔   cup blanched, finely ground almonds

Work all the ingredients together with
your hands until you have a smooth, stiff
paste. To form the cookies, break off a
small chunk—a spoonful or a bit more—
and roll into a ball between the palms of
your hands. Flatten into a round, and you
will have a circle with fine, cracked edges.
Arrange these on a baking sheet and press
a design in the top if you wish. Bake at
325 degrees for about 25 minutes or until
golden in color.

They go very nicely with Fresh Fruit
Compote (page 280).

apricot mousse

2 cups dried apricots
⅓ cup sugar
¼ cup water
3 egg whites, stiffly beaten
1 cup whipping cream
½ tsp. vanilla extract
2 Tbs. sugar
grated lemon peel

Cook 2 cups (loosely packed) of small, dried apricots in water for about 45 minutes, or until they are very soft and can be mashed easily. Keep the water level minimal so that no draining is necessary. Simply let it cook down when the apricots are soft enough. Press the apricots through a coarse sieve or purée them in a blender.

Cook the sugar and water together until the syrup spins a thread, then add it very slowly to the beaten egg whites, beating all the while. Carefully fold in the apricot mixture.

Whip the cream with a little sugar and vanilla until it is just stiff enough to form peaks. Fold it into the apricot mixture, along with a little grated lemon peel (to your taste).

Turn the mixture into a buttered mold and freeze for about 4 to 6 hours. To unmold, dip it up to the rim in hot water for a few minutes (longer than for gelatin), then cover with a plate and turn over. This mousse will have a rougher surface than an aspic or custard, and will be softer than most mousse. Serve immediately or return to the refrigerator to chill.

Serves 8 to 10.

raspberry fool

2 cups Crème Anglaise made with
    cream (see below)
1 qt. fresh raspberries
sugar as needed
¾ cup whipping cream
½ tsp. vanilla extract

Prepare the Crème Anglaise, as directed, using light cream instead of milk and allowing the cream to thicken somewhat more than usual. Use the maximum amount of large egg yolks and stir over a low heat for a longer time to make a thicker sauce. Chill the Crème Anglaise.

Wash the fresh raspberries and press them through a sieve, leaving behind only a mass of seeds. Sweeten the purée lightly with sugar if you feel that it needs some.

Sweeten the whipping cream with about 2 tablespoons of sugar and add the vanilla. Whip until it holds soft peaks.

Combine the raspberry purée and the Crème Anglaise thoroughly. Then fold in the whipped cream lightly and stir once or twice, leaving ribbons of raspberry mixture and whipped cream not altogether combined.

Spoon the fool into chilled dessert glasses. Chill well before serving. Serves 8.

crème anglaise: basic custard sauce

2 cups milk
4 to 5 egg yolks (depending on egg
    size)
6 Tbs. sugar
½ tsp. salt
½ tsp. vanilla extract

Scald the milk and keep it hot in the top of a double boiler. In a bowl, beat the egg yolks with the salt and sugar until they are fluffy. Still beating with a whisk, pour the hot milk into the egg yolks. Return the mixture to the double boiler and heat it gently, stirring often, until it thickens enough to coat a spoon. Add the vanilla (or other) flavoring and strain.
Serve this sauce warm or cool over puddings, sweet soufflés, etc.

basic shortcrust pastry

2 cups hard-wheat white flour
    (preferably unbleached)
½ tsp. salt
½ tsp. sugar
¾ cup butter
lemon juice
1 to 3 Tbs. iced water

Mix the flour, salt, and sugar in a bowl. Cut in the butter, using two knives or a pastry cutter, until the mixture resembles coarse corn meal. Sprinkle over it a few drops of lemon juice and a very small amount of iced water—absolutely no more than 3 tablespoons—and toss lightly until it begins to come together. Form it quickly into a ball and chill before rolling it out.

Roll it out quickly on a lightly floured board—making two circles, slightly larger than the pie dish. This recipe makes two 9-inch crusts or one double crust.

If the pie shell is to be prebaked (or baked "blind," as this procedure is often called), prick the bottom with a fork in several places, put a piece of foil in the shell and about a cup of dried beans on the foil. Bake it for 12 to 15 minutes in a hot oven—425 degrees. Remove the foil and store the beans, which may be used over and over again for this purpose.

pastry brisée

2 cups flour
⅔ cup butter
salt
1 Tbs. sugar

This pastry crust is very delicate and crumbly in texture—the shortest of the shortcrusts. It is recommended for any kind of quiche or savory cheese pie.

Sift together the flour, sugar, and a good pinch of salt, and cut in the butter until the mixture resembles coarse sand. You may also rub the butter in with your fingertips. Add no water. Work it into a ball, wrap, and put away to chill for an hour or more.

This pastry is too crumbly for rolling out, so you must press it into the buttered pie dish with your fingers until you have a smooth crust of even thickness. Finish the edges as you normally do, prick the bottom with a fork, and bake for 10 minutes at 450 degrees. Fill as desired and finish baking.

pastry brisée sweet

1 cup flour
⅓ cup sugar
¼ lb. butter
pinch of salt

Sift together the flour, sugar, and salt. Cut in the butter with a pastry blender until it has the texture of coarse sand. Continue working it with your hands until you can pat the dough into a ball. Put it away to chill for an hour or two. Press it into a 10-inch pie pan with your fingers until it is even and fairly smooth. Finish the edges as usual. Prick the bottom with a fork for steam-escape holes.

For a prebaked crust, put a layer of foil in the bottom and fill it with some dry beans. Bake at 450 degrees for about 10 minutes, reduce heat to 350 degrees and bake another 15 to 20 minutes. If the edges get too dark, cover them with a little foil.

pastry sucrée *(Rich)*

¼ cup butter
1 cup white flour
¼ cup sugar
pinch of salt
1   whole egg
2   egg yolks

Cut the butter into the flour until the mixture resembles coarse sand. Mix together the egg, egg yolks, salt, and sugar, and combine with the flour-butter mixture. Put it away to rest in the refrigerator for at least 1 hour.

To line the pie pan or the tart shells with this pastry, press it into the form with your fingertips—rub some butter on your fingers first and work carefully to ensure an even thickness. Prick the bottom of the crust with little holes so the steam can escape (this is very important, or your pie crust might have exactly the shape of a derby hat) and bake in a 400-degree oven for 5 minutes only—if it is to be baked again with filling—or for about 20 minutes—if the filling does not require baking.

This is enough for one 9-inch or 10-inch crust, and is especially recommended for fresh fruit tarts and other such sweet pies. Be careful not to bake it too long.

holidays, traditions, and some new thoughts

There are some of us who more or less lapsed into vegetarianism without noticing quite when and how it happened. That is the natural way, and the transition can be a very smooth one—indeed almost effortless—until we inevitably arrive at our first vegetarian Thanksgiving or Christmas. Then come rushing back all the time-honored customs, all the memories of family celebrations, all the compulsive planning of festivity, and the certain explosion of baking and cookery in all good kitchens. For, indeed, all our happiest traditions are inextricably bound up with the preparation and sharing of food, and the pull of tradition is mighty. This can be a difficult moment for the new vegetarian—but it needn't be! On the contrary, I say welcome it. Here is a tale of success—a boast, if you will:

My first break with obligatory holiday tradition came at Thanksgiving, the year that I had, for some time, been really a vegetarian. It was truly and plesasantly memorable. I think part of the trick was to indulge ourselves in as many traditions as possible: the few that were missing were hardly missed. But more important, there was an unmistakable excitement—a spirit of renaissance—in breaking some new ground. When you know that you are very probably establishing new traditions for your family and friends, everything becomes very much more interesting and, more important—you, most of all!

We looked forward to our Thanksgiving since early autumn. The close friends we invited to share it with us (not all of them vegetarians) felt the mood. Some came early to help cook, and the house was full of a very old-fashioned kind of holiday industry. Curiously, or perhaps not, the absence of that uninspired national preoccupation with turkey left room for more considerable sentiments: friendship, thanksgiving, and a general enjoyment of all things good.

That meal began, amid genial toasting with a venerable, ruby-red Margaux, with Roast Chestnut Soup—a rich and mellow liquid, flavored with red wine and cognac, it emerged as instant tradition with us. Gracefully following it was Curried Lentil and Tomato Salad in pineapple boats. The third course consisted of crisp Almond Croquettes bathed in creamy Béchamel sauce, accompanied by Cranberry-Cumberland Sauce and Potatoes in Wine. Chilled Cider-Spiced Apples ended the first part of that debauch.

Four hours later, in a mood of lackadaisical hilarity, we had some pumpkin pie, coffee, and a ceremonial pipe. Any spirit of celebration which in years past had grown stale and fallen victim to habit, had been that day rousingly revived.

CHRISTMAS

I especially love Christmas. Eleven months out of the year I don't hold much with custom for custom's sake, but, come December, I'm helpless. The fever seizes me. At any rate, if there ever was a time for sentimentality and traditional merrymaking, one that has transcended religious orientation, Christmas must be that time. The effect seems salutary: even people who ordinarily are as colorful and gay as groundworms, who would dare not consider a flamboyant gesture, hang long strings of brightly colored lights around their houses, trim Christmas trees, and talk to strangers.

When I was small, all the aunts and uncles, cousins and close friends came to our house for Christmas Eve supper, the solemn and joyous festivity called *Vigilia*. Cooking and baking, it seemed, had been going on for weeks, and all manner of cakes and sugar-plums were stored in great boxes in the pantry. By noon we were scrubbed and dressed and frantically racing around the house, thinking evening would never come. Finally it did, with all the guests in turn arriving, coming in quickly from the wind, smelling of snow and perfume, with cold cheeks to kiss, silk and velvet to touch, bright eyes, and arms full of gaily wrapped packages—but these were spirited away by the con-spiring adults to the living room, where the children weren't allowed to look.

Just before supper, a beautiful ceremony took place. Each person present held a piece of *oplatek,* a special paper-thin wafer sent from Poland. One by one, everybody would break a piece of *oplatek* with everybody else in a slowly moving group around the table, embracing and exchanging personal good wishes.

Then began the interminable courses of the meal. At the ages of four or five, or even seven, food was not nearly so interesting a thing as what was behind the closed doors across the hall. But the big people loved it, and twelve or twenty of them sat there gently clinking crystal and porcelain, and laughing and talking much more than they ate, it seemed.

The Polish *Vigilia,* interestingly, is traditionally a meatless meal. My fondest association was then, and still is, with the complex and beautiful vegetable salad which started the meal, flanked on all sides by simpler relishes, and the superbly elegant, clear beet broth with mushroom dumplings that followed it. The salad, comprised of a dozen ingredients at least, seasoned with authority, and bound together with a fine homemade mayonnaise sauce (bearing no resemblance to commercial mayonnaise) is always decorated with such artistry that only the artist, whoever it may be that year, dare plunge the serving spoon into it. The beet broth, called *barszcz,* is a perfectly clear, aromatic liquid, the color of dark rubies. It begins with a delicate vegetable broth, to which are added beets and the strong perfume of dark mushrooms. Those same mushrooms fill twisted little pastry pockets to make *uszki*—the dumplings.

Both of these recipes, carefully translated into specific measurements from the more general methods used by my mother and our Polish friends, are included in this book. I also have written down a third Christmas Eve dish, the Baked Sauerkraut with Peas. A good homemade kraut is preferred; it is seasoned with the most savory mushrooms, a rich sour cream sauce, and covered with whole yellow peas. The dish is then baked to a succulent and hearty marriage of flavors, and served with an assortment of dark and light breads.

Poppy-seed struçla is the moist and sweet confection served with coffee at the end of the meal. This, however, is only a prelude to the delights of *bakalia*. Huge trays or platters, arranged on a separate table or sideboard somewhere not far from the Christmas tree, are laden with every variety of cake and confection, dried fruits in abundance, traditional cookies, candies, nuts, and fresh fruit.

When the peering and impatient, insistent eyes of the children were at last enough to drive the adults from the table, the company removed *en masse* to the living room or parlor. There, as the doors were swung open, the glorious sight of the lighted and sparkling tree, reigning quietly over a sea of Christmas packages, was finally revealed; up to that time, the room was not for children's eyes. Then the old carols were sung, greedy little fingers paused with indecision over the *bakalia* trays, more toasts were drunk, and gifts exchanged, opened, and admired. On a few special Christmas Eves, a red-cheeked, white-whiskered, profoundly imposing Santa Claus took an hour or so to carefully distribute the gifts. Other years, he didn't have time to stop so long, and some lucky member of the family assumed the ceremonial task. Many hours later, a hardy group departed through the snow to midnight mass, while smaller people— much-tamed now—wearily allowed themselves to be transferred from finery to feather-beds.

a suggested christmas eve dinner menu, in the polish tradition

Relish Tray   Pickles and Peppers
Holiday Vegetable Salad
Barszcz z Uszkami
(clear beet broth with stuffed dumplings)
Baked Sauerkraut with Peas
Poppy Seed Strucla, Coffee
Pastries, Nuts, Fruits, Candies

We now celebrate Christmas Eve in the same time-honored way, though the number at table has been cut by distances. On Christmas Day, in less formal fashion, the feasting begins anew. Friends are always expected to unexpectedly visit, glasses of eggnog may be raised, and, late in the afternoon, is served a gala Christmas dinner, well embroidered with English and American traditions.

a suggested christmas day dinner menu

Giant Stuffed Mushrooms
(with a seasoned bread stuffing)
Chestnut Paté in a Crust
Cranberry-Cumberland Sauce   Spiced Nectarines
Pineapple Glazed Yams
Vegetable Salad Vinaigrette
Steamed Plum Pudding
Pastries   Coffee   Cognac

nutmeat paté in brioche

Paté:

2½ Tbs. butter
2　small cloves garlic, minced
1　chopped onion
¼ tsp. ground cumin
¼ tsp. thyme
¼ tsp. marjoram
¼ tsp. paprika
2　Tbs. flour
¾ cup vegetable broth
½ cup red wine
1½ cups broken, shelled chestnuts
2½ cups broken, shelled walnuts
½ cup broken, shelled pecans
1　cup diced celery
1　Tbs. Worcestershire sauce
1　Tbs. cognac
2　eggs, lightly beaten
2　Tbs. chopped fresh parsley
1　tsp. salt
fresh-ground black pepper
　　to taste
½ cup dry breadcrumbs
　　(more if needed)
4　oz. grated Gruyère cheese

Brioche:

3　packages yeast
½ tsp. sugar
¾ cup lukewarm milk
4　cups flour, more as needed
2　tsp. salt
10 large egg yolks
½ cup butter, well softened

Paté: Melt the butter in a medium-size, heavy-bottomed skillet and sauté the onion and garlic in it. When the onion turns transparent, stir in the cumin, thyme, majoram, paprika, and the flour. Allow the roux to cook for a few minutes, then add the vegetable broth and the wine, stirring with a whisk. When the sauce thickens, remove it from the heat and set aside.

Put the nutmeats and the celery through the medium blade of a food mill. Stir in the sauce and all the remaining ingredients. Taste and correct seasoning.

Prepare the brioche dough: Butter a loaf pan and preheat the oven to 400 degrees. Sprinkle the yeast and sugar on the milk and let it stand for about 10 minutes. Put 3 cups of the flour in a large bowl with the salt, egg yolks, and the well-softened butter. Add the yeast mixture and mix well to make a soft dough. Turn out onto a lightly floured board and knead in 1 more cup of flour. Knead for 10 to 15 minutes, until the dough no longer sticks to your hands.

Transfer the dough to a lightly buttered bowl and flip it over so that all sides are greased. Cover the bowl with a tea towel and leave the dough in a warm place to rise for 1½ to 2 hours. Punch it down, knead for 2 or 3 minutes, and let it rise again until it is double in size. Punch down once more and roll it out into a rectangle about 12 inches x 15 inches.

Pile the paté mixture carefully in an oblong shape down the center of the brioche rectangle, leaving several inches at each end and enough room on the long sides to wrap the dough around the paté. Fold the 2 long sides over the top so that they overlap about an inch, brush the edges with a little water, and seal the overlapping edges firmly. Trim the ends, tuck them up as if wrapping a package, and seal. Pinch the seams securely. Place the loaf in the pan, seam side down, and brush the top with a little beaten egg yolk. Decorate the loaf with pastry cutouts made from the trimmings and brush the decoration with egg yolk. Bake for 20 minutes at 400 degrees, then for 40 minutes more at 350 degrees.

Variation: Peel and core 2 or 3 small green apples and fit them inside the paté as you arrange it on the brioche dough. The centers of the apples should be filled with paté and they should be covered with paté on all sides. Proceed as above. When the loaf is sliced, you should have perfectly centered apple rings in the centers of the slices.

Serve hot or chilled; 10 to 12 servings.

struçla

Here is a recipe that my mother has made at Christmastime ever since I can remember. It is a lot of work, but so worth it. This recipe makes 4 to 5 large loaves or 9 to 10 small ones. They go fast and make splendid gifts.

Dough:
3   packages yeast
½   cup warm water
1½ cups warm milk
9½ to 10 cups unbleached white flour
10 egg yolks
5   egg whites
1½ cups sugar
1   tsp. salt
2   tsp. vanilla extract
½   tsp. lemon extract
1   Tbs. rum
grated peel of 1 orange
½   cup butter
egg yolk and water, beaten

Poppy Seed Filling:
1½ lb. poppy seeds
boiling water
1   lb. sugar

1   cup chopped almonds
1   egg white
1   cup raisins
2   Tbs. honey (more if needed)
almond extract

To make the dough: In a large bowl, dissolve the yeast in the warm water and stir in the warm milk and 4 cups of the flour. When the mixture is smooth, put it aside in a warm place.

In another bowl beat together the egg yolks, egg whites, sugar, salt, vanilla, lemon extract, rum, and grated orange rind. Beat this mixture until it is pale and very smooth. When the yeast mixture is puffed up and spongy, stir in the eggs with a wooden spoon. Gradually add about 4 more cups flour, stirring vigorously. Melt the butter, allow it to cool, and stir it in.

The dough will be rather stiff at this point. Put aside the spoon and plunge into the bowl with your hand as you gradually add another 1½ cups flour. Slap the dough against the bowl, pull it up, and slap down again. Proceed in this fashion for about ½ hour or until the dough is very elastic, blistering, and no longer wants to stick to the bowl or your hand. Cover the bowl with a tea towel and let the dough rise until double in size.

When the dough has risen, punch it down and turn out on a well-floured surface. Divide it into as many parts as you want to make loaves. Knead each portion a little, then roll out into an oval shape about ½-inch thick. Spread a generous amount of poppy seed filling (or walnut filling on the next page) over the dough, leaving a 1-inch border all the way around. Starting at one narrow end, roll the dough rather tightly to the other and pinch the seam and ends securely. Place seam side down on a buttered cookie sheet and let rise until double. You can place two large loaves lengthwise on one sheet, or three small ones across the sheet. Bake only one sheet of loaves at a time, placing it on the center rack of the oven.

Just before baking, brush the loaves with a mixture of beaten egg yolk and water. Bake in a preheated 375-degree oven for about 25 to 35 minutes, depending on the size of the loaves. They are done when golden brown all over. The struçla can be decorated with a glaze of powdered sugar and water, and with bits of candied fruits and nuts.

To make the Poppy Seed Filling: Prepare the filling the night before you make the struçle.

Place the poppy seeds in a large bowl and cover with boiling water. Let stand at least 1 hour. Drain off the water. Put the seeds through the fine blade of a food mill two or three times, until the meal starts to look milky. Add the sugar and put through the mill again.

Add the chopped almonds, the egg white, raisins, honey, and almond extract. Mix well and taste. Add more honey if necessary. The filling should be moist and sweet.

walnut filling for struçla

3 egg whites
⅛ tsp. salt
1 cup sugar
1½ cups ground walnuts
½ tsp. almond extract

Beat the egg whites lightly. Mix all ingredients thoroughly. Spread the filling on the dough according to the instructions on the preceding page.

pineapple glazed yams

4 large yams
4 Tbs. butter
½ cup brown sugar
1 tsp. salt
1 tsp. grated orange rind
1 cup crushed pineapple
2 tsp. cornstarch

Peel the yams, slice them thickly, and boil them in salted water for about 10 minutes. Melt the butter in a large, heavy skillet and stir in the brown sugar, salt, orange rind, and pineapple. Dissolve the cornstarch in about 2 tablespoons of cold water and stir it into the pineapple mixture.

When the mixture is well blended and thickened, add the yams and turn them over until all the slices are coated evenly. Continue cooking over a medium flame until the yams are quite tender and well glazed. Serve hot.

Serves 6.

spiced nectarines

2   qt. firm, ripe nectarines (or small peaches)
whole cloves
2½ cup brown sugar
1   cup cider vinegar
2-inch stick of cinnamon, broken

Wash the fruit carefully. Scald and peel it if you wish, although nectarines don't really need peeling. Stick 1 whole clove into each piece of fruit.

Heat the sugar, vinegar, cinnamon, and 1 tablespoon of cloves in an enameled kettle. When it comes to a boil, add the fruit and cook until just tender, about 10 minutes. Place the fruit in hot, sterilized glass jars and pour the syrup over it to within ½ inch of the top. Seal at once and let stand for several weeks.

Serve as a garnish for rich or milk-flavored foods.

spiced nuts

1   cup sugar
1   tsp. powdered cinnamon
1   tsp. finely grated orange peel
⅛ tsp. mace
½ cup milk
1   tsp. butter
1   tsp. pure vanilla extract
2   cups walnut halves

Combine the sugar, cinnamon, orange peel, mace, and milk. Cook until the mixture reaches the soft-ball stage—236 degrees on the candy thermometer. Remove from heat and add the butter. Let it stand for a few minutes, then add the vanilla and nuts.

Stir until thick and turn out on waxed paper. Quickly separate the nuts from one another and allow them to dry.

pierniki *(Polish Spice Cookies)*

1 to 1½ cups honey
4 to 5 cups flour
pinch of black pepper
½ tsp. cinnamon
½ tsp. nutmeg
½ tsp. cloves
½ tsp. allspice
4 eggs
1 cup sugar
1 tsp. soda, dissolved in a little water

Heat the honey until it boils, then allow it to cool to lukewarm. Sift the flour with the spices.

Beat the eggs with the sugar until thick. Add the soda, the honey, and the flour. Mix well.

Roll out the dough on a lightly floured board to ¼-inch thickness. Cut cookies in whatever shapes you like. Bake them on buttered sheets in a 350-degree oven for about 10 to 15 minutes, or until *just* lightly browned.

The *pierniki* may be decorated with a thin glaze made of confectioner's sugar, water, almond or vanilla extract, and a drop of food coloring.

fruited piernik *(Polish Pastry)*

1½ cups honey
1 cup sugar
1 package yeast
½ cup beer
1 Tbs. butter
4 cups flour
4 eggs
¾ cup chopped dates
2 Tbs. finely chopped, candied ginger
½ cup chopped walnuts
½ cup chopped dried apricots
½ tsp. each: cloves, allspice, cinnamon, dried, grated orange peel
4 Tbs. cocoa

Heat the honey until it boils, then add the sugar and bring the mixture to a boil again. Cool.

Dissolve the yeast in the warm beer and add it to the honey. Beat in the butter, flour, and eggs. Add all the remaining ingredients and stir well.

Spread the batter evenly in a buttered, oblong cake pan, or into buttered molds. Bake at 350 degrees for about 40 to 45 minutes. To serve, slice very thinly.

pannetone *(Sweet Italian Christmas Bread)*

1   cup milk
½   cup sugar
½   cup butter
¼   tsp. salt
¼   cup warm water
1   package yeast
2   eggs, beaten
1   tsp. anise seeds, crushed in a mortar
½   cup raisins
½   cup mixed candied orange and
       lemon peel
¼   cup maraschino cherries, drained
5   cups flour

Scald the milk. Stir in the butter, sugar, and salt. Cool to lukewarm.

In a large bowl, dissolve the yeast in the warm water and stir in the milk mixture, the eggs, the crushed anise seeds, the fruit, and half the flour. Beat until very smooth. Add the remaining flour and work it in to make a stiff dough. Knead on a lightly floured board until smooth.

Form the dough into a ball and place it in a greased bowl, turning it over once. Cover the bowl and let the dough rise in a warm place until double in size, about 2 hours. Punch it down and let it rest 10 minutes.

Shape the dough into 2 even balls. Place each one on a buttered baking sheet, cover with a towel, and let rise again until doubled. Bake the loaves for about 40 minutes at 350 degrees.

tyrolean leckerli

½ cup candied orange peel
⅓ cup candied lemon peel
1½ cups unblanched almonds
¾ cup honey
1¼ cups sugar
1 Tbs. grated fresh lemon peel
¼ cup lemon juice
1½ Tbs. Kirsch
4 cups sifted white flour
1 tsp. baking soda
1 tsp. salt
1 tsp. cinnamon
¼ tsp. cloves
¼ tsp. nutmeg

Put the candied peel and almonds through the food grinder with a fine blade.

Heat the honey and sugar in a medium saucepan until it just boils, stirring well. Add the fresh lemon peel and the lemon juice, then set it aside to cool for about 10 minutes. Add the ground peel and almonds.

Sift the flour with the soda, salt, and spices. Add the honey mixture and knead until thoroughly combined.

Divide the dough into 4 parts and roll them out, one at a time, to ¼-inch thickness, from which rectangular cookies can be cut. Place them about 1 inch apart on lightly greased cookie sheets and bake at 350 degrees for about 10 minutes.

Dust the cookies with confectioner's sugar. Store them in tightly covered tins or jars.

nut cake

3½ cups flour
½ tsp. salt
2 tsp. baking powder
1 cup butter
2 cups sugar
6 eggs
¾ cup milk
¼ cup Marsala wine or sherry
7 cups walnuts and pecans, in halves
   and large pieces
butter and brown paper for pans

This recipe makes 2 loaf cakes or 1 large tube cake. Prepare your pans by buttering them and lining them with buttered brown paper.

Sift the flour with the salt and baking powder. Beat the butter and sugar together until light and fluffy—then beat in the eggs, one at a time.

Combine the milk with the Marsala. Alternating the milk-marsala mixture with the flour mixture, beat them both into the batter. Stir the nuts into the batter, and turn it into the pans.

Bake the cakes for about 2½ hours in a preheated, 275-degree oven. Cool them completely, then wrap them in cheesecloth soaked in more Marsala for a few days.

stollen

This is a quick-bread version of *stollen*—also a German recipe—and better, I think, than the yeast *stollen*. It keeps moisture longer, and is much less trouble to make.

2½ cups flour
2 tsp. baking powder
¾ cup sugar
½ tsp. salt
½ tsp. mace
seeds of 5 to 6 cardamom pods, crushed
¾ cup ground blanched almonds
½ cup butter
1 cup softened cream cheese
1 egg
½ tsp. vanilla extract
⅓ tsp. almond extract
2 Tbs. brandy
½ cup currants
½ cup golden raisins
¼ cup chopped candied lemon peel
melted butter (optional)
confectioner's sugar

Sift together the flour, baking powder, sugar, salt, mace, and crushed cardamom seeds. Stir in the ground almonds. Cut the butter in with a pastry blender until the mixture resembles coarse sand.

In a blender, cream the egg with the cream cheese, vanilla, almond extract, and brandy. Pour it into a bowl and stir in the dried fruit. Gradually stir in the flour mixture, until everything is well-blended.

Work the dough into a ball and turn it out on a lightly floured board. Knead it for a few minutes, just until it is smooth. Shape it into an oval, about 10 inches long and 8 inches wide. With the blunt edge of a knife, crease it just off center, lengthwise. Fold the smaller side over the larger and place the *stollen* on an ungreased baking sheet.

You may want to brush it lightly with melted butter before baking. Bake the *stollen* in a preheated 350-degree oven for about 45 minutes. Allow it to cool slightly before dusting it with confectioner's sugar.

eggnog

12 eggs, separated
1½ cups powdered sugar
1   qt. rich milk
1   cup cognac
1   cup dark rum
1   large orange
1   lemon
1   qt. heavy cream
grated nutmeg

Beat the egg yolks and sugar until thick, then stir in the milk, cognac, and rum. Beat the egg whites until they just hold a peak, and fold them in. Put this mixture away to chill for a few hours.

Peel the orange and cut off the white pulp from the inside of the peel until only the pure orange rind is left. Cut this into matchsticks, as thin as possible and about 1½ inches long. Grate the fresh lemon rind.

Whip the cream until it only just begins to thicken, not so much that it actually holds peaks. Stir this half-whipped cream into the milk and egg mixture, and beat a few more strokes with the whisk. Stir in the lemon rind and half the orange rind. Pour the eggnog into a serving bowl. Over the top of it, sprinkle the remaining orange rind and plenty of grated nutmeg.

Serves 25 to 30.

index

A Note About the Author

Anna Thomas was born in Stuttgart, Germany, in 1948, and came to this country as a child. She has been a student most of her life—for the past four years at UCLA in the film department, where she is now producing and directing her third short film. She has supported her interest in film-making by writing press releases, working as a waitress, clerking, modeling—and writing a cookbook. She is strongly committed to the women's liberation movement and has been involved in its activities.

A Note About the Type

The text of this book was set in Zenith, the film version of Optima, a typeface designed by Hermann Zapf from 1952–55 and issued in 1958. In designing Optima, Zapf created a truly new type form—a cross between the classic roman and a sans-serif face. So delicate are the stresses and balances in Optima that it rivals sans-serif faces in clarity and freshness and old-style faces in variety and interest.